T/REFERENCE BOOKS ON DATA COMMUNICATIONS AND COMPUTER ARCHITECTURE
(Available from Macmillian Publishing Co.)

DATA AND COMPUTER COMMUNICATIONS, SECOND EDITION

A broad but detailed survey, covering four main areas: (1) data communications, including transmission, media, signal encoding, link control, and multiplexing; (2) communication networks, including circuit- and packet-switched, local, packet radio, and satellite; (3) communications architecture, including the OSI model and related protocols; and (4) ISDN.

LOCAL NETWORKS: AN INTRODUCTION, THIRD EDITION

An in-depth presentation of the technology and architecture of local networks. Covers topology, transmission media, medium access control, standards, internet-working, and interface issues.

COMPUTER ORGANIZATION AND ARCHITECTURE, SECOND EDITION

A unified view of this broad field. Covers fundamentals such as CPU, control unit, microprogramming, instruction set, I/O, and memory. Also covers advanced topics such as RISC and parallel organization.

ISDN: AN INTRODUCTION

An in-depth presentation of the technology and architecture of integrated services digital network (ISDN). Covers the integrated digital network (IDN), ISDN services, architecture, signaling system no. 7 (SS7), and detailed coverage of the 1988 CCITT standards.

BUSINESS DATA COMMUNICATIONS

A comprehensive presentation of data communications and telecommunications from a business perspective. Covers voice, data, image, and video communications and applications technology, and includes a number of case studies.

All of these books include a glossary, a list of acronyms, homework problems, and recommendations for further reading. These books are suitable as references, for self-study, and as textbooks.

Handbook of
COMPUTER-COMMUNICATIONS
Standards

Handbook of
COMPUTER-
COMMUNICATIONS
Standards

Volume 3, Second Edition

The TCP/IP Protocol Suite

William Stallings, Ph.D.
Paul Mockapetris
Sue McLeod
Tony Michel
Craig Partridge
Keith McCloghrie

HOWARD W. SAMS & COMPANY
A Division of Macmillan, Inc.
11711 North College, Suite 141, Carmel, IN 46032 USA

International Standard Book Number: 0-672-22696-0
Library of Congress Catalog Card Number: 87-14062

Acquisitions Editor: Scott Arant
Development Editor: C. Herbert Feltner
Manuscript Editor: Kathy Grider-Carlyle
Indexer: Northwind Editorial Services
Compositor: Compset, Inc.

Printed in the United States of America

For Tricia Antigone

Contents

Preface

The Department of Defense (DOD) has promulgated a set of military standards for computer communications protocols. These protocols are required on virtually all military procurements. In addition, most existing computer and terminal concentration equipment in use within the DOD is being upgraded to incorporate these standards. Although DOD is committed to the adoption and use of international standards, their military standards will be the dominant means of computer communications within the military for some years to come. Furthermore, these protocols have achieved widespread acceptance outside of the DOD, particularly in commercial local network installations.

OBJECTIVES

This book is one of a series of books that provides a comprehensive treatment of computer communications standards. The series systematically covers the major standards topics, providing the introductory and tutorial material not found in the actual standards documents. The books function as a primary reference for those who need an understanding of the technology, implementation, design, and application issues that relate to the standards. The books also function as companions to the standards documents for those who need to understand the standards for implementation or product assessment purposes.

In terms of content, the objectives for this and the other volumes are:

- Clear tutorial exposition
- Discussion of relevance and value of each standard

- Analysis of options within each standard
- Explanation of underlying technology
- Manageable and consistent treatment of a variety of standards
- Comparative assessment of alternative standards and options

This volume, Volume 3, covers the five military standard protocols that have been issued by the DOD. The book begins by introducing the four-layer communications architecture that is the framework within which these standards fit. Following the introduction of this architecture, a chapter is devoted to each of the standards.

In contrast with the other books in this series, several of the chapters in this book were written by contributors. Each contributor is intimately familiar with the topic under discussion: biographies of the main author and the contributing authors are found at the end of the book.

INTENDED AUDIENCE

This book is intended for a broad range of readers interested in computer-communications architecture and protocols:

- *Students and professionals in data processing and data communications:* This book is intended as a basic tutorial and reference source for all of the DOD military protocol standards, which together cover many of the basic areas of importance in computer communications.
- *Computer and information system customers and managers:* The book provides the reader with an understanding of what features and structures are needed in a communications capability, as well as a knowledge of the mechanisms and services of the military standards. This information provides a means of assessing specific implementations and vendor offerings.
- *Designers and implementers:* The book discusses critical design issues as they relate to the military standards.

RELATED MATERIALS

A videotape course that covers the material of this text is available from the Media Group, Boston University, 565 Commonwealth Avenue, Boston, MA 02215: telephone (617) 353-3227.

Data and Computer Communications, Second Edition (1988, Macmillan) covers fundamental topics in computer communications and protocols, as well as related topics such as communication networks and data communications. This is one of a number of books that the author has written for Macmillan; these are described on the inside front cover of this book.

THE SECOND EDITION

Since the publication of the first edition of this book, interest in the DOD protocols has continued to grow. The number of vendors that market TCP/IP-based products has expanded dramatically and there is increasing use of these protocols in non-military, commercial applications. The purpose of this revised edition is to expand the scope of coverage to make this book a more useful reference for the many users and developers concerned with the practical application of these protocols.

The principal change in this addition is the addition of coverage of protocols that are not military standards, but that are nevertheless considered essential to the practical use of these protocols in a real configuration. The additional protocols that are covered are:

- Address Resolution Protocol (ARP)
- Reverse Address Resolution Protocol (RARP)
- Exterior Gateway Protocol (EGP)
- Simple Network Management Protocol (SNMP)
- User Datagram Protocol (UDP)

In addition, coverage of the internet control message protocol (ICMP) and of the RFC 822 specification for electronic mail format have been expanded. All of these protocols are based on formal, well-defined specifications although they have not been made into military standards, and all are widely used. In recognition of this expanded coverage, the title of the book has been changed from *DOD Protocol Standards* to *TCP/IP Protocol Suite*.

In addition to this new material, there have been some slight revisions and expansions, most notably in Chapter 2.

This new edition boasts two new contributors, Craig Partridge and Keith McCloghrie, who have written the chapter on network management. Their depth of knowledge on the subject is evident in this chapter. This contribution, as well as Craig's critical and constructive review of the first edition, is most welcome.

1

The Department of Defense Communications Architecture

This chapter has two purposes. First, it introduces the communications architecture which is the framework for the TCP/IP protocol suite. Second, it serves as an overview of the remainder of the book, as the protocols to be examined in the following chapters can be described in the context of the communications architecture.

We begin with a brief discussion of the motivation that led the U.S. Department of Defense (DOD) to develop its own protocol standards and communications architecture. We also describe the widespread use of these protocols in nonmilitary areas. Then, this four-layer architecture is examined. Next, we provide an overview of the five military standard protocols that fit into the architecture and whose description forms the bulk of the book. We then look briefly at other protocols which are essential to the functioning of the TCP/IP suite and which are also examined later in the book. Finally, the relationship of the DOD protocol standards to international standards is examined.

1.1 MOTIVATION

Two trends relating to computer communications within the DOD have motivated the need for military standard communication protocols and for a communications architecture:

- The rapid proliferation of computers and other signal processing elements throughout the military and the requirement for the use of multiple vendor equipment.
- The rapid proliferation of communication networks throughout the military and the need for a variety of networking technologies.

The decreasing cost and increasing power of computer hardware has led to an increasing use of minicomputers and microcomputers to handle a wide variety of tasks. Reinforcing this trend is the superiority of a distributed data processing environment to the traditional mainframe-based centralized data processing installation. The advantages of the distributed approach include improved performance, higher application availability, and improved survivability. The emphasis on resource distribution leads, however, to a corresponding emphasis on resource interconnection and resource sharing. Users need to be able to exchange data, files, and messages. Expensive resources, such as a laser printer or a large mass storage device, need to be shared among a community of users. Complicating this need for interconnection is the requirement within the federal government for competitive procurement. The result is that, even within fairly small organizational units within DOD, there is data processing equipment from multiple vendors. Traditionally, the communications software developed by one vendor will not interoperate with that of other vendors.

At the same time, there has been a rapid growth in the use of data communications networks within DOD. In particular, there has been explosive growth in the use of local networks in recent years. Differences in both requirements and environments for these networks have resulted in the use of a variety of network designs, including packet-switched networks, packet radio networks, and a variety of local networks. Again, these networks involve a variety of vendors.

Thus, we have a situation in which there is a large number of different computers, located on different networks, but with a requirement to communicate with each other. In general terms, two technical requirements must be met:

1. End systems (computers, terminals) must share a common set of communication protocols so they can interoperate.
2. The suite of protocols used for this purpose must support an internetworking capability in a mixed-network environment.

Faced with these requirements, the DOD, through the Defense Communications Agency (DCA), has issued a set of military standard protocols [STAL86], listed in Table 1.1. These standards can be viewed as fitting within a framework, or communications architecture, which is described in the next section.

With the promulgation of military standards, DOD has chosen to

Table 1.1.   DOD MILITARY STANDARD PROTOCOLS

MIL-STD-1777   Internet Protocol (IP)
  Provides a connectionless service for end systems to communicate across one
  or more networks. Does not assume the networks to be reliable.
MIL-STD-1778   Transmission Control Protocol (TCP)
  A reliable end-to-end data transfer service. Equivalent to the ISO Class 4
  transport protocol.
MIL-STD-1780   File Transfer Protocol (FTP)
  A simple application for transfer of ASCII, EBCDIC, and binary files.
MIL-STD-1781   Simple Mail Transfer Protocol (SMTP)
  A simple electronic mail facility.
MIL-STD-1782   TELNET Protocol
  Provides a simple scroll-mode terminal capability.

meet the requirements listed previously by mandating the use of a common set of protocols on all DOD equipment rather than allowing smaller organizational units within DOD to adopt their own individual solutions or relying on some de facto standard such as IBM's System Network Architecture (SNA). There are a number of advantages to this reliance on DOD-wide standards:

- *Interoperability:* If the same set of protocols are implemented on all DOD data processing equipment, then, for the functions provided by those protocols, interoperability is achieved.
- *Vendor productivity and efficiency:* Vendors wishing to sell to DOD can concentrate on developing the standard protocols and need not devote resources to special purpose protocol conversion capabilities needed to interoperate with other proprietary schemes.
- *Competition:* Without standards, DOD managers, to preserve interoperability, will tend to purchase new equipment from the same vendor as the equipment already installed. Thus, smaller firms and firms new to the DOD marketplace cannot compete effectively.
- *Procurement simplification:* Procurement decisions can be based on the relative cost and performance of competing vendors, without having to consider protocol conversion costs, with the attendant installation delays.

Possible disadvantages of the use of military standard protocols are their potential to inhibit innovation and other (perhaps superior) solutions, and their potential to limit the choices available to the customer for a specific product or functional capability. The protocols that have been standardized by DOD, however, were all developed by DOD as part of the ARPANET research project [LEIN85]. Consequently, these protocols were designed and evolved to meet specific DOD requirements.

There is one other disadvantage that must be mentioned. Primarily because of a need to satisfy immediate operational requirements, DOD could not wait for the promulgation and vendor implementation of international standards. Thus, the standards issued by DOD and described in this book do not conform to international standards. Because of the increasingly widespread acceptance and use of these international standards, this lack of conformance places an additional implementation burden on vendors and tends to limit competition of DOD procurements. Furthermore, the international standards continue to evolve to incorporate new and more sophisticated functions and services, whereas the DOD standards are essentially static.

For these reasons, DOD has committed to migrating from the DOD protocol standards to international standards. This process, however, will be a slow and painful one because of the large installed base of equipment within DOD using the military standards. Thus, it is certain that the military standard protocols described in this book will be the dominant mode of operation within DOD into the early 1990s and that these protocols will remain important well into the 1990s.

We return briefly to the subject of international standards later in this chapter.

1.2 NONMILITARY USE OF THE DOD PROTOCOL SUITE

An interesting and generally unexpected development has been the increasingly widespread use of the TCP/IP protocol suite in nonmilitary applications. Since the introduction of IBM's System Network Architecture in 1974, followed by the introduction of competing communications architectures by other computer vendors, most computer customers have relied on these proprietary systems. Ultimately, these vendors and their customers are evolving towards the use of international standards based on the Open Systems Interconnection (OSI) architecture. However, to the surprise of most observers, many customers have chosen to make an interim step to the TCP/IP protocol suite.

This trend has been confirmed by several studies, as illustrated in Figures 1.1 through 1.3. The most direct measure is shown in Figure 1.1. This 1987 survey of 300 user organizations and customers attempted to determine the present and planned use of the TCP/IP protocol suite. As can be seen, the utilization is shifting away from predominantly the defense industry and related university programs to the commercial environment.

This introduction of a large new market for TCP/IP products has spurred a substantial growth in vendor offerings. If we look at simply the number of vendors offering TCP/IP hardware and/or software (Figure 1.2), we see that it has grown from just a few defense contractors in the late 1970s to nearly 200 vendors by 1988. This number continues to grow.

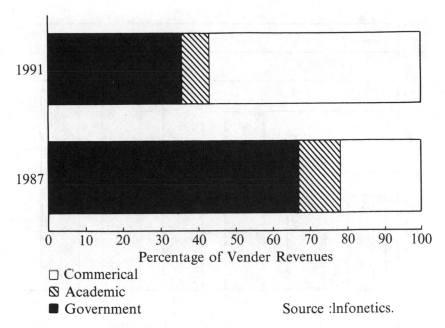

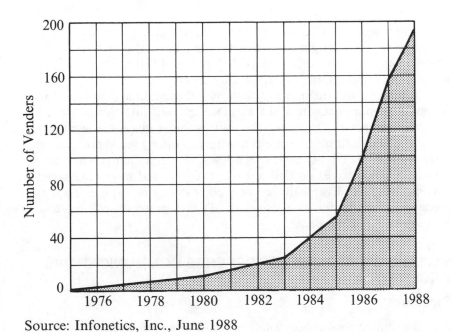

Source: Infonetics, Inc., June 1988

Figure 1.2.   Number of TCP/IP vendors.

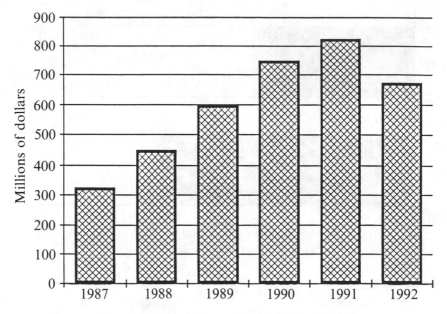

Source: Newton-Evans Research Co., March 1988

Figure 1.3. TCP/IP expenditure forecast.

Correspondingly, TCP/IP-related expenditures have grown and are projected to continue to grow at least through 1991. As with the military environment, we can expect the TCP/IP protocol suite to be a major factor in the commercial realm well into the 1990s.

It remains to attempt to explain why these military protocols have found favor in a commercial marketplace that should, on the face of it, prefer international standards. The motivation is much the same as for DOD: the TCP/IP protocol suite is a mature, working set of protocols that provides interoperability and a high level of functionality. The international standards based on OSI are still evolving and have only recently become available. Eventually, commercial customers will express a preference for OSI, but for the present, the TCP/IP protocol suite has a solid position in the marketplace.

1.3 THE DEPARTMENT OF DEFENSE COMMUNICATIONS ARCHITECTURE

Structure

Any distributed application, such as file transfer or electronic mail, requires a complex set of communications functions for proper operation. Many of these functions, such as reliability mechanisms, are common across many or even all applications. Thus, the communications task is viewed as consisting of a modular architecture, in which the various elements of the architecture perform the various required functions.

The DOD communications architecture [CERF83, PADL83] is based on a view of data communications that involves three agents: processes, hosts, and networks. *Processes* are the fundamental entities that communicate. One example is a file transfer operation. In this case, a file transfer process in one system is exchanging data with a file transfer process in another system. Another example is remote logon. In this case, a user terminal is attached to one system and controlled by a terminal-handling process in that system. The user may be remotely connected to a time-sharing system; then data is exchanged between the terminal-handling process in one computer and the time-sharing system in the other. Processes execute on *hosts* (computers), which can often support multiple simultaneous processes. Hosts are connected by *networks,* and the data to be exchanged are transmitted by the network from one host to another.

These three concepts yield a fundamental principle of the DOD communications architecture: the transfer of data from one process to another involves first getting the data to the host in which the process resides and then getting it to the process within the host. Therefore, a communications network facility needs to be concerned only with routing data between hosts, and the hosts are concerned with directing data to processes.

With these concepts in mind, it is natural to organize the communications task into four relatively independent layers [LEIN85]:

- Network access layer
- Internet layer
- Host-to-host layer
- Process layer

The *network access layer* is concerned with the exchange of data between a host and the network to which it is attached. The sending host must provide the network with the address of the destination host, so that the network may route the data appropriately. The sending host may also wish to invoke certain services that might be provided by the network, such as priority. The specific protocol used at this layer will depend on the type of network to be used; different protocols have been developed for circuit-switched networks (e.g., X.21), packet-switched networks (e.g., X.25), local networks (e.g., the IEEE 802 protocols), and others. Thus, it makes sense to separate those functions having to do with network access into a separate layer. By doing this, the remainder of the communication software, above the network access layer, needs not be concerned with the specifics of the network to be used. The same higher-layer software should function properly regardless of the particular network to which the host is attached.

The network access layer is concerned with routing data between two devices attached to the same network. In those cases where two hosts are attached to different networks, procedures are needed to allow data to traverse multiple networks. This is the function of the *internet layer.* An internet protocol is used at this layer to provide the routing function across multiple networks. This protocol is implemented not only in the hosts but also in gateways. A gateway is a processor that connects two networks and whose primary function is to relay data from one network to the other on its route from the source to the destination host.

Regardless of the nature of the processes that are exchanging data (e.g., file transfer, remote logon), there is usually a requirement that data be exchanged reliably. That is, we would like to be assured that all of the transmitted data arrives at the destination process and that the data arrives in the same order in which it was sent. As we shall see, the mechanisms for providing reliability are essentially independent of the nature of the processes. Therefore, it makes sense to collect those mechanisms in a common layer shared by all processes; this is referred to as the *host-to-host layer.*

Finally, the *process layer* contains those protocols needed to support the various applications. For each different type of application, such as file transfer, a protocol is needed that is peculiar to that application [POST85].

Within this architecture, DOD has issued the protocol standards defined in Table 1.1. Figure 1.4 illustrates the architecture and how the protocols fit into it. Note that these standards fit into the upper three layers of the architecture. At the network access layer, systems may be interfaced to a variety of networks. By and large, DOD relies on national and international standards at this layer, such as X.25 (FIPS 100) for packet-switched networks and IEEE 802 (FIPS 107) for local networks.

Operation

Figure 1.5 suggests the way in which these protocols may be configured for communications. Each host contains software at the network access, internet, and host-to-host layers, and software at the process layer for one or more processes. Gateways between networks need the network access layer to interface to the networks to which they attach, and the internet layer to be able to perform the routing and relaying function. For successful communication, every entity in the overall system must have a unique address. Actually, two levels of addressing are needed. Each host on network must have a unique global network address; this allows the data to be delivered to the proper host. Each process within a host must have an address that is unique within the host; this allows the host-to-host protocol (TCP) to deliver data to the proper process. These latter

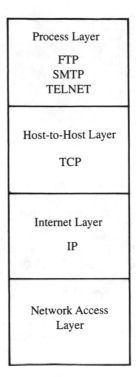

Figure 1.4. DOD communications architecture and protocol standards.

addresses are known as *ports*. The subject of addressing is considered in more detail in the next section (section 1.4).

Let us trace a simple operation. Suppose that a process, associated with port 1 at host *A*, wishes to send a message to another process, associated with port 2 at host *B*. The process at *A* hands the message over to its host-to-host layer with instructions to send it to host *B*, port 2. The host-to-host layer hands the message over to the internet layer with instructions to send it to host *B*. Note that the internet layer need not be told the identity of the destination port. All that it needs to know is that the data is intended for host *B*. Finally, the internet layer hands the message over to the network access layer with instructions to send it to gateway *X* (the first *hop* on the way to *B*).

To control this operation, control information as well as user data must be transmitted, as suggested in Figure 1.6. Let us say that the sending process generates a block of data and passes this to its host-to-host layer protocol, TCP. TCP may break this block into two smaller pieces to make it more manageable. To each of these pieces TCP appends a TCP header. The combination of data from the process layer and control information from TCP is known as a *TCP segment*. The header in each segment contains control information to be used by the peer TCP protocol

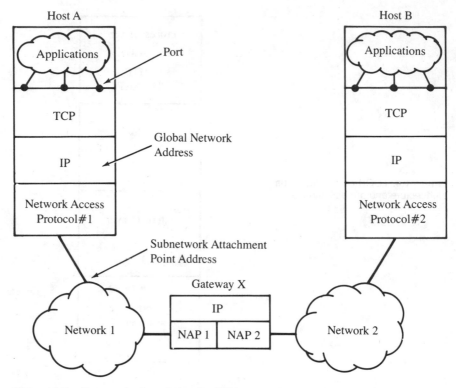

Figure 1.5.   Communications using the DOD protocols.

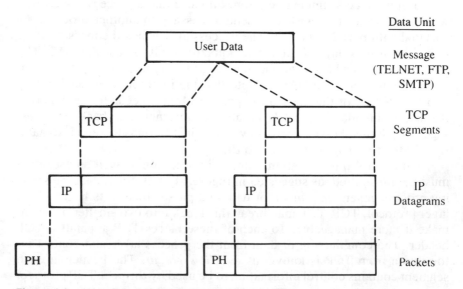

Figure 1.6.   User data and protocol control information.

entity at host *B*. Examples of items that may be stored in this header include:

- *Destination port:* When the destination TCP receives the segment, it must know to whom the data are to be delivered.
- *Sequence number:* Because TCP is sending a sequence of segments, it numbers them sequentially so that if they arrive out of order, the destination TCP entity may reorder them.
- *Checksum:* The sending TCP includes a code that is a function of the contents of the remainder of the segment. The receiving TCP performs the same calculation and compares the result with the incoming code. A discrepancy results if there has been some error in transmission (see Appendix B).

The next step is for TCP to hand each segment over to the internet layer, with instructions to transmit it to the destination host. These segments must be transmitted across one or more networks and relayed through the intermediate gateways. As before, this operation requires the use of control information. In this case the internet protocol (IP) appends an IP header to each segment it receives from TCP; the result is called an *IP datagram*. An example of an item stored in the IP header is the destination host address.

Finally, each IP datagram is presented to the network access layer for transmission across the first network in the journey to the destination. The network access layer appends its own header, creating a *packet*. The packet is transmitted from the host to the network; the packet header contains the information that the network needs to transfer the data across the network. Examples of items that may be stored in this header include:

- *Destination subnetwork address:* The network must know to which attached device the packet is to be delivered.
- *Facilities requests:* The network access protocol might request the use of certain network facilities, such as priority.

When the data are received at the other host, the reverse process occurs. At each layer, the corresponding header is removed, and the remainder is passed on to the next higher layer, until the original process data are delivered to the destination process.

Protocol Interfaces

Each layer interacts with the immediate adjacent layers. At the source, the process layer makes use of the services of the host-to-host layer and provides data down to that layer. A similar relationship exists at the interface of the host-to-host and internet layers, and at the interface of the internet and network access layers. At the destination, each layer delivers data up to the next higher layer.

This use of each individual layer is not required by the model [PADL83]. As Figure 1.7 suggests, it is possible to develop applications that directly invoke the services of any one of the layers. Most applications require a reliable end-to-end protocol and thus make use of TCP. Some special-purpose applications, however, may be developed that do not need the services of TCP and make use of IP directly. Applications

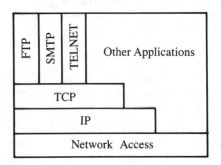

Figure 1.7. DOD protocol interfaces.

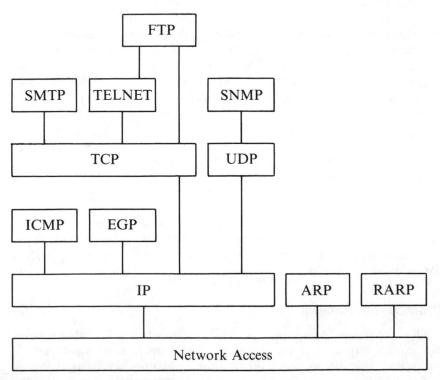

Figure 1.8. Protocol dependencies.

that do not involve internetworking and that do not need TCP could be developed to invoke the network access layer directly.

Incidentally, Figure 1.7 also underscores the important point that the DOD communications architecture is not limited to the five military standard protocols. Rather, a variety of applications and other processes may make use of this architecture. Figure 1.8 shows the relationship among the various protocols discussed in this book.

1.4 PROTOCOL MECHANISMS

A fundamental aspect of any communications architecture is that one or more protocols operate at each layer of the architecture and that two peer protocols at the same layer but in different systems cooperate to achieve the communication function. Before continuing with an examination of each of the protocols in the DOD communications architecture, it is helpful to consider some of the key protocol mechanisms that are common to many protocols:

- Segmentation and reassembly
- Encapsulation
- Connection control
- Addressing

Segmentation and Reassembly

A protocol is concerned with exchanging streams of data between two entities. Usually, the transfer can be characterized as consisting of a sequence of blocks of data of some bounded size. At the process level, we can refer to a logical unit of data transfer as a message. Now, whether the application process (e.g., TELNET, FTP, SMTP) sends data in messages or in a continuous stream, lower level protocols may need to break up the data into blocks of smaller bounded size. This function is called *segmentation*. For convenience, we refer to a block of data exchanged between two entities via a protocol as a *protocol data unit* (PDU).

There are a number of motivations for segmentation, depending on the context. Among the typical reasons for segmentation:

- The communications network may only accept blocks of data up to a certain size. For example, the Defense Data Network (DDN) accepts packets up to a maximum size of 1024 octets [DCA83c].
- Error control may be more efficient with a smaller PDU size. If an error is detected, only a small amount of data may need to be retransmitted.
- More equitable access to shared transmission facilities, with shorter delay, can be provided. For example, without a maximum block size, one station could monopolize a shared medium.

- A smaller PDU size may mean that receiving entities can allocate smaller buffers.
- An entity may require that data transfer comes to some sort of *closure* from time to time, for checkpoint and restart/recovery operations.

There are several disadvantages to segmentation that argue for making blocks as large as possible:

- Each PDU, as we shall see, contains a fixed minimum amount of control information. Hence the smaller the block, the greater the percentage overhead.
- PDU arrival may generate an interrupt that must be serviced. Smaller blocks result in more interrupts.
- More time is spent processing smaller, more numerous PDUs.

All of these factors must be taken into account by the protocol designer to determine the minimum and maximum PDU size.

The counterpart of segmentation is *reassembly*. Eventually, the segmented data must be reassembled into messages appropriate to the application. If PDUs arrive out of order, the task is complicated.

The process of segmentation was illustrated in Figure 1.6, which shows process data being divided into two segments by TCP, at the host-to-host level. Actually, the segmentation function can occur at any of the three layers of the architecture below the process layer.

At the network access layer, a PDU received from the internet layer can be sent across the network as a sequence of packets. The network access protocol splits the internet datagram into a number of parts and places a packet header on each one. These packets will be reassembled into a single internet datagram on the other end of the network for delivery to the internet protocol.

At the internet layer, the same function may be performed: splitting a TCP segment into pieces and appending an IP header to each one. At this layer, the reassembly function is complicated by the fact that the various IP datagrams may take different routes across the multiple-network environment from source to destination. This implies that datagrams may arrive out of order. Furthermore, some datagrams may be lost in transit, making reassembly impossible.

Segmentation can occur in more than one of the three layers for the same user message. In many situations, the originating end system has latitude in deciding where segmentation should actually be performed. The key determining criteria are the maximum packet sizes permitted by the networks to be traversed and the processing efficiencies of segmentation at the different layers. This degree of freedom can be exploited to optimize the operation provided that the originator has information about the characteristics of the networks to be traversed.

Encapsulation

Each PDU contains not only data but also control information. Indeed, some PDUs consist solely of control information and no data. The control information falls into three general categories:

- *Address:* The address of the sender and/or receiver may be indicated.
- *Error detecting code:* Some sort of code is often included for error detection (see Appendix B).
- *Protocol control:* Additional information is included to implement other protocol functions.

The addition of control information to data is referred to as *encapsulation.* Data are accepted or generated by an entity and encapsulated into a PDU containing that data plus control information.

Encapsulation was illustrated in Figure 1.6. Figure 1.9 shows the combined use of encapsulation, segmentation, and reassembly. In this figure, a data unit is segmented into three PDUs before transmission. Upon reception, the PDU headers are stripped off and the segmented data units are reassembled for delivery to the next higher layer.

Connection Control

An entity may transmit data to another entity in an unplanned fashion and without prior coordination. This is known as *connectionless data transfer.* Although this mode can be useful, it is less common than *connection-oriented data transfer.*

Connection-oriented data transfer is preferred (even required) if stations anticipate a lengthy exchange of data and/or certain details of their

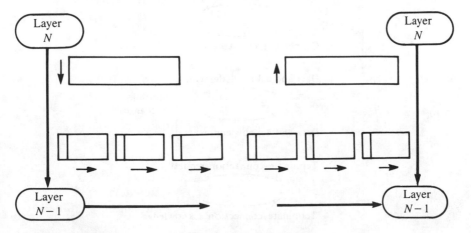

Figure 1.9.   Encapsulation, segmentation, and reassembly.

protocol must be worked out dynamically. A logical association, or *connection*, is established between the entities. Three phases occur (Figure 1.10):

- Connection establishment
- Data transfer
- Connection termination

With more sophisticated protocols, there may also be connection interrupt and recovery phases to cope with errors and other sorts of interruptions.

During the connection establishment phase, two entities agree to exchange data. Typically, one station will issue a connection request (in connectionless fashion) to the other. A central authority may or may not be involved. In simpler protocols, the receiving entity either accepts or rejects the request and, in the former case, the connection is immediately established. In more complex proposals, this phase includes a negotiation concerning the syntax, semantics, and timing of the protocol. Both entities must, of course, be using the same protocol. But the protocol may allow certain optional features and these must be agreed on by means of negotiation. For example, the protocol may specify a PDU size of *up to* 8000 bytes; one entity may wish to restrict this to 1000 bytes.

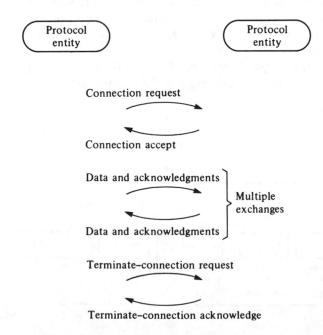

Figure 1.10.   The phases of a connection-oriented data transfer.

After connection establishment, the data transfer phase is entered. During this phase both data and control information (e.g., flow control, error control) is exchanged. Finally, one side or the other wishes to terminate the connection and does so by sending a termination request. Alternatively, a central authority might forcibly terminate a connection.

Within the DOD architecture, the network access layer may provide either a connectionless or a connection-oriented protocol, corresponding to whether the network does or does not offer a connection-oriented service. The internet protocol is connectionless; this is desirable to provide an internetworking capability. TCP is connection-oriented to support reliable transfer of data. As FTP, SMTP, and TELNET all make use of TCP, they are connection-oriented as well.

Addressing

For two processes to communicate, they must somehow be able to identify each other. This identification is needed for three reasons:

1. An entity (e.g., FTP) may simultaneously engage in dialogues with more than one remote entity. Each remote correspondent must be uniquely identifiable to keep track of the state of the various dialogues.
2. Certain protocols (again, FTP is an example) may require identification of their remote correspondent for purposes of access control.
3. The lower layers of the architecture (host-to-host, internet, network access) must be provided with sufficient information to be able to route data units through the communications facility and deliver them to the intended destination.

The DOD communications architecture is intended to support an environment in which there are multiple networks, multiple hosts on each network, and multiple processes in each host. This requires a complex addressing scheme. The elements of such a scheme are suggested in Figure 1.5.

Let us consider this addressing scheme from the bottom up. First, each network must maintain a unique address for each host attached to that network. This allows the network to route packets through the network and deliver them to the intended host. We can call that address the *subnetwork attachment point address*. The term subnetwork is used to identify a physically distinct network that may be part of a complex of networks interconnected by gateways.

At the internet level, it is the responsibility of the internet protocol to deliver datagrams across multiple networks from source to destination. Hence, the internet protocol must be provided with a *global network address* that uniquely identifies each host. It would appear convenient to provide this address in the form of (*network, host*), where the parameter *network* identifies a particular network and the parameter *host* identifies a particular host attached to that network. It would appear convenient for the host parameter in the global network address to be identical to the subnetwork attachment point address for that host. Unfortunately, this may not always be possible. Different networks use different addressing formats and different address lengths. Furthermore, a host may enjoy more than one link into the same network. Accordingly, we must assume that the host parameter has global significance and the subnetwork attachment point address has significance only within a particular network. In this case, the internet protocol must translate from the global address to the locally-significant address to transmit a datagram across a network.

Finally, once a data unit is delivered to a host, it is passed to the host-to-host layer for delivery to the ultimate user (process). Because there may be multiple users, each is identified by a *port* number that is unique within the host. Thus, the combination of port and global network address uniquely identifies a process within an environment of multiple networks and multiple hosts. This three-level address (network, host, port) is referred to as a *socket*.

1.5 MILITARY STANDARD PROTOCOLS

Within the DOD, the Defense Communications Agency (DCA) is responsible for the development of long-haul communications standards, including protocol standards [SELV85]. In this section, we provide a brief overview of each of the five protocol standards issued by DCA. The next five chapters examine each of these standards in detail.

Internet Protocol

Long haul packet switched networks and local networks grew out of a need to allow the computer user to have access to resources beyond those available in a single system. In a similar fashion, the resources of a single network are often inadequate to meet users' needs. Because the networks that might be of interest exhibit so many differences, it is impractical to consider merging them into a single network. Rather, what is needed is the ability to interconnect various networks so that any two stations on any of the constituent networks can communicate.

An interconnected set of networks is referred to as an *internet*. Each constituent network supports communication among a number of attached devices. In addition, networks are connected by devices that are referred to generically as gateways. Gateways provide a communication path so that data can be exchanged between networks.

As Figure 1.5 indicates, IP is implemented in each endpoint computer and in each gateway. IP running in a host computer accepts data in segments from TCP and sends them out across the internet and through as many gateways as needed, until they reach the intended destination. IP provides what is known as unreliable connectionless service. That is, some PDUs may never get through and those that do may arrive out of sequence. It is up to TCP to assure reliable data delivery.

The operation of IP can be described as follows. Consider two hosts, *A* and *B,* on different networks in the internet. Host *A* is sending data to host *B.* The process starts in host *A.* The IP module in host *A* constructs a datagram, consisting of data from TCP plus control information used by IP. The datagram is then sent across *A's* network to the appropriate gateway. When the gateway receives a datagram, it must make a routing decision. There are two possibilities:

1. The destination host *B* is connected directly to one of the networks to which the gateway is attached. If so, the IP module in the gateway sends the datagram across that network to *B.*
2. To reach the host, one or more additional gateways must be traversed. If so, the datagram is sent across a network to the next gateway on the proper route.

Thus, the IP module in a host or gateway must have information allowing it to make this routing decision. In addition, it must be able to employ the appropriate network access protocol to be able to send data across networks to which it is attached.

Transmission Control Protocol

TCP provides a reliable mechanism for the exchange of data between processes in different computers. The protocol ensures that data are delivered error free, in sequence, with no loss or duplication. The transport service relieves higher level software of the burden of managing the intervening communications facility. Because the transport protocol provides for high quality service, and because it may need to deal with a range of communications services, it is one of the most complex of all communications protocols.

The basic service provided by TCP is the transfer of data between two transport users, such as a file transfer protocol (FTP) or a simple mail transfer protocol (SMTP). Data are passed from a transport user to TCP. TCP encapsulates those data into a segment, which contains the user data plus control information, such as the destination address. To achieve reliable data transfer, outgoing segments are numbered sequentially and subsequently acknowledged, by number by the destination TCP module. If segments arrive out of order, they can be reordered based on sequence number. If a segment is lost, it will not be acknowledged, and the sending TCP module will retransmit it.

Beyond this basic service, there are a number of other services offered by TCP:

- *Quality of service:* TCP allows the transport user to specify the quality of transmission service to be provided. TCP will attempt to optimize the use of the underlying IP and network resources to the best of its ability to provide the collective requested services. Parameters that may be specified include precedence and delay.
- *Urgent delivery:* Some data submitted to TCP may have special urgency. TCP will attempt to have the transmission facility transfer the data as rapidly as possible. At the receiving end, TCP will notify the user of the receipt of urgent data. Thus, this is in the nature of an interrupt mechanism, and is used to transfer occasional urgent data, such as a break character from a terminal or an alarm condition.
- *Security:* A security classification or range may be used to label data provided to TCP. This may influence the route taken by the data and whether it is encrypted.

File Transfer Protocol

The purpose of FTP is to transfer a file or a portion of a file from one system to another, under command of an FTP user. Typically, FTP is used interactively by an on-line user. The user's communication with FTP is mediated by the operating system, which contains input/output (I/O) drivers. If the user on system *A* wishes access to a file on system *B,* then *A*'s FTP communicates with *B*'s FTP. The user connects to the local FTP to transfer all or part of a file. There are three possibilities. The user at system *A* may wish a file at system *B* to be transferred to system *A*. This would give the user local access to the contents of a file. The user may have prepared a file locally (at system *A*) and wish it sent to system *B*. Finally, the user may request that a file be exchanged between system *B* and a third system, *C*. This is referred to as third-party transfer and involves the FTP entities at *A, B,* and *C*.

FTP must interact with three entities, as depicted in Figure 1.11. First, there must be a user interface to accept requests from an interactive user or, possibly, a program. Of course, this interaction only takes place at the requesting system. The remote FTP in a file transfer event does not interact with a user. Second, FTP must be able to communicate with other FTPs to achieve file transfer. This is done by using the services of TCP. Finally, to transfer a file, FTP must be able to get at the file. For this, an interface is needed to the local file management system.

FTP provides a number of options. Text files that use either ASCII or EBCDIC character codes may be transferred; in addition, a transparent bit stream type can be employed to allow any sort of data or text file

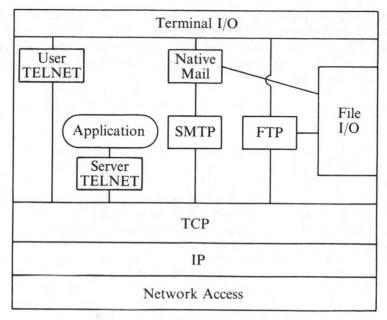

Figure 1.11. Conceptual structure for DOD protocol implementation.

to be sent. This latter option is useful primarily for exchanging files between systems from the same vendor. Data compression can be invoked
to reduce communications costs. Finally, FTP provides mechanisms for
controlling user access; to access files on a given system, a user may be
required to have an authorized password/identifier for that system.

Simple Mail Transfer Protocol

SMTP provides the basis for a network electronic mail facility. Typically,
an electronic mail facility runs on a single system. For each user with
access to the system, a mailbox exists. When a user signs on to a system,
he or she can send mail by placing a message in the mailbox of another
user, and receive mail by reading messages in the user's own mailbox.
Typically, mailboxes are maintained through the file management system.
Each mailbox is a directory that may contain text files, which are messages. Users may prepare messages through an editor or a word processor. Such a single system facility can be referred to as the native mail
facility, provided as an application on a particular system.

SMTP provides a mechanism for transferring messages among
separate systems. With SMTP, a user can send mail not only to other
users on the same system, but to users anywhere in the network or
internet.

Figure 1.11 indicates the context for SMTP. SMTP accepts messages prepared by the native mail facility and delivers messages to that facility. It makes use of TCP to send and receive messages across the network. The SMTP standard does not specify the user interface. Thus, the user sees the same interface whether sending local mail (native) or remote mail (SMTP).

TELNET

TELNET is a protocol used to link terminals to applications. It can be characterized as follows:

1. It specifies a network standard terminal. Thus, characteristics of specific terminals are mapped into the standard. This allows terminals from a variety of vendors to be connected to a variety of hosts.
2. It specifies the protocol between terminal and hosts. This allows certain terminal characteristics to be negotiated (e.g., line width, page size, full-duplex versus half-duplex, remote versus local echo).
3. It provides reliable data exchange by means of TCP.
4. It allows a user at a terminal to control an application in a remote host as if the user were a local user of that host.

TELNET actually is implemented in two modules: User TELNET and Server TELNET. User TELNET interacts with the terminal I/O module on the system. It converts the characteristics of real terminals to the network standard and vice versa. Server TELNET interacts with process and applications. It acts as a surrogate terminal handler so that remote terminals appear as local to the process or application.

TELNET is intended primarily for asynchronous scroll mode terminals. However, it includes a binary transmission option that allows it transparently to pass any terminal traffic. In this latter case, there is no conversion to a network standard; interoperability is the responsibility of the TELNET users.

1.6   OTHER PROTOCOLS IN THE TCP/IP PROTOCOL SUITE

The five military standard protocols are the core of the TCP/IP protocol suite. However, these five protocols do not provide all of the functions required for full computer networking. Other protocols are used as supplements to the five core protocols to provide the additional necessary functionality. These protocols are not formal military standards. Rather, they have been issued as "Requests for Comment" and designated with an RFC number by DOD. The most important of these protocols are examined in this book. In each case, with the exception of SNMP, the supplemental protocol is covered in the same chapter as the most nearly related military standard protocol. In this section, we provide a brief overview.

Internet Control Message Protocol

The Internet Protocol (IP) provides the functions necessary for gateways and hosts to cooperate in the movement of datagrams from a source host to a destination host. However, it does not support any other exchange of information among hosts and gateways. For all but the simplest internet configurations, information must be exchanged concerning the topology and level of congestion of the internet. For example, if a gateway may forward a datagram through one of two gateways, it must make a routing decision. This decision will depend on the "health" of each gateway (one may be down) and the relative delay through each gateway. Thus, information must be exchanged among all devices that support IP that will allow dynamic routing decisions. One such protocol is the Internet Control Message Protocol (ICMP).

ICMP is a protocol that uses IP to send status messages from a gateway or destination host to the source host. The messages are of two types: error and information. Each message refers to a previously transmitted IP datagram. An example of an error message is the *Destination Unreachable* message. A gateway would return this message to the source host if the datagram in question contains a destination network or destination host address unknown to the gateway. An example of an information message is the *Echo Request/Echo Reply* message pair. This pair of messages allows a source host to perform a loopback test with a gateway or destination host.

Address Resolution Protocol and Reverse Address Resolution Protocol

An IP datagram contains the internet address, or global network address, of a destination host. However, once the datagram reaches the network to which the destination host is attached, the subnetwork attachment point address of the host is needed for actual delivery. Unless the mapping from internet address to subnetwork attachment point address is already known (e.g., preconfigured), some mechanism is needed by which this mapping can be discovered. One approach that is useful on local area networks is the Address Resolution Protocol (ARP). With ARP, a station (host, gateway) broadcasts a request for a subnet address. The request message contains the internet address. The host on the network that has that internet address will replay with an ARP message containing the subnet address.

The Reverse Address Resolution Protocol (RARP) allows a host to discover its internet address. This situation may arise with a diskless workstation that has no permanent means of storing its internet address.

Exterior Gateway Protocol

The Exterior Gateway Protocol (EGP) operates between gateways. In particular, it is used in a situation in which an internet consists of a number of "autonomous systems." Each autonomous system is a portion of the internet managed by a particular organization. Routing within an autonomous system is the responsibility of the controlling organization, and proprietary protocols may be used to support routing. EGP is a way in which neighboring gateways in different autonomous systems can exchange general information about which networks are reachable via a particular gateway.

User Datagram Protocol

The User Datagram Protocol (UDP) operates at the same level as TCP. It provides a connectionless service for the exchange of messages between hosts, avoiding the overhead of TCP's reliability mechanisms. UDP is useful for some transaction-oriented applications such as network management.

Simple Network Management Protocol

The Simple Network Management Protocol (SNMP) is an application-level protocol that provides support for the exchange of network management messages and information among hosts, including a host that supports a network management, or network control, center. The protocol provides a limited repertoire of functions and is aimed at optimizing the processing of a few simple operations upon which network management can be built. This approach has the virtue that it allows rapid implementation of a useful, if rudimentary, network management capability. At the same time, it allows for small, efficient implementation which places minimal burden on the internet and its hosts. SNMP is designed to operate over UDP.

1.7   DEPARTMENT OF DEFENSE STANDARDS AND INTERNATIONAL STANDARDS

The military standard protocols have been a success for DOD. A wide variety of products are coming into the market. Most major computer vendors support the DOD protocols. Also there are a number of communications boards, especially for local networks, that provide TCP and IP, thereby relieving a host system of that burden.

Thus, DOD is in the process of achieving its interoperability objectives. Unfortunately, these standards have come to a fruition at a time when international standards, developed within the framework of the Open Systems Interconnection (OSI) Reference Model, are maturing and receiving widespread support by both vendors and customers.

Figure 1.12 compares the four-layer DOD communications architecture to the better known OSI model. For the reader unfamiliar with this model, Appendix A provides a brief tutorial. More detail on the model and OSI-related standards may be found in Volume 1 of this series.

There are two principal reasons why DOD chose to develop its own protocols and architecture rather than adopt the developing international standards [ENNI83]:

1. The DOD protocols were specified and have enjoyed extensive use before ISO and CCITT standardization of alternative protocols. Because DOD's need was immediate, it was deemed impractical to wait for the international protocol standards to evolve and stabilize.
2. DOD-specific requirements, such as robustness and security, have a major impact on the design of protocols and on architecture. These

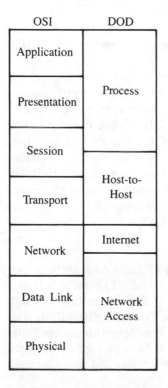

Figure 1.12. A comparison of the OSI and the DOD communications architecture.

Table 1.2. COMPARISON BETWEEN MILITARY STANDARD PROTOCOLS AND
INTERNATIONAL STANDARD PROTOCOLS

MIL-STD-1777	DIS 8473
Internet Protocol (IP)	Protocol for Providing the Connectionless-Mode Network Service
MIL-STD-1778	ISO 8073
Transmission Control Protocol (TCP)	Connection Oriented Transport Protocol Specification
MIL-STD-1780	DIS 8571
File Transfer Protocol (FTP)	File Transfer, Access and Management (FTAM)
MIL-STD-1781	X.400
Simple Mail Transfer Protocol (SMTP)	Message Handling System
MIL-STD-1782	DIS 9041
TELNET Protocol	Virtual Terminal Protocol (VTP)

requirements were, at least initially, not addressed well in the international standards.

As the international standards have evolved, they have reached a point where they can satisfy DOD requirements at least as well as the existing DOD standards. Specifically, Table 1.2 lists a set of international standards that correspond to the military standards. Compared with TCP and IP, the corresponding international standards provide equivalent functionality. These standards are examined in Volume 1 of this series. Compared with SMTP, X.400 provides greater capability. Furthermore, X.400 has been a standard since 1984 and is available from a number of vendors. Finally, compared with FTP and TELNET, the corresponding international standards provide greater capability; however, these standards are relatively new and, as of this writing, still not widely available. These three standards (X.400, FTAM, VTP) are described briefly in [STAL88] and are described in detail in a forthcoming volume of this series.

Motivation for Transition to OSI

DOD has made a commitment to transition from their own architecture and protocol standards to the OSI architecture and OSI-related international standards. A major milestone that led to this commitment was a report issued in 1985 by the National Research Council (NRC) [NRC85].

The NRC report was the result of a study commissioned by DOD and the National Bureau of Standards (NBS) in May of 1983. The study was done by representatives of industry, government, and the academic community, under NRC sponsorship. Its objective was to resolve differences between DOD and NBS on a data communications transport protocol standard. Specifically, the issue was whether or not the ISO transport standard could meet DOD's requirements instead of TCP, and, if so, how could DOD migrate to this standard.

The study produced three findings:

1. DOD objectives can be met by international standards.
2. TCP and ISO transport are functionally equivalent.
3. There are significant benefits for DOD in using standard commercial products.

The report recommended that DOD migrate not only to ISO transport, but to international standards in general. A major motivation is cost. The cost for the development, procurement, and maintenance will be lower for products based on international standards because the broader demand for those products leads to economies of scale and greater competition.

In addition to the cost benefit cited in the report, there are three functional benefits:

1. There are a number of useful commercial products integrated with OSI-related standards, and this benefit will become more significant as more and more products based on OSI become available.
2. There are limitations to FTP, SMTP, and TELNET compared with their OSI counterparts.
3. OSI-related standards are being developed in areas not covered by DOD standards, such as document architecture, network management, and transaction processing.

Transition to OSI

Because of the reasons cited previously, DOD is committed to making a transition from its own standards to OSI-based standards. Although there has been no official schedule published, the general strategy for this transition has emerged, and DOD has enlisted the support of the NBS in accomplishing the transition [NBS86]. There are three phases:

- *Phase I:* Mandatory use of DOD military standards on procurements that involve networking and distributed processing
- *Phase II:* Adoption of corresponding international standards as co-standards to DOD military standards
- *Phase III:* Exclusive use of the international standards

During Phase II, systems that implement the DOD protocols must coexist with systems that implement the OSI protocols. To provide

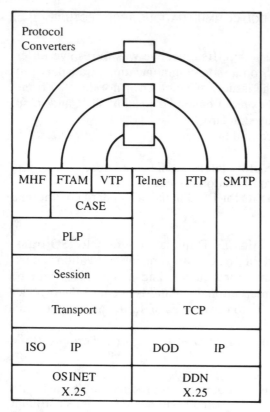

Figure 1.13. OSI/DOD intermediate system.

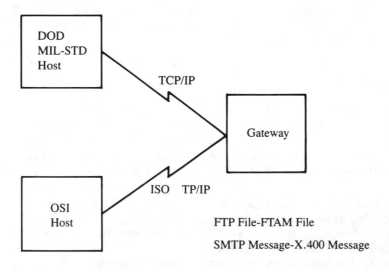

Figure 1.14. Use of an application-level gateway.

interoperability, an application gateway will be employed [TANG86, WALL86]. Figure 1.13 shows the architecture of the gateway and Figure 1.14 depicts its use. As illustrated, data could be exchanged between hosts by routing it through a gateway that does a conversion at the application level. A number of these gateways would be deployed to handle the required traffic.

As was mentioned earlier in this chapter, this migration process will take many years. In the meantime, the DOD military standard protocols will remain the basis for computer communications within the DOD.

2

Internet Protocol

Packet-switched and packet broadcasting networks grew out of a need to allow the computer user to have access to resources beyond that available in a single system. In a similar fashion, the resources of a single network are often inadequate to meet users' needs. Because the networks that might be of interest exhibit so many differences, it is impractical to consider merging them into a single network. Rather, what is needed is the ability to interconnect various networks so that any two stations on any of the constituent networks can communicate.

An interconnected set of networks is referred to as an *internet,* and the concept is illustrated in Figure 2.1. Each constituent network supports communication among a number of attached devices. In addition, networks are connected by devices that we refer to generically as *gateways*. Gateways provide a communication path so that data can be exchanged between networks.

We begin our examination of internetworking with a look at the requirements for an internetworking facility. Following this, the operation of the internet protocol (IP) is described in functional terms. Details of the IP standard are then presented. Finally, we look at those protocols that are related to the use of IP: ICMP, ARP, and EGP.

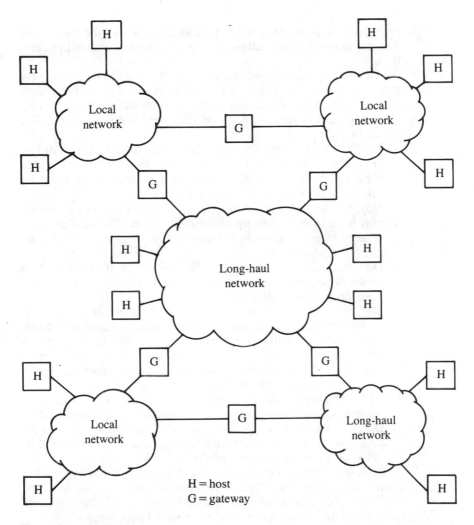

Figure 2.1. An internet.

2.1 REQUIREMENTS FOR AN INTERNETWORKING FACILITY

Although a variety of approaches have been taken to provide internet-work service, the overall requirements on the internetworking facility can be stated in general terms. These include:

1. Provide a link between networks.
2. Provide for the routing and delivery of data between processes on different networks.

3. Provide an accounting service that keeps track of the use of the various networks and gateways and maintains status information.
4. Provide the services listed above in such a way as not to require modifications to the networking architecture of any of the constituent networks. This means that the internetworking facility must accommodate a number of differences among networks. These include:
   a. *Different addressing schemes:* The networks may use different endpoint names and addresses and directory maintenance schemes. Some form of global network addressing must be provided, as well as a directory service.
   b. *Different maximum packet size:* Packets from one network may have to be broken up into smaller pieces for another. This is segmentation, usually referred to as *fragmentation* in the internet context.
   c. *Different network access mechanisms:* The network access protocol between station and network may be different for stations on different networks.
   d. *Different timeouts:* Typically, a connection-oriented transport service will await an acknowledgment until a timeout expires, at which time it will retransmit its segment of data. In general, longer times are required for successful delivery across multiple networks. Internetwork timing procedures must allow successful transmission that avoids unnecessary retransmissions.
   e. *Error recovery:* Intranetwork procedures may provide anything from no error recovery up to reliable end-to-end (within the network) service. The internetwork service should not depend on nor be interfered with by the nature of the individual network's error recovery capability.
   f. *Status reporting:* Different networks report status and performance differently. Yet it must be possible for the internetworking facility to provide such information on internetworking activity to interested and authorized processes.
   g. *Routing techniques:* Intranetwork routing may depend on fault detection and congestion control techniques peculiar to each network. The internetworking facility must be able to coordinate these to adaptively route data between stations on different networks.
   h. *User access control:* Each network will have its own user access control technique (authorization for use of the network). These must be invoked by the internetwork facility as needed. Furthermore, a separate internetwork access control technique may be required.
   i. *Connection, connectionless:* Individual networks may provide connection-oriented (e.g., virtual circuit) or connectionless (datagram) service. It may be desirable for the internetwork service not to depend on the nature of the connection service of the individual networks.

2.2   INTERNET PROTOCOL OPERATION

The DOD IP, MIL-STD-1777, was developed as part of the DARPA Internet Project [POST81a]. This project has resulted in the creation of an internet that includes DOD, contractor, and academic networks. As of late 1986, the DOD internet consisted of over 150 interconnected networks (Figure 2.2). The internet includes the two unclassified segments of the Defense Data Network (DDN), MILNET and ARPANET. Table 2.1 lists characteristics of some of the constituent networks [HIND83].

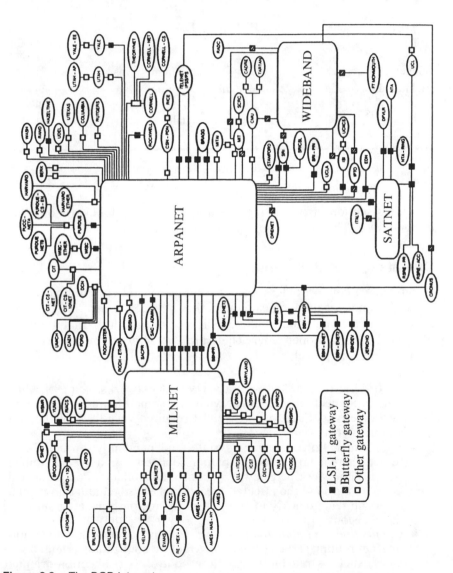

Figure 2.2.   The DOD internet.

Table 2.1. DARPA INTERNET NETWORK CHARACTERISTICS

Network Type	Message Size (Octets)	Speed*	Delay†	Guaranteed Delivery	Notes
ARPANET	1008	Medium	Medium	Yes	
SATNET	256	Low	High	No	Satellite network
Pronet	2048	High	Low	Yes	Local area network
Ethernet	1500	High	Low	Yes	Local area network
Telenet	128	Low	Medium	Yes	
Packet radio	254	Medium	Medium	No	Varying topology
Wideband	2000	High	High	No	Satellite Network

*Low speed is <100 kbps; medium speed is 100 kbps to 1 Mbps; high speed is >1 Mpbs.
†Low delay is <50 ms; medium delay is 50 to 500 ms; high delay is >500 ms.

This section discusses the operation of IP and looks at some key design issues. The next section describes the standard itself.

Operation of an IP Internet

IP provides a connectionless, or datagram, service between hosts. That is, IP does not set up a logical connection between hosts, and does not guarantee that all data units will be delivered or that those that are delivered will be in the proper order. There are a number of advantages to the connectionless approach:

- *Flexibility:* IP can deal with a variety of networks, some of which offer a connection-oriented service and some of which offer a connectionless service. In essence, IP requires very little of the constituent networks.
- *Robustness:* Each datagram is routed independently through the internet; there is no predefined path associated with a logical connection. If a network or gateway becomes unavailable, datagrams can be routed around the affected area. Similarly, the datagram mechanism can react quickly to congestion by making per-datagram routing decisions.
- *Connectionless application support:* For applications that do require internet routing services but do not require connection-oriented services, such as reliability and flow control, a connection-oriented protocol would introduce unwanted processing overhead. For appli-

cations that need such services, these are provided by running a transmission control protocol (TCP) on top of IP.

Figure 2.3 illustrates the basic operation of IP. It traces the transfer of user data from host A on network 1 to host B on network 2 via an intervening gateway. The two hosts share a common application protocol (e.g., file transfer protocol) and TCP. The two hosts and the gateway all implement IP. We can trace the operation of this architecture on a single block of user data in Figure 2.3b, which is keyed to event times marked in Figure 2.3a. At some time t_0, the user of TCP in host A presents a block of data to TCP. TCP encapsulates this data with a TCP header and passes the resulting segment to IP (t_1). IP adds its own header and passes the resulting datagram to the network access protocol (NAP-1), which is used to access network 1 (t_2). The network access protocol adds its own header and transmits the resulting packet across the network (t_3) to the gateway

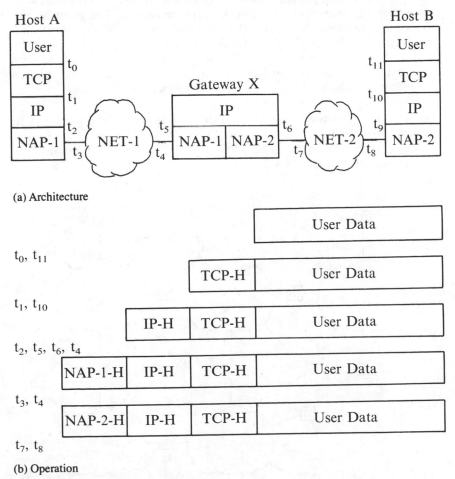

(a) Architecture

(b) Operation

Figure 2.3. Data encapsulation with IP.

(t_4). The gateway strips off the packet header and delivers the resulting datagram to IP (t_5). The remainder of the steps are essentially a mirror image of the first six steps, used for the next hop.

With this example in mind, we describe briefly the sequence of steps involved in sending a datagram between two hosts on different networks. The process starts in the sending host. The station wants to send an IP datagram to a host in another network. The IP module in the host constructs the datagram with a global network address and recognizes that the destination is on another network. So the first step is to send the datagram to a gateway (example: host A to gateway X in Figure 2.3. To do this, the network access protocol module appends to the IP datagram a header appropriate to the network that contains the subnetwork address of the gateway. For example, for an X.25 network, a layer 3 packet encapsulates the IP datagram to be sent to the gateway.

Next, the packet travels through the network to the gateway, which receives it via a network access protocol. The gateway unwraps the packet to recover the original datagram. The gateway analyzes the IP header to determine whether this datagram contains control information intended for the gateway, or data intended for a host farther on. In the latter instance, the gateway must make a routing decision. There are four possibilities:

1. The destination host is attached directly to one of the networks to which the gateway is attached. This is referred to as *directly connected*. For example, in Figure 2.4, all hosts labeled S0 are directly connected to gateway G1.

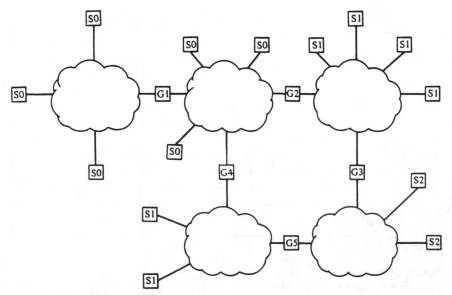

Figure 2.4. Example of internet connectivity.

2. The destination host is on a network that has a gateway that directly connects to this gateway. This is known as a *neighbor gateway*. In Figure 2.4, G2 is a neighbor gateway of G1, and all hosts labeled S1 are one *hop* from G1.
3. To reach the destination host, more than one additional gateway must be traversed. This is known as a *multiple-hop* situation. In Figure 2.4, all stations labeled S2 are in this category.
4. The gateway does not know the destination address.

In case 4, the gateway returns an error message to the source of the datagram. For cases 1 through 3, the gateway must select the appropriate route for the data, and insert them into the appropriate network with the appropriate address. For case 1, the address is the destination station address. For cases 2 and 3, the address is a gateway address. Remember, we are speaking here of a lower layer address (subnetwork attachment point).

Before actually sending data, however, the gateway may need to fragment the datagram to accommodate a smaller maximum packet size limitation on the outgoing network. Each fragment becomes an independent IP datagram. Each new datagram is wrapped in a lower layer packet for transmission. The gateway then queues each packet for transmission. It may also enforce a maximum queue-length size for each network to which it attaches to avoid having a slow network penalize a faster one. Once the queue limit is reached, additional datagrams are simply dropped, or queued for an alternate route.

The process described continues through zero or more gateways until the datagram reaches the destination host. As with a gateway, the destination host recovers the IP datagram from its network wrapping. If fragmentation has occurred, the IP module in the destination host buffers the incoming data until the original data field is reassembled. It then passes this block of data to a higher layer. The higher layer (e.g., TCP) is responsible for the proper sequencing of a stream of datagrams and for end-to-end error and flow control.

Design Issues

With that thumbnail sketch of the operation of an IP-controlled internet, we can now go back and examine some design issues in greater detail:

- Addressing
- Routing
- Datagram lifetime
- Fragmentation and reassembly
- Error control
- Flow control

Addressing. A distinction is generally made among names, addresses, and routes. A name specifies what an object is, an address specifies where it is, and a route indicates how to get there. The distinction between names and addresses can be a useful concept, but it is also an arbitrary one. For a single network, an application program uses a name to identify a referent (process, station); the host translates the name into an address understood by the network; and the network may use a route to reach the referent.

In an internet, the distinction is less clear. Applications continue to use names and individual networks continue to use addresses and, if necessary, routes. To transfer data through a gateway, two entities must be identified: the destination network and the destination host. The gateway requires the address of the network to perform its function. This address can be specified in a number of ways:

- The application can refer to a network by a unique number; in effect, the name and the address are the same.
- The internet logic in the host can translate a network name into a network address.
- A global addressing scheme can be used. That is, there is a unique identifier for each host in the internet. For routing purposes, each gateway would need to derive network addresses from host addresses.

The latter technique has been proposed by the developers of Ethernet [DALA81]. They recommend a 48-bit station address. This is an address space sufficient to accommodate over 10^{14} unique referents, therefore, it is likely to be sufficient for the foreseeable future. The primary advantages of this approach are that it permits stations to move from one network to another and that it allows address recognition at the station to be *hardwired*. The main disadvantages are that some central facility must manage the assignment of names and that unnecessarily long address fields must be carried across multiple networks.

Therefore, typically, a gateway will receive an internet packet with a referent in the form *Net.Host,* where *Net* is a network address. The identifier *Host* is usually both a name and an address. To the higher-layer software in the host that generated the packet, *Host* is an address, translated from an application-level name. However, when it comes time for a gateway to deliver a datagram to a host on an attached network, *Host* must be translated into a subnetwork attachment point address. This is so because different networks will have different address field lengths. Hence, *Host* is treated as a name by the gateway.

The referent *Net.Host* can be considered a two-level hierarchical identifier of a host in the internet. The Ethernet developers (interestingly, the same ones interested in global station addresses) have proposed a third level of addressing to identify, at the internet level, an individual service access point (SAP) at a host [BOGG80, DALA82]. Thus, the internet identifier would be of the form *Net.Host.SAP*. With this identifier, an internet protocol can be viewed as process to process rather than host to host. With *SAP* in the internet layer, the internet protocol is responsible for multiplexing and demultiplexing datagrams for software modules that use the internet service. The advantage of this approach is that the next-higher layer could be simplified, a useful feature for small microprocessor devices. There are some problems in this approach, particularly when local networks are involved, where there is likely to be a proliferation of station types. Perhaps the most significant problem relates to the use of *well-known* ports, which allow ready access to common services. For example, TCP port 23 is the remote login service. Devices not using TCP, but using some other higher-level protocol, would have other well-known ports. If ports were implemented as SAPs at the IP level, the assignment of well-known ports would have to be centralized. For a further discussion, see [CLAR82].

Finally, an important service that must somehow be provided in the internet is a directory service. The station software must be able to determine the *Net.Host* identifier of a desired destination. One or more directory servers are needed, which themselves are well known. Each server would contain part or all of a name/address directory for internet hosts.

Routing. Routing is generally accomplished by maintaining a routing table in each host and gateway that gives, for each possible destination network, the next gateway to which the IP datagram should be sent.

Table 2.2 shows the routing table for the BBN gateway, which is part of the DOD internet. If a network is directly connected, it is so indicated. Otherwise, the datagram must be directed through one or more gateways (one or more hops). The table indicates the identity of the next gateway on the route (which must share a common network with this gateway or host) and the number of hops to the destination.

The routing table may be static or dynamic. A static table, however, could contain alternate routes if a gateway is unavailable. A dynamic table is more flexible in responding both to error and congestion situations. In the DOD internet, for example, when a gateway goes down, all of its neighbors will send out a status report, allowing other gateways and hosts to update their routing tables. A similar scheme can be used to control congestion. This is particularly important because of the mismatch in capacity between local and long-haul networks.

Routing tables may also be used to support other internet services, such as security and priority. For example, individual networks might be classified to handle data up to a given security classification. The routing mechanism must assure that unencrypted data of a given security level is not allowed to pass through networks not cleared to handle such data.

Another routing technique is source routing. The source station

Table 2.2.   INTERNET ROUTING TABLE*

Network Name	Net Address	Route†
SATNET	4	Directly connected
ARPANET	10	Directly connected
BBN-NET	3	1 hop via RCC 10.3.0.72 (ARPANET 3/72)
Purdue-Computer Science	192.5.1	2 hops via Purdue 10.2.0.37 (ARPANET 2/37)
INTELPOST	43	2 hops via Mills 10.3.0.17 (ARPANET 3/17)
DECNET-TEST	38	3 hops via Mills 10.3.0.17 (ARPANET 3/17)
Wideband	28	3 hops via RCC 10.3.0.72 (ARPANET 3/72)
BBN-Packet Radio	1	2 hops via RCC 10.3.0.72 (ARPANET 3/72)
DCN-COMSAT	29	1 hop via Mills 10.3.0.17 (ARPANET 3/17)
FIBERNET	24	3 hops via RCC 10.3.0.72 (ARPANET 3/72)
Bragg-Packet Radio	9	1 hop via Bragg 10.0.0.38 (ARPANET 0/38)
Clark Net	8	2 hops via Mills 10.3.0.17 (ARPANET 3/17)
LCSNET	18	1 hop via MIT LCS 10.0.0.77 (ARPANET 0/77)
BBN-Terminal Concentrator	192.1.2	3 hops via RCC 10.3.0.72 (ARPANET 3/72)
BBN-Jericho	192.1.3	3 hops via RCC 10.3.0.72 (ARPANET 3/72)
UCLNET	11	1 hop via UCL 4.0.0.60 (SATNET 60)
RSRE-NULL	35	1 hop via UCL 4.0.0.60 (SATNET 60)
RSRE-PPSN	25	2 hops via UCL 4.0.0.60 (SATNET 60)
San Francisco-Packet Radio-2	6	1 hop via C3PO 10.1.0.51 (ARPANET 1/51)

*Network table for BBN gateway.
†Names and acronyms identify gateways in the INTERNET system.
Source: [SHEL82].

specifies the route by including a sequential list of gateways in the datagram. This, again, could be useful for security or priority requirements.

Finally, we mention a service related to routing: route recording. To record a route, each gateway appends its address to a list of addresses in the datagram. This feature is useful for testing and debugging purposes.

Datagram Lifetime.   If dynamic or alternate routing is used, the potential exists for a datagram or some of its fragments to loop indefinitely through the internet. This is undesirable for two reasons. First, an endlessly circulating datagram consumes resources. Second, we will see in Chapter 3 that a reliable transport protocol depends on there being an upper bound on datagram lifetime. To avoid these problems, each datagram can be marked with a lifetime. Once the lifetime expires, the datagram is discarded.

A simple way to implement lifetime is to use a hop count. Each time that a datagram passes through a gateway, the count is decremented. Alternatively, the lifetime could be a true measure of time. This requires that the gateways somehow know how long it has been since the datagram or fragment last crossed a gateway, to know by how much to decrement the lifetime field. This would seem to require some global clocking mechanism.

The advantage of using a true time measure is that it can be used in the reassembly algorithm described next. The IP protocol gets the best of both worlds in the following way: The lifetime field in the header is set to some multiple of 1 second. However, each gateway automatically subtracts 1 second, which is the same as treating it as a hop count. It is only during reassembly that the lifetime is interpreted as a unit of time.

Fragmentation and Reassembly.   Individual networks within an internet will generally be diverse and, in particular, specify different maximum (and sometimes minimum) packet sizes. It would be inefficient and unwieldy to try to dictate uniform packet size across networks. Thus, gateways may need to fragment incoming datagrams into smaller pieces before transmitting on to the next network.

If datagrams can be fragmented (perhaps more than once) in the course of their travels, the question arises as to where they should be reassembled. The easiest solution is to have reassembly performed at the destination only. The principal disadvantage of this approach is that packets can only get smaller as data moves through the internet. This may seriously impair the efficiency of some networks. On the other hand, if intermediate gateway reassembly is allowed, the following disadvantages result:

1. Large buffers are required at gateways, and there is the risk that all of the buffer space will be used up storing partial datagrams.

2. All fragments of a datagram must pass through the same gateway. This inhibits the use of dynamic routing.

In IP, fragments are reassembled at the destination host. The IP fragmentation technique requires the following fields in the datagram header:

- ID
- Data length
- Offset
- More flag

The *ID* is some means of uniquely identifying a host-originated datagram. In IP, it consists of the source and destination addresses, an identifier of the protocol layer that generated the data, and a sequence number supplied by that protocol layer. The *Data Length* is the length of the data field in octets, and the *Offset* is the position of a fragment in the original datagram in multiples of 64 bits.

The source host IP layer creates a datagram with Data Length equal to the entire length of the data field, with Offset = 0, and a More Flag set to False. To fragment a long datagram, an IP module in a gateway performs the following tasks:

1. Create two new datagrams and copy the header fields of the incoming datagram into both.
2. Divide the data into two approximately equal portions along a 64-bit boundary, placing one portion in each new datagram. The first portion must be a multiple of 64 bits.
3. Set the Data Length of the first datagram to the length of the inserted data, and set the More Flag to True. The Offset field is unchanged.
4. Set the Data Length of the second datagram to the length of the inserted data, and add the length of the first data portion divided by eight to the Offset field. The More Flag remains the same.

Table 2.3 gives an example. The procedure can be generalized to an *n*-way split.

To reassemble a datagram, there must be sufficient buffer space at the reassembly point. As fragments with the same ID arrive, their data fields are inserted in the proper position in the buffer until the entire datagram is reassembled, which is achieved when a contiguous set of data exists starting with an *Offset* of zero and ending with data from a fragment with a false *More Flag*.

Because IP does not guarantee delivery, one eventuality that must be dealt with is that one or more of the fragments may not get through. Some means is needed to decide to abandon a reassembly effort to free up buffer space. The IP standard recommends that the datagram lifetime

Table 2.3.   FRAGMENTATION EXAMPLE

Original datagram
   Data Length = 472
   Offset   = 0
   More   = 0
First Fragment
   Data Length = 240
   Offset   = 0
   More   = 1
Second fragment
   Data Length = 232
   Offset   = 30
   More   = 0

field in each fragment header be used. When the first fragment of a datagram arrives at a destination host, the host IP module assigns to it a reassembly timer. The timer is set to the minimum of some predefined value and the lifetime field of the incoming fragment. During the reassembly process, this timer runs down. As each new fragment arrives, the timer is set to the minimum of its current value and the lifetime field of the incoming fragment. If the timer expires before all fragments are received, the partially reassembled datagram is discarded.

Finally, as was pointed out in Chapter 1, fragmentation can occur at various levels of the architecture. This is illustrated in Figure 2.5. User data may be handed down to TCP in larger blocks and broken up by TCP into smaller segments. As we have just been discussing, a gateway may fragment an IP datagram to create two or more smaller IP datagrams. In this case, the original IP header is replicated in each new datagram, with some modifications.

An alternative is to perform the fragmentation at the network access level. In this case, an IP datagram is handed down to a lower-level protocol (e.g., X.25). At the lower level, the datagram is broken up into two or more pieces, each of which becomes the data field in a separate network-level packet. Note that the IP header is not replicated but appears only in the first packet. This is because the destination network-level module will reassemble the original datagram before handing up to its IP module. Hence, IP only deals with the full datagram.

When fragmentation is done at the network access level, reassembly occurs at the other end of the network hop, whereas IP-level fragmentation typically results in reassembly only at the destination host. The choice of where to do the fragmentation will depend on performance and resource considerations.

Error Control.   The internetwork facility does not guarantee successful delivery of every datagram. When a datagram is discarded by a gateway,

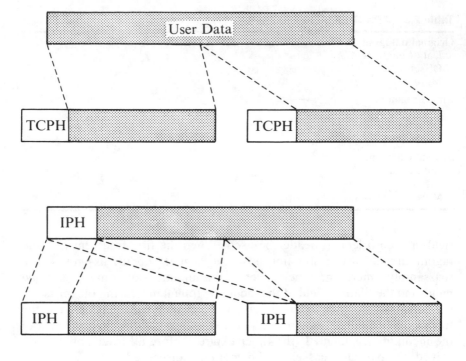

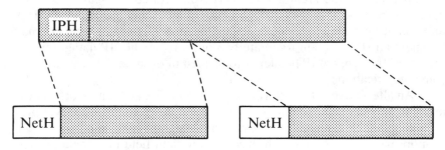

Figure 2.5. Fragmentation possibilities.

the gateway should attempt to return some information to the source, if possible. The source internet protocol entity may use this information to modify its transmission strategy and may notify higher layers. To report that a specific datagram has been discarded, some means of datagram identification is needed.

Datagrams may be discarded for a number of reasons, including lifetime expiration, congestion, and bit error. In the latter case, notification is not possible because the source address field may have been damaged.

Flow Control.   Internet flow control allows gateways or receiving stations, or both, to limit the rate at which they receive data. For the connectionless type of service we are describing, flow control mechanisms are limited. The best approach would seem to be to send flow control packets, requesting reduced data flow, to other gateways and source stations. This can be done using the ICMP protocol, discussed in Section 2.4.

2.3   THE DEPARTMENT OF DEFENSE INTERNETWORK PROTOCOL STANDARD

Having looked at the general operation of IP, we now turn to a description of the standard (MIL-STD-1777). As with any protocol standard, IP is specified in two parts:

- The interface with a higher layer (e.g., TCP), specifying the services that IP provides.
- The actual protocol format and mechanisms, specifying host–gateway and gateway–gateway interaction.

IP Services

The IP protocol, as is the case with most protocol standards, is precisely defined. The definition includes the format of the protocol data units (datagrams in the case of IP) exchanged between entities, the semantics of each field in each data unit, and the allowable sequencing of protocol actions.

The service provided by a layer is much less explicitly defined. The reason for this is that, generally, adjacent layers in the same system reside on the same operating system and are implemented by the same vendor. The standards must leave the implementor free to implement adjacent layers and the interface between those layers in the most efficient manner possible. As the interaction between layers takes place within a single system, a precise and explicit standard is not needed. Accordingly, the service specification is presented in functional terms only.

The services to be provided across an interface between adjacent layers are expressed in terms of primitives and parameters. A primitive specifies the function to be performed, and the parameters are used to pass data and control information. The actual form of a primitive is implementation dependent. An example is a subroutine call.

Two primitives are used to define the IP service. These are listed in Table 2.4, and their use is illustrated in Figure 2.6. In this example, host A is sending data to host B through a single gateway and two subnetworks. The sending IP user (usually TCP) makes use of the SEND prim-

Table 2.4.   IP SERVICE PRIMITIVES AND PARAMETERS

SEND (source address, destination address, protocol, type of service indicators,
   identifier, don't fragment indicator, time to live, data length, option data,
   data)

DELIVER (source address, destination address, protocol, type of service
   indicators, data length, option data, data)

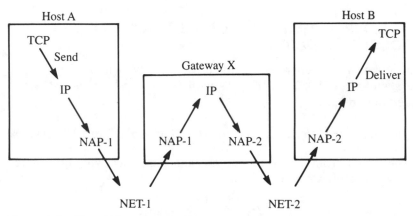

Figure 2.6.   Use of IP service primitives.

itive to request that IP construct a datagram to send data across the internet to the intended destination. The IP protocol entities in the two
hosts and in the gateway cooperate to deliver the datagram to the IP entity
in host *B,* which provides the data, plus control information associated
with the data, to the IP user in host *B* via the DELIVER primitive.

   The parameters associated with the two primitives are:

- *Source address:* The global network address of the sending host.
  This address appears in the SEND primitive, even though the IP
  entity presumably knows its own address. If a host has more than
  one address, this allows the IP user to select the source address to
  be used in the DELIVER primitive.
- *Destination address:* The global network address of the recipient
  host.
- *Protocol:* Specifies the recipient protocol entity (an IP user). This
  will usually be TCP, but, as mentioned earlier, other protocols may
  directly access IP services. Hence, this indicator is needed so that
  the destination IP entity can deliver the data to the appropriate IP
  user.
- *Type of service indicators:* Used to specify the treatment of the data
  unit in its transmission through component networks.
- *Identifier:* Value optionally provided by the sending IP user, distin-

guishing this portion of data from others sent by this user. The identifier, along with the source and destination addresses and the user protocol, identify the data unit uniquely. This parameter is needed for reassembly and error reporting.

- *Don't fragment indicator:* At the IP level, segmentation is referred to as fragmentation. This indicates whether IP can fragment data to accomplish delivery. This can be used if it is known that the receiving host does not wish to reassemble internet fragments.
- *Time to live:* Indicates the maximum lifetime of data within the internet, measured in one-second increments.
- *Data length:* Length of data being transmitted.
- *Option data:* Options requested by the user. Discussed below.
- *Data:* User data to be transmitted.

Note that the following parameters are present in the SEND primitive but not in the DELIVER primitive: identifier, don't fragment indicator, and time to live. These parameters provide instructions to IP that are not the concern of the recipient IP user.

The type of service parameter is used by the sending IP user to request a particular quality of service. Table 2.5 list the options that may be specified. If selected, this parameter is passed down to the network access protocol and mapped into subnetwork-specific transmission parameters. On each subsequent hop, the gateway starting the hop will also pass this parameter down for use across the next network hop. Not every subnetwork supports all transmission services, but each network access protocol on the delivery path should make its best effort to match the available subnetwork services to the desired service quality. It is to be expected that the use of these options may increase the cost (in some sense) of the service.

In addition to the service quality options, there are a number of options that may be specified by the sending user. These are specified in the

Table 2.5. IP SERVICE QUALITY OPTIONS

Precedence	A measure of a datagram's relative importance. Eight levels of precedence are used. IP will attempt to provide preferential treatment for higher importance datagrams.
Reliability	A measure of the level of effort desired to ensure delivery of this datagram. One of two levels (normal, high) may be specified.
Delay	A measure of the importance of prompt delivery of this datagram, from the point of view of delay. One of two levels (normal, low) may be specified.
Throughput	A measure of the importance of prompt delivery of this datagram, from the point of view of throughput. One of two levels (normal, high) may be specified.

option data parameter, and are listed in Table 2.6. The options are handled as follows:

- *Security labeling:* If the option is selected in the SEND primitive, then the security label is provided in the DELIVER primitive.
- *Source routing:* Routing may be strict (only identified gateways may be visited) or loose (other intermediate gateways may be visited). In either case, the list of specified gateways is included in the DELIVER primitive.
- *Route recording:* If this option is specified in the SEND primitive, then the DELIVER primitive will contain a list of the gateways visited.
- *Stream identification:* The stream identifier specified in the SEND primitive is provided in the DELIVER primitive.
- *Timestamping:* The sending user may request one of three options: (1) each gateway visited records the time it received the datagram; (2) each gateway visited records both the time and its internet address; or (3) the sender prespecifies gateway addresses and only those listed record the time. In any case the list of timestamps and addresses, if present, is provided in the DELIVER primitive.

The motivation for some of these options has already been discussed. The security option might be used by gateways in making routing decisions. The timestamp option could be used by a network manager to monitor the performance of various components of the internet.

Table 2.6.   IP SERVICE OPTIONS

Security Labeling	Used by hosts needing to transmit security information throughout the internet in a standard manner.
Source Routing	Host may specify loose or strict source routing, by selecting a set of gateways to be visited in transit.
Route Recording	Records gateways encountered in transit.
Stream Identification	Names reserved resources used for stream service. Provides a way for a stream identifier to be carried both through stream-oriented subnetworks and subnetworks not supporting the stream concept. A stream identifier indicates that there will be other datagrams from this source to this destination at regular frequent intervals. IP attempts to minimize delay and delay variability through reservation of network resources.
Timestamping	Allows timing information to be gathered as a datagram travels through the internet to its destination.

IP Protocol

The IP protocol is best explained with reference to the IP datagram format, shown in Figure 2.7. We begin with a description of the elements of the format, followed by a discussion of the IP operation on the datagram.

Datagram Format.   The fields in the IP datagram are:

- *Version (4 bits):* Version number, included to allow evolution of the protocol. Either header format or semantics might change.
- *Internet header length (IHL) (4 bits):* Length of header in 32-bit words. The minimum value is five. Thus, a header is at least 20 octets long.
- *Type of service (8 bits):* Specifies reliability, precedence, delay, and throughput parameters.
- *Total length (16 bits):* Total datagram length, including header, in octets.
- *Identification (16 bits):* Together with source address, destination address, and user protocol, intended to uniquely identify a datagram. Thus, the identification must be unique for the datagram's source, destination, and user protocol for the time during which the datagram will remain in the internet.
- *Flags (3 bits):* One bit, the More flag, used for fragmentation and reassembly. Another bit, if set, prohibits fragmentation. This facility may be useful if it is known that the destination does not have the capability to reassemble fragments. An example is to down-line load a small microprocessor. If this bit is set, however, the datagram may be discarded if it exceeds the maximum size of an en route network. When the bit is set, it may be advisable to use source routing to avoid networks with small maximum packet sizes. The third bit is currently not used.

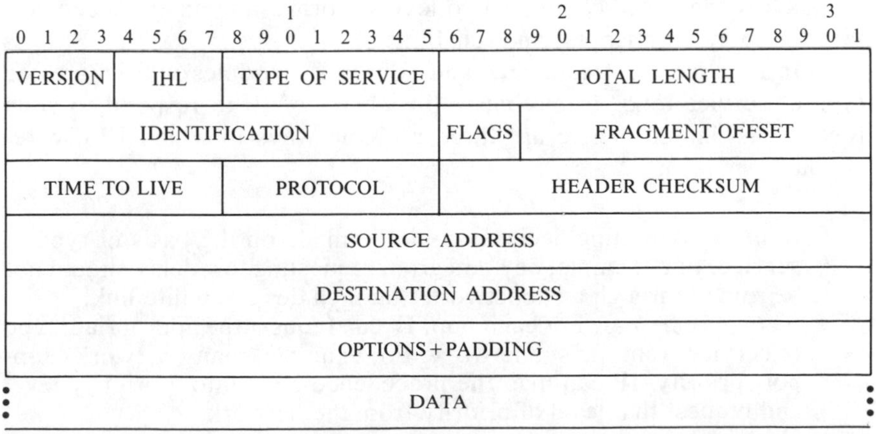

VERSION	IHL	TYPE OF SERVICE	TOTAL LENGTH	
IDENTIFICATION			FLAGS	FRAGMENT OFFSET
TIME TO LIVE		PROTOCOL	HEADER CHECKSUM	
SOURCE ADDRESS				
DESTINATION ADDRESS				
OPTIONS + PADDING				
DATA				

Figure 2.7.   Internet protocol format.

- *Fragment offset (13 bits):* Indicates where in the datagram this fragment belongs. It is measured in 64-bit units. This implies that fragments (other than the last fragment) must contain a data field that is a multiple of 64 bits long.
- *Time to live (8 bits):* Measured in 1-second increments.
- *Protocol (8 bits):* Indicates the next level protocol that is to receive the data field at the destination.
- *Header checksum (16 bits):* Explained later.
- *Source address (32 bits):* Coded to allow a variable allocation of bits to specify the network and the station within the specified network (7 and 24, 14 and 16, or 21 and 8).
- *Destination address (32 bits):* As for source address.
- *Options (variable):* Encodes the options requested by the sender.
- *Padding (variable):* Used to ensure that the internet header ends on a 32-bit boundary.
- *Data (variable):* The data field must be a multiple of eight bits in length. Total length of data field plus header is a maximum of 65,535 octets.

It should be easy to see how the services specified above map into the fields of the IP data units.

Several of the fields listed warrant elaboration. The *type of service* field allows the user to provide guidance to its own IP module and to en route gateways. Figure 2.8a shows the encoding of this field. The precedence indicator ranges from the lowest level of *Routine* to the highest level of *Network Control*. The *Network Control* level is intended for use only within a subnetwork. For example, if a subnetwork management entity needs to send control information to a host attached to the same network, this precedence level could be used. The *Internetwork Control* level is intended for use by gateway control originators only. This might be used by gateways exchanging routing information. The remaining parameters allow the specification of two levels: normal and an enhanced service for delay, throughput, and reliability.

In practice most gateways and source IP modules will ignore the type of service field. In any case, the ability of IP to respond to such requests is limited. There are three possible ways in which IP can respond:

- *Routing:* A routing decision could be made on the basis of type of service. For example, any datagram requesting low delay should not be routed through a subnetwork that includes a satellite link.
- *Network services:* For each hop, IP can request the appropriate type of service from the subnetwork. For example, many networks support priority. IP can map the precedence code into a priority level and request that level of priority from the network.
- *Queuing discipline:* If a gateway has a number of datagrams queued to transmit over a particular network, it can transmit them according to precedence.

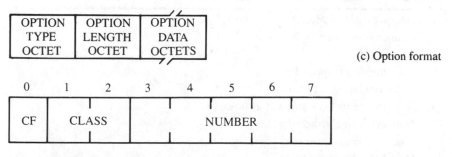

0	1	2	3	4	5	6	7
PRECEDENCE			D	T	R	O	O

Bits 0-2:   Precedence
Bit   3:   Delay
Bits   4:   Throughput
Bits   5:   Reliability
Bit   6-7:   Reserved for Future Use

Precedence
  111-Network Control
  110-Internetwork Control
  101-CRITIC/ECP
  100-Flash Override
  011-Flash
  010-Immediate
  001-Priority
  000-Routine

Delay
  0-normal
  1-low
Throughput
  0-normal
  1-high

Reliability
  0-normal
  1-high

(a) Type of service field

0	1	2
0	D F	M F

Bit 0: reserved, must be zero
Bit 1: (DF) 0 = May Fragment, 1 = Don't Fragment.
Bit 2: (MF) 0 = Last Fragment, 1 = More Fragments.

(b) Control flags field

OPTION TYPE OCTET	OPTION LENGTH OCTET	OPTION DATA OCTETS

(c) Option format

0	1	2	3	4	5	6	7
CF	CLASS		NUMBER				

bit 0 - copy flag
     0 = not copied, 1 = copied
bits 1-2 - option class
     000 = control
     001 = reserved for future use
     010 = debugging and measurement
     011 = reserved for future use
bits 3-7 - option number (defined in the following table)

**(d) Fields in the
option-type octet**

Figure 2.8.   Formats of some IP fields.

The *protocol* field indicates to which IP-user this data is to be delivered. Although TCP is the most common user of IP, other protocols can access IP. For common protocols that use IP, specific protocol numbers have been assigned and should be used. Table 2.7 lists these assignments. Any other protocol number depends on mutual agreements between the correspondents.

The *header checksum* field is used to perform error detection. The general process of error detection is discussed in Appendix B. For each hop, the sending IP entity performs a calculation on the bits in the IP header, excluding the header checksum field, and places the result in the header checksum field. The IP entity at the other end of the hop performs the same calculation and compares the result with the value in the header checksum field. If there is a discrepancy, then an error has occurred (one or more bits have been altered in transit), and the IP entity discards the datagram. The calculation is a simple *one's-complement addition,* described in Appendix B. Note that a new checksum must be calculated at each gateway for retransmission of the datagram, because some header fields may change (e.g., time to live, fragmentation-related fields).

The *source address* and *destination address* fields each contain a 32-bit global network address (see Figure 1.2), consisting of a network identifier and a host identifier. The address is coded to allow a variable allocation of bits to specify network and host, as depicted in Figure 2.9. This encoding provides flexibility in assigning addresses to hosts and al-

Table 2.7.   ASSIGNED PROTOCOL NUMBERS

1	Internet Control Message Protocol
3	Gateway-to-Gateway Protocol
5	Stream
6	Transmission Control Protocol
8	Exterior Gateway Protocol
9	Any private interior gateway protocol
11	Network Voice Protocol
17	User Datagram Protocol
20	Host Monitoring Protocol
22	Xerox Network System Internet Datagram Protocol
27	Reliable Datagram Protocol
28	Internet Reliable Transaction Protocol
29	ISO Class 4 Transport Protocol
30	Bulk Data Transfer Protocol
61	Any host internet protocol

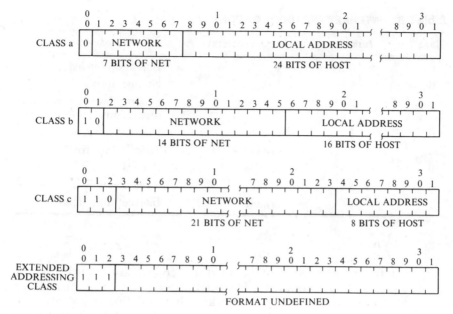

Figure 2.9. IP address formats.

lows a mix of network sizes on the internet. In particular, the three network classes are best suited to the following conditions:

- *Class A:* Few networks, each with many hosts.
- *Class B:* Medium number of networks, each with a medium number of hosts.
- *Class C:* Many networks, each with a few hosts.

In a particular environment, it may be best to use addresses all from one class. For example, a corporate internetwork that consists of a large number of departmental local area networks may need to use Class C addresses exclusively. However, because of the format of the addresses, it is possible to mix all three classes of addresses on the same internet; this is what is done in the case of the DOD internet. A mixture of classes is appropriate for an internet that consists of a few large networks, many small networks, plus some medium-sized networks.

The *options* field has a variable length, depending on the number and type of options associated with the datagram. The field consists of a sequence of options, each of which is encoded as depicted in Figure 2.8c and d; Table 2.8 indicates the coding used. Each option begins with an option-type octet, which consists of three subfields:

- *Copy flag:* Indicates whether this option is to be copied into all fragments on fragmentation. If not, it only appears in the header of the

Table 2.8.   INTERNET PROTOCOL OPTIONS

Class	Number	Length (octets)	Description
0	0	1	End of option list
0	1	1	No operation
0	2	11	Security level and handling restrictions
0	3	variable	Loose source routing
0	9	variable	Strict source routing
0	7	variable	Record route
0	8	4	Stream identifier
2	4	variable	Internet timestamp

first fragment. Options that must be copied are security, strict source routing, and stream identifier. Loose source routing, route recording, and timestamping appear only in the first fragment.
- *Option class:* The timestamp option is considered a debugging option; the others are control options.
- *Option number:* Identifies the specific option.

Figure 2.10 shows the format for specifying the security option. The security field specifies the classification level of the data (e.g., unclassified, confidential, secret, top secret). The compartments field is set if the data is compartmented. The handling restrictions field contains values for control and release markings. The transmission control code provides a means to segregate traffic and define controlled communities of interest among subscribers.

Operation on Datagrams.   Based on the previous description, we can summarize the steps taken by each IP module. To begin, the IP entity in the sending host receives a SEND primitive from an IP user, and performs the following steps:

1. Constructs an IP datagram based on the parameters accompanying the SEND primitive (see Table 2.4).
2. Performs a checksum calculation and adds the result to the datagram header.
3. Makes a routing decision. Either the destination host is attached to the same network or a gateway must be selected for the first hop.
4. Passes the IP datagram down to the network access protocol for transmission over the network.

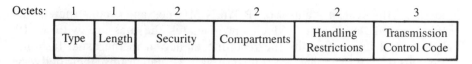

Figure 2.10.   Security option format.

For each datagram that passes through a gateway, the gateway performs the following functions:

1. Performs a checksum calculation. If there is no match, then discards the datagram.
2. Decrements the time-to-live parameter. If the time has expired, discards the datagram.
3. Makes a routing decision.
4. Fragments the datagram, if necessary.
5. Rebuilds the IP header, including new time-to-live, fragmentation, and checksum fields.
6. Passes the IP datagram or datagrams down to the network access protocol for transmission over the network.

Finally, when a datagram is received by the IP entity in the destination host, the following functions are peformed:

1. Performs a checksum calculation. If there is no match, then discards the datagram.
2. If this is a fragment, buffers until the complete datagram is reassembled.
3. Passes data and parameters from the header to the user in a DELIVER primitive.

2.4   INTERNET CONTROL MESSAGE PROTOCOL

The internet control message protocol (ICMP), defined in RFC 792 [POST81b], is an integral part of the DOD protocol suite. Although it is not a formal military standard, it is a required companion to IP. That is, all systems that implement IP must also provide ICMP. ICMP provides a means for transferring messages from gateways and other hosts to a host. In essence, it provides feedback about problems in the communication environment. Examples of its use are: when a datagram cannot reach its destination, when a gateway does not have the buffering capacity to forward a datagram, and when a gateway can direct the host to send traffic on a shorter route. In most cases, an ICMP message is sent in response to a datagram, either by a gateway en route or by the intended destination host.

ICMP is considered to be at the internet level of the protocol architecture. However, it is a user of IP. An ICMP message is constructed and then passed down to IP, which encapsulates the message with an IP header and then transmits the resulting datagram in the usual fashion. Because ICMP messages are transmitted in IP datagrams, their delivery is not guaranteed and their use can not be considered reliable.

Figure 2.11 shows the general format of ICMP messages. The fields are:

- *Type (8 bits):* Identifies the particular ICMP message.
- *Code (8 bits):* Used to specify parameters of the message that can be encoded in a few bits.
- *Checksum (16 bits):* Checksum of the entire ICMP message. This is the same checksum used for IP, and is described in Appendix B.
- *Parameters (32 bits):* Used to specify more lengthy parameters.
- *Information (variables):* Provides additional information related to the message.

In those cases in which the ICMP message refers to a prior datagram, the information field includes the entire IP header plus the first 64 bits of the data field of the original datagram. This enables the source host to match the incoming ICMP message with the prior datagram. The reason for including the first 64 bits of the data field is to enable the IP module in the host to determine which upper-level protocols were involved. In particular, the first 64 bits would include the TCP header or other transport-level header (see Figure 1.3).

Thirteen types of messages have been defined:

- Destination unreachable
- Time exceeded
- Parameter problem
- Source quench
- Redirect
- Echo
- Echo reply
- Timestamp
- Timestamp reply

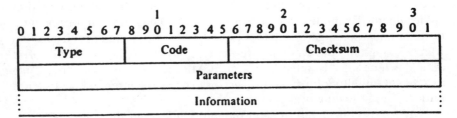

Figure 2.11. ICMP format.

- Information request
- Information reply
- Address request
- Address reply

Figure 2.12 shows the specific formats of these messages, and Table 2.9 lists the type number and codes of each message.

The *destination unreachable* message covers a number of contingencies. A gateway may return this message if it does not know how to reach the destination network. In some networks, an attached gateway may be able to determine if a particular host is unreachable and return the message. The destination host itself may return this message if the user protocol or a port is unreachable. This could happen if the corresponding field in the IP header was set incorrectly. If the datagram specifies a source route that is unusable, a message is returned. Finally, if a gateway must fragment a datagram but the *Don't Fragment* flag is set, a message is returned. The message includes the entire IP header plus the first 64 bits of the original datagram in the information field.

A gateway will return a *time exceeded* message if the lifetime of the datagram expires. A host will send this message if it cannot complete reassembly within a time limit.

A syntactic or semantic error in an IP header will cause a *parameter problem* message to be returned by a gateway or host. For example, an incorrect argument may be provided with an option. The parameter field contains a pointer to the octet in the original header where the error was detected.

The *source quench* message provides a rudimentary form of flow control. Either a gateway or a destination host may send this message to a source host, requesting that it reduce the rate at which it is sending traffic to the internet destination. On receipt of a source quench message, the source host should cut back the rate at which it is sending traffic to the specified destination until it no longer receives source quench messages. The source quench message can be used by a gateway or host which must discard datagrams because of a full buffer. In that case, the gateway or host will issue a source quench message for every datagram that it discards. In addition, a system may anticipate congestion and issue source quench messages when its buffers approach capacity. In that case, the datagram referred to in the source quench message may well be delivered. Therefore, receipt of a source quench message does not imply delivery or nondelivery of the corresponding datagram.

A gateway sends a *redirect* message to a host on a directly connected gateway to advise the host of a better route to a particular destination. The following is an example of its use. A gateway, *G1*, receives a datagram from a host on a network to which the gateway is attached. The gateway, *G1*, checks its routing table and obtains the address for the next

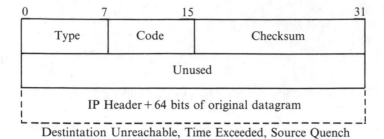

Destintation Unreachable, Time Exceeded, Source Quench

Parameter Problem

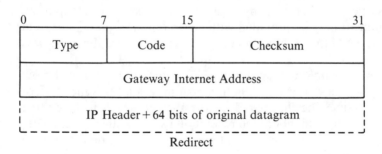

Redirect

Echo, Echo Reply

Figure 2.12.   ICMP formats.

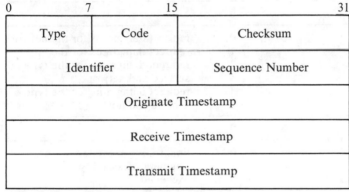

```
0            7          15                      31
┌──────────┬──────────┬────────────────────────┐
│   Type   │   Code   │        Checksum         │
├──────────┴──────────┼────────────────────────┤
│     Identifier      │    Sequence Number      │
├─────────────────────┴────────────────────────┤
│            Originate Timestamp                │
└───────────────────────────────────────────────┘
```

Timestamp

```
0            7          15                      31
┌──────────┬──────────┬────────────────────────┐
│   Type   │   Code   │        Checksum         │
├──────────┴──────────┼────────────────────────┤
│     Identifier      │    Sequence Number      │
├─────────────────────┴────────────────────────┤
│            Originate Timestamp                │
├───────────────────────────────────────────────┤
│            Receive Timestamp                  │
├───────────────────────────────────────────────┤
│            Transmit Timestamp                 │
└───────────────────────────────────────────────┘
```

Timestamp Reply

```
0            7          15                      31
┌──────────┬──────────┬────────────────────────┐
│   Type   │   Code   │        Checksum         │
├──────────┴──────────┼────────────────────────┤
│     Identifier      │    Sequence Number      │
└─────────────────────┴────────────────────────┘
```

Information Request, Information Reply, Address Mask Request

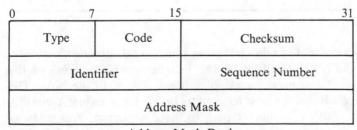

```
0            7          15                      31
┌──────────┬──────────┬────────────────────────┐
│   Type   │   Code   │        Checksum         │
├──────────┴──────────┼────────────────────────┤
│     Identifier      │    Sequence Number      │
├─────────────────────┴────────────────────────┤
│               Address Mask                    │
└───────────────────────────────────────────────┘
```

Address Mask Reply

Figure 2.12. ICMP formats (continued).

Table 2.9. ICMP MESSAGE TYPES

Name	Type	Code	Code Interpretation
Echo Reply	0	0	
Destination Unreachable	3	0	network unreachable
		1	host unreachable
		2	protocol unreachable
		3	port unreachable
		4	fragmentation needed and don't-fragment flag set
		5	source route failed
Source Quench	4	0	
Redirect	5	0	redirect datagrams for the network
		1	redirect datagrams for the host
		2	redirect datagrams for the type of service and network
		3	redirect datagrams for the type of service and host
Echo	8	0	
Time Exceeded	11	0	time to live exceeded in transit
		1	fragment reassembly time exceeded
Parameter Problem	12	0	pointer indicates the error
Timestamp	13	0	
Timestamp Reply	14	0	
Information Request	15	0	
Information Reply	16	0	
Address Mask Request	17	0	
Address Mask Reply	18	0	

gateway, *G2*, on the route to the datagram's internet destination network, *X*. If *G2* and the host identified by the internet source address of the datagram are on the same network, a redirect is sent to the host. The redirect message advises the host to send its traffic for network *X* directly to gateway *G2* as this is a shorter path to the destination. The gateway forwards the original datagram to its internet destination (via *G2*). The address of *G2* is contained in the parameter field of the redirect message. In the case of this example, the code associated with the message is 0, meaning that datagrams for any host on the destination network should be redirected to the named gateway (*G2*). Code 1 indicates that only datagrams for the specific destination host should be redirected. Code 2 indicates that only those datagrams for the same destination network as the original destination network with the same type of service should be redirected. Finally, code 3 limits the redirect advice to the same direction host with the same type of serivce.

The *echo* and *echo reply* messages provide a mechanism for testing that communication is possible between entities. The recipient of an echo message is obligated to return the message in an echo reply message. An identifier and sequence number are associated with the echo message to be matched in the echo reply message. The identifier might be used like a port to identify a particular session and the sequence number might be incremented on each echo request sent.

The *timestamp* and *timestamp reply* message provide a mechanism for sampling the delay characteristics of the internet. The sender of a timestamp message may include an identifier and sequence number in the parameters field and include the time that the message is sent (originate timestamp). The receiver records the time it received the message and the time that it transmits the reply message in the timestamp reply message. If the timestamp message is sent using strict source routing, then the delay characteristics of a particular route can be measured.

The *information request* and *information reply* messages can be used by a host to discover the address of the network to which it is attached, in the following way. The host sends an information request message with the network portion of the source address field of the IP header set to 0. The use of 0 is interpreted as "this network." The replying IP module should send the reply with the addresses fully specified.

The *address mask request* and *address mask reply* messages are useful in an environment that includes what are referred to as *subnets*. The concept of subnet was introduced to address the following requirement. Consider an internet which includes one or more wide-area networks and a number of sites, each of which has a number of local area networks (LANs). We would like to allow arbitrary complexity of interconnected LAN structures within an organization, while insulating the overall internet against explosive growth in network numbers and routing complexity. One approach to this problem is to assign a single network number to all of the LANs at a site. From the point of view of the rest of the internet, there is a single network at that site, which provides for simple addressing and routing. To allow the gateways within the site to function properly, each LAN is assigned a subnet number. The host portion of the internet address is partitioned into a subnet number and a host number to accommodate this new level of addressing.

Within the subnetted network, the local gateways must route on the basis of an extended network number consisting of the network number and the subnet number. The bit positions containing this extended network number are indicated by the address mask. The address mask request and address mask reply messages allow a host to learn the address mask for the LAN to which it connects. The host broadcasts an address mask request message on the LAN. The gateway on the LAN responds with an address mask reply that contains the address mask. The use of the address mask allows the host to determine whether an outgoing datagram is destined for a host on the same LAN (send directly) of another LAN (send datagram to gateway). It is assumed that some other means (e.g., manual configuration) is used to create address masks to make them known to the local gateways.

2.5   ADDRESS RESOLUTION

Address Resolution Protocol

In section 1.3, we discussed the distinction between internet address and subnetwork addresses (Figure 1.2). Clearly, to deliver a datagram to a destination host, a mapping must be made from the internet address to the subnetwork address for that last hop. The internet protocol deals only with the internet address. If a datagram traverses one or more gateways between source and destination hosts, then the mapping must be done in the final gateway, which is attached to the same network as the destination host. If the datagram is being transmitted from one host to another host on the same network, then the source host must do the mapping. In the following discussion, we will use the term *system* to refer to the entity responsible for the mapping.

The question arises as to how the mapping to subnetwork address can be accomplished. A number of approaches are possible:

- The system can maintain a local table of internet and subnetwork addresses for possible correspondents. This approach is rather rigid and does not accommodate easy and automatic additions of new hosts to a network.
- The subnetwork addresses can be a subnet of the network address. As we have seen, the typical internet address includes a host address field (Figure 2.8). However, the entire internet address is 32 bits long and for some networks the host address field is longer. For example, Ethernet addresses are 48 bits long.
- A centralized directory can be maintained on each network which contains the internet-subnetwork address mappings. This is actually a rather good solution and much research is being done in this area.
- The address resolution protocol. This is a simpler approach than the centralized-directory approach and is well-suited to local area networks.

The *address resolution protocol* (ARP) [ARP82] provides a method for systems on a local area network (LAN) to discover the subnetwork address of hosts on the LAN for which the internet address is known. Although the protocol was designed with Ethernet in mind, it will work with any LAN. It exploits the broadcast property of a LAN: namely, that a transmission from any device on the network is received by all other devices on the network.

The ARP works as follows:

1. Each system on a LAN maintains a table of known internet-subnetwork address mappings.
2. When a subnet address is needed, ARP is used directly on top of the LAN protocol (e.g., Ethernet, IEEE 802) to broadcast a request. The broadcast message contains the internet address in question.
3. Other hosts on the network listen for ARP messages and reply when a match occurs. The reply includes both the internet and subnetwork address of the target host.
4. The request includes the requesting host's internet address and subnetwork address. Any interested host can copy this information into a local directory, avoiding the need for a later ARP message.
5. The ARP message can also be used simply to broadcast a host's internet and subnetwork address, for the benefit of others on the network. This would be done when a host first attaches to the network.

Figure 2.13 shows the format of the ARP message. The fields are as follows:

- *Network type:* Indicates which network (e.g., Ethernet).
- *Protocol type:* The protocol that needs the address resolution. This indicates the form of internet address needed to the target machine.

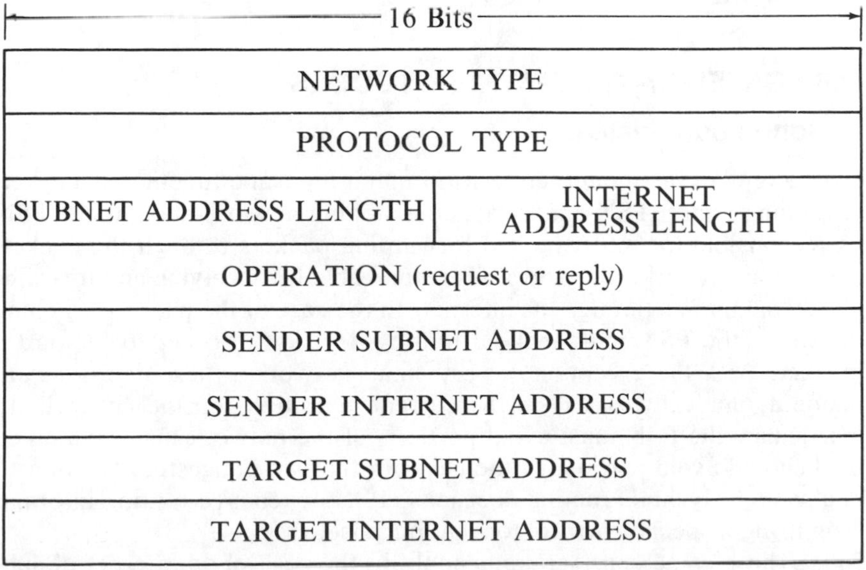

←——————— 16 Bits ———————→	
NETWORK TYPE	
PROTOCOL TYPE	
SUBNET ADDRESS LENGTH	INTERNET ADDRESS LENGTH
OPERATION (request or reply)	
SENDER SUBNET ADDRESS	
SENDER INTERNET ADDRESS	
TARGET SUBNET ADDRESS	
TARGET INTERNET ADDRESS	

Figure 2.13.   ARP format.

- *Subnet address length:* Length in octets of each subnet address. For Ethernet, this value is 6.
- *Internet address length:* Length in octets of each internet address length. For IP, this is 4. However, ARP could be used with other protocols, such as the ISO internet protocol.
- *Operation:* Specifies request or reply.
- *Sender subnet address:* Provided by requestor and repeated in the reply message.
- *Sender internet address:* Provided by requestor and repeated in the reply message.
- *Target subnet address:* Provided in the reply message.
- *Target internet address:* Provided by requestor and repeated in the reply message.

Reverse Address Resolution Protocol

The opposite of the problem addressed by ARP is the situation in which subnetwork address is known but not the internet address. An example of this situation is a diskless workstation. When the workstation is booted up, it may know its subnetwork address if this is in effect a hardware address, but it will not know its internet address. If there is a *server* on the LAN which maintains such informaiton, then the host can learn its internet address by sending a *request reverse* message. This message has the format of Figure 2.13, with the code in the operation field indicating request reverse. The server, upon receipt of this message, replies with a request reply message, which fills in the missing internet address. The protocol for this operation is known as the reverse address resolution protocol (RARP) [FINL84].

2.6   GATEWAY–GATEWAY PROTOCOLS

Autonomous Systems

The gateways in an internet perform much the same function as packet-switching nodes (PSNs) in a packet-switching network. Just as the PSN is responsible for receiving and forwarding packets through the packet-switching network, the gateway is responsible for receiving and forwarding IP datagrams through the internet. In the case of the packet-switching network, the PSN must make a routing decision in order to forward a packet. With the exception of very small networks, these decisions are made dynamically, based on the current conditions on the network. In particular, the PSN must avoid portions of the network that have failed and should avoid portions of the network that are congested. In order to make such dynamic routing decisions, PSNs exchange routing information using a special protocol for that purpose.

These same considerations apply in the case of an internet of subnetworks connected by gateways. In order for the gateways to function effectively, they need to have information about the status of the internet, in terms of which networks can be reached by which routes, and the delay characteristics of various routes.

In considering the routing function of gateways, it is important to distinguish two concepts:

- *Routing information:* Information about the topology and delays of the internet.
- *Routing algorithm:* The algorithm used to make a routing decision for a particular datagram, based on current routing information.

A gateway–gateway protocol can be used for the purpose of exchanging routing information. In general, however, such protocols do not assume or dictate a particular routing algorithm. A general-purpose protocol will provide sufficient information to support a variety of routing algorithms.

In order to proceed in our discussion of gateway-gateway protocols, we need to introduce the concept of an *autonomous system*. An autonomous system is an internet connected by homogenous gateways; generally the gateways are under the administrative control of a single entity. An *interior gateway protocol* (IGP) passes routing information between gateways within an autonomous system. The protocol used within the autonomous system does not need to be implemented outside of the system. This flexibility allows IGPs to be custom-tailored to specific applications and requirements.

It may happen, however, that an internet will be constructed of more than one autonomous system. For example, all of the local area networks at a site, such as a military base or campus, could be linked by gateways to form an autonomous system. This system might be linked through a wide-area network, such as the DDN, to other aotonomous systems. The situation is illustrated in Figure 2.14. In this case, the routing algorithms and routing tables used by gateways in different autonomous systems may differ. Nevertheless, the gateways in one autonomous system need at least a minimal level of information concerning networks outside the system that can be reached. The protocol used to pass routing information between gateways in different autonomous systems is referred to as an *exterior gateway protocol* (EGP).

We can expect that an EGP will need to pass less information and be simpler than an IGP, for the following reason. If a datagram is to be transferred from a host in one autonomous system to a host in another autonomous system, a gateway in the first system need only determine the target autonomous system and devise a route to get into that target system. Once the datagram enters the target autonomous system, the gateways within that system can cooperate to finally deliver the data-

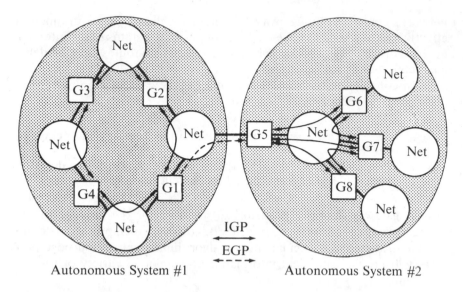

Figure 2.14. Application of EGP and IGP.

gram. For this reason, more progress has been made in standardizing on an EGP that on an IGP. In the remainder of this section, we look at the most widely used EGP, RFC 904 [MILL84].

Exterior Gateway Protocol

Functions. The EGP was designed to allow gateways in different autonomous systems to cooperate in the exchange of routing information. The protocol operates in terms of commands and responses, which are sent inside IP datagrams. The repertoire of commands and responses is summarized in Table 2.10.

Three functional procedures are involved in EGP:

- Neighbor acquisition
- Neighbor reachability
- Network reachability

Two gateways are considered to be neighbors if they share the same subnetwork. If the two gateways are in different autonomous systems, they may wish to exchange routing information. For this purpose, it is necessary to first perform *neighbor acquisition*. In essence, neighbor acquisition occurs when two neighboring gateways in different autonomous systems agree to regularly exchange routing information. A formal acquisition prodecure is needed since one of the gateways may not wish to participate. For example, the gateway may be overburdened and does not want to be responsible for traffic coming in from outside the system. In

Table 2.10. EGP COMMANDS AND RESPONSES

	Command		Corresponding response	
Name	**Interpretation**		**Name**	**Interpretation**
Request	Request gateway become a neighbor		Confirm	Confirm neighbor relationship
			Refuse	Refuse neighbor relationship
Cease	Request termination of neighbor relationship		Cease-ack	Confirm termination
Hello	Request neighbor confirm neighbor reachability		I-H-U	Confirm reachability
Poll	Request neighbor provide network reachability information		Update	Provide network reachability update
			Error	Error

the neighbor acquisition process, one gateway sends a request message to the other, which may either accept or refuse the offer. The protocol does not address the issue of how one gateway knows the address or even the existence of another gateway, nor how it decides that it needs to exchange routing information with that particular gateway. These issues must be dealt with at configuration time or by active intervention of a network manager.

To perform neighbor acquisition, one gateway sends a *Request* command to another. If the target gateway accepts the request, it returns a *Confirm* response. Otherwise, it returns a *Refuse* response. After a neighbor relationship has been established, either side may terminate the relationship with a *Cease* message, for which the appropriate response is a *Cease-ack* message.

Once a neighbor relationship is established, the *neighbor reachability* procedure is used to maintain the relationship. Each partner needs to be assured that the other partner still exists and is still engaged in the neighbor relationship. For this purpose, the two gateways periodically exchange *Hello* and *I-H-U* (I heard you) messages. Either gateway may issue a Hello command and the partner gateway is obligated to reply as soon as possible with an I-H-U response.

The final procedure specified by EGP is *network reachability*. As with neighbor reachability, network reachability involves a periodic command/response pair. In this case, one gateway sends a *Poll* command and its partner responds with an *Update* response. The Update response contains a list of networks that can be reached by the responding gateway,

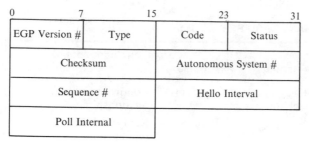

Neighbor Acquistion

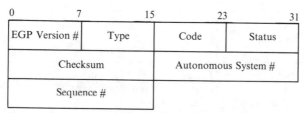

Neighbor Reachability

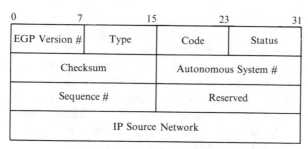

Poll

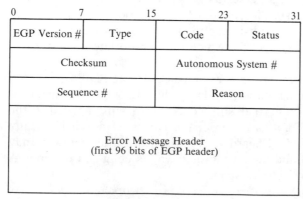

Error Response/Indication

Figure 2.15. EGP formats.

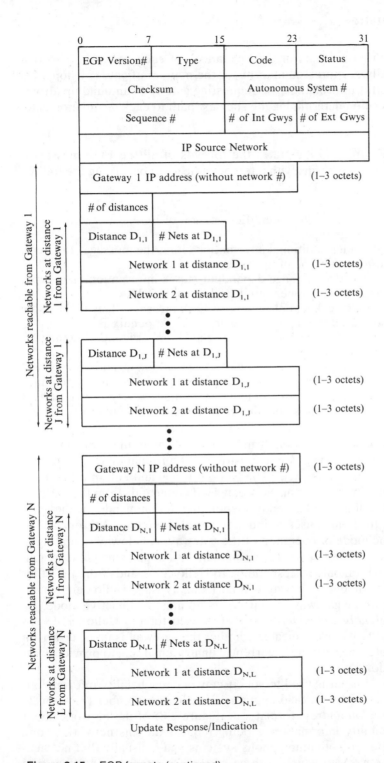

Figure 2.15. EGP formats (continued).

together with an estimate of the "distance" of each network. This distance typically is expressed in terms of the number of gateway hops. On the basis of this information, the requesting gateway can build up a routing table based on determining the shortest path to each destination gateway.

Formats.   Figure 2.15 illustrates the formats of all the EGP messages. Each message type begins with a ten-octet header concerning the following fields:

- *EGP Version Number:* Identifies version of EGP.
- *Type:* Message type.
- *Code:* Provides additional information about the message. In effect, it identifies a subtype of message.
- *Status:* Provides message-dependent status information. The type, codes and status numbers are listed in Table 2.11.
- *Checksum:* Checksum of the entire EGP message. This is the same checksum used for IP, and is described in Appendix B.
- *Autonomous System Number:* Assigned number identifying the particular autonomous system.
- *Sequence Number:* Used to synchronize commands and responses. A gateway establishes an initial sequence number during neighbor acquisition, and may increment the number for each subsequent command. Responses contain the last sequence number received.

The *neighbor acquisition* format is used for all of the commands and responses relating to neighbor acquisition and termination (request, confirm, refuse, cease, cease-ack). The Hello Interval and Poll Interval fields specify the minimum intervals between such commands from the partner. This is used to limit the burden of responding to commands for the gateway. The status field is used to indicate a problem (codes 3 through 7) or to declare the mode of operation of the gateway. A gateway operating in passive mode will not send Hello commands, and gains neighbor reachability information only by responding to Hello commands from the other side. In active mode, a gateway will periodically issue Hello commands. At least one of the gateways in a partnership must be in active mode.

The *neighbor reachability* format is used for the Hello/I-H-U exchange. The status field indicates whether the gateway is up or down. In the down state, the gateway is currently unable/unwilling to provide routing information.

The *poll* format is used to solicit network reachability information. The IP Source Network field contains the network number (7,14, or 21 bits depending on address format; see Figure 2.8) of the network about which reachability information is being requested. This network is one that is common to both autonomous systems and is usually (but not necessarily) a network to which both gateways are attached. In effect, the poll message is asking the question: For all gateways on the specified

Table 2.11.   EGP MESSAGE TYPES

Name	Type	Code	Interpretation	Status	Interpretation
Neighbor Acquisition	3	0	Request command	0	Unspecified
		1	Confirm response	1	Active mode
		2	Refuse response	2	Passive mode
		3	Cease command	3	Insufficient resources
		4	Cease-ack response	4	Administratively prohibited
				5	Going down
				6	Parameter problem
				7	Protocol violation
Neighbor Reachability	5	0	Hello command	0	Indeterminate
		1	I Hear You response	1	Up state
				2	Down state
Poll	2	0		0	Indeterminate
				1	Up state
				2	Down state
Update Response/ Indication	1	0		0	Indeterminate
				1	Up state
				2	Down state
				128	Unsolicited message bit
Error Response/ Indication	8	0		0	Indeterminate
				1	Up state
				2	Down state
				128	Unsolicited message bit

network, what networks can be reached by each gateway and what are the distances involved?

At first glance, the question seems too broad. The requesting gateway will necessarily want to know which networks are reachable via the responding gateway, but why ask about other gateways? This is best explained with reference to Figure 2.14. In this example, gateway *G1* in autonomous system 1 and gateway *G5* in autonomous system 2 implement EGP and acquire a neighbor relationship. When *G5* sends a poll request to *G1*, *G1* responds by indicating which networks it could reach and the distances (network hops) involved. *G1* also provides the same information on behalf of *G2*. That is, *G1* tells *G5* what networks are reachable via *G2* at what distances. In this example, the reason that *G5* does not interrogate *G2* directly is that *G2* does not implement EGP. Typically, most of the gateways in an autonomous system will not implement EGP. Only a few gateways will be assigned the responsibility for communicating with gateways in other autonomous systems. A final point: *G1* is in possession of the necessary information about *G2* because *G1* and *G2* share an interior gateway protocol (IGP).

With this background, we can now describe the *update* format. The bulk of the message consists of a number of blocks, one for each gateway for which a report is provided. The block begins with the internet address of the gateway that is the subject of that block. Only the local address portion (see Figure 2.8) of the address is provided. The network portion is provided in the IP source network field of the Update message. The remainder of the block consists of a list of reachable networks grouped according to their distance from this gateway. First, the number of different distances is specified. The remainder of the block consists of a number of sub-blocks, one for each distance. Each sub-block begins with a field specifying the distance, followed by a field that specifies the number of networks that are reachable at that distance. Finally, the network address of each network at that distance is listed. In Figure 2.15, the notation $D_{i,j}$ has the interpretation: the jth distance in the block for gateway i.

Two fields in the update message remain to be explained. These fields list the number of internal and external gateways provided in this update report. All gateways, of course, must directly attach to the network specified in the poll command and be repeated in the update response. Internal gateways are those that are in the same autonomous system as the responding gateway. External gateways are those in other autonomous systems whose routing information is known to the responding gateway. This latter situation may arise when one network supports gateways from more than two autonomous systems (DDN is an example of such a network).

The *error* format is used to provide information about a variety of error conditions and may be used in response to any command. The reason field may contain one of the following identifiers:

0   Unspecified
1   Bad EGP header format
2   Bad EGP data field format
3   Reachability information unavailable
4   Excessive polling rate
5   No response received to a poll

The last field of the error message contains the first 12 octets of the message that caused the error detection.

3

Transmission Control Protocol

The transmission control protocol (TCP) is an example of what is usually referred to as a transport protocol. The transport protocol is the keystone of the whole concept of a computer-communications architecture. Within the structure of a communications architecture, the transport protocol can provide a reliable mechanism for the exchange of data between processes in different computers. A transport protocol typically ensures that data is delivered error free, in sequence, with no loss or duplication. The transport service relieves higher-level software of the burden of managing the intervening communications facility. Because the transport protocol provides for high-quality service and because it may need to deal with a range of communications services, it can be one of the most complex of all communications protocols.

We begin our discussion with an examination of the services provided by TCP and the formal specification of these services. Next, we examine the key protocol mechanisms employed in TCP. Details of the standard are then presented. Then, implementation options allowed within the standard are explained. Finally, another protocol that operates at the same level as TCP, namely UDP, is also examined.

3.1 TRANSMISSION CONTROL PROTOCOL SERVICES

Overview

In general, the service provided by TCP is the reliable end-to-end transport of data between host processes. More specifically, the standard calls out the following categories of service (Table 3.1):

- Multiplexing
- Connection management
- Data transport
- Special capabilities
- Error reporting

Multiplexing.   A TCP entity within a host can simultaneously provide service to multiple processes using TCP. A process within a host using

Table 3.1.   SUMMARY OF TCP SERVICES

Multiplexing	Supports multiple users by use of ports
Connection Management	
Connection Establishment	Establishes connection between unconnected pair of sockets with specified security and precedence
Connection Maintenance	Maintains connection for transport of data
Connection Termination	Provides graceful close and abort
Data Transport	
Full-duplex	Delivers simultaneous bidirectional data flow between the two sockets of the connection
Timely	Delivers within user-specified timeout or notifies user and terminates connection
Ordered	Delivers data in same sequence that it was provided by source user
Labeled	Security and precedence level of the connection associated with each data transfer
Flow Controlled	Flow of data across the connection is regulated
Error Checked	Data will be delivered free of error
Special Capabilities	
Data Stream Push	Pushes data through connection and delivers it to user
Urgent Data Signaling	Expedites transfer and delivery of data
Error Reporting	Reports service failure

TCP services is identified with a *port*. A port, when concatenated with an internet address, forms a *socket,* which is unique throughout the internet. Service by TCP is provided by means of a logical connection between a pair of sockets.

An example may clarify these concepts. Figure 3.1 shows three hosts attached to an internet. Each host has an internet address. Furthermore, the TCP entity within each host supports multiple ports, each within its own port number. TCP provides communication between ports. Assume that a process or application *X* in host *A* wished to send a message to a process in host *C*. *X* may be a report generator program in minicomputer *A*. *C* may be a host server that controls a high-quality printer. *X* attaches itself to port 2 and requests a connection to host *C*, port 1 (*C* may have only one port if it is a single printer). *A*'s TCP then transmits a connection request to the TCP entity in *B*, indicating a desire to connect to port 1. It transmits this request by means of an internet protocol (IP) SEND primitive (scc Table 2.4), which specifies *A* as the source address and *C* as the destination address. Once the logical connection is set up, all data from *X* for that connection will be assembled into TCP segments (see Figure 1.6) for transmission to host *C*, port 1. Data in incoming seg-

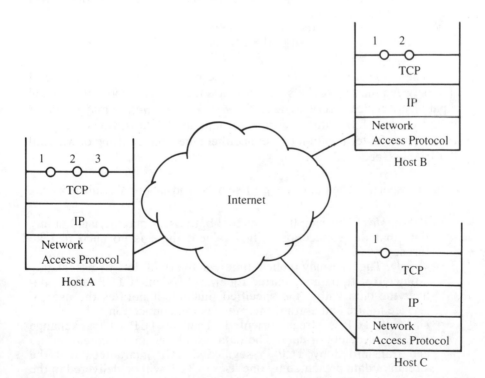

Figure 3.1. Multiplexing example.

ments addressed to port 2 from host *C*, port 1 is delivered to *X*. Similarly, *C*'s printer is declared busy and accepts data only from host *A*, port 2.

At the same time, process *Y* in *A* could attach to port 1 and exchange data with a process at port 1 in *B*. This is an example of multiplexing. Multiple users within a host can employ the services of TCP to engage in data exchange with remote processes.

Connection Management.   Section 1.4 introduced the concept of connection control (see Figure 1.10). Connection management in TCP consists of three services: connection establishment, connection maintenance, and connection termination. The *connection establishment* service allows two TCP users to set up a logical connection between their respective sockets. A logical connection is endowed with certain properties that endure for the lifetime of the connection. The most notable of these are security and precedence levels, which are specified by the two TCP users at the time of connection establishment. A connection between two TCP users may be set up if:

- No connection between the two sockets currently exists. From a given socket, it is possible to simultaneously maintain more than one connection, but only one connection to any specific remote socket at a time is permitted.
- Internal TCP resources are sufficient.
- Both users have agreed to the connection.

The *connection maintenance* service provides for the exchange of data between the two sockets and supports the data transport and special capability services described next. *Connection termination* may be either abrupt or graceful. With an abrupt termination, data in transit may be lost. A graceful termination prevents either side from shutting down until all data have been delivered.

Data Transport.   The data transport service consists of six subservices:

- *Full-duplex:* This simply means that both users may transmit at any time that the connection is maintained; there is no need to take turns.
- *Timely:* The user may request timely delivery of data by associating a timeout with data submitted for transmission. If TCP fails to deliver the data within the specified timeout, it notifies the user of service failure and abruptly terminates the connection.
- *Ordered:* TCP is stream oriented. That is, TCP users exchange streams of octets of data. The data are placed in allocated buffers and transmitted by TCP in segments. TCP guarantees that the stream of data presented by one user to TCP will be delivered in the same order to the destination user.

- *Labeled:* TCP establishes a connection only if the security desig-nation provided by both users requesting the connection match. If the precedence levels do not match, the higher level is associated with the connection. All data transferred over the connection carries the associated security and precedence levels. These are provided to IP for transfer of segments across the internet.
- *Flow controlled:* TCP regulates the flow of data to prevent internal TCP congestion that could lead to service degradation and failure, and in response to the buffer allocation provided by the user.
- *Error controlled:* TCP makes use of a simple checksum (see Appen-dix B), and delivers data that is free of errors within the probabilities supported by the checksum.

Special Capabilities. TCP supports two special capabilities associated with the transfer of data over an established connection: data stream push and urgent data signaling.

- *Data stream push:* Ordinarily, TCP decides when sufficient data has accumulated to form a segment for transmission. The sending TCP user can require TCP to transmit all outstanding data up to and in-cluding that labeled with a push flag. On the receiving end, TCP will ordinarily buffer incoming data and deliver it from time to time to the destination user. When data marked with a push flag is received, TCP immediately delivers all buffered data up to the push flag to the destination user. A sending user might request this service if it has come to a logical break in the data.
- *Urgent data signaling:* This provides a means of informing the des-tination TCP user that significant or "urgent" data is in the incoming data stream. It is up to the destination user to determine appropriate action.

Error Reporting. TCP will report service failure stemming from cata-strophic conditions in the internetwork environment for which TCP can-not compensate.

TCP Service Primitives

As with IP, the services provided by TCP are defined in terms of primi-tives and parameters. The services provided by TCP are considerably richer than those provided by IP, and hence the set of primitives and parameters is considerably more complex. Tables 3.2 and 3.3 list the TCP service primitives. Service request primitives are issued by a TCP user to TCP, and service response primitives are issued by TCP to a user. Table 3.4 defines the parameters associated with these primitives.

Figure 3.2 shows the context for use of the TCP service primitives and parameters. Users of TCP, at the process level, exchange request and response primitives with TCP. Many of these primitives trigger an ex-

Table 3.2.   TCP SERVICE REQUEST PRIMITIVES

Primitive	Parameters	Description
Unspecified Passive Open	source port, [timeout], [timeout-action] [precedence], [security-range]	Listen for connection attempt at specified security and precedence from any remote destination
Fully Specified Passive Open	source port, destination port, destination address, [timeout], [timeout-action], [precedence], [security-range]	Listen for connection attempt at specified security and precedence from specified destination
Active Open	source port, destination port, destination address, [timeout], [timeout-action], [precedence], [security]	Request connection at a particular security and precedence to a specified destination
Active Open With Data	source port, destination port, destination address, [timeout], [timeout-action], [precedence], [security], data, data length, PUSH flag, URGENT flag	Request connection at a particular security and precedence to a specified destination and transmit data with the request
Send	local connection name, data, data length, PUSH flag, URGENT flag, [timeout], [timeout-action]	Transfer data across named connection
Allocate	local connection name, data length	Issue incremental allocation for receive data to TCP
Close	local connection name	Close connection gracefully
Abort	local connection name	Close connection abruptly
Status	local connection name	Query connection status

Note: Square brackets indicate optional parameter

change of TCP segments between hosts. These segments are submitted by TCP to IP in a SEND primitive and delivered by IP to TCP in a DE-LIVER primitive (see Table 2.4).

Connection Establishment.   The first four service request primitives are used to open a new connection. Connections can be opened in one of two modes: active and passive. In passive mode, a user has requested TCP to listen for an incoming connection request for the specified port. The Passive Open specifies the minimum desired precedence level and the range of security levels that are acceptable. The Passive Open may be either fully specified or unspecified. In the former case, the user specifies a particular socket from which it will accept a connection. A connection is

Table 3.3.   TCP SERVICE RESPONSE PRIMITIVES

Primitive	Parameters	Description
Open ID	local connection name, source port, destination port,* destination address*	Informs user of connection name assigned to pending connection requested in an Open primitive
Open Failure	local connection name	Reports failure of an Active Open request
Open Success	local connection name	Reports completion of a pending Open request
Deliver	local connection name, data, data length, URGENT flag	Reports arrival of data
Closing	local connection name	Reports that remote TCP user has issued a Close and that all data sent by remote user has been delivered
Terminate	local connection name, description	Reports that the connection has been terminated and no longer exists; a description of the reason for termination is provided
Status Response	local connection name, source port, source address, destination port, destination address, connection state, receive window, send window, amount awaiting ACK, amount awaiting receipt, urgent state, precedence, security, timeout	Reports current status of connection
Error	local connection name, description	Reports service request or internal error

*Not used for Unspecified Passive Open

established when a matching Active Open (explained later) is executed at the specified remote socket. With an Unspecified Passive Open, the user is declaring a willingness to establish a connection with any caller. Such a primitive would be issued by a server process that is available for service for unknown other processes.

With an Active Open, the user requests that TCP attempt to open a connection with a specified remote socket, at given precedence and security levels. A connection can be opened if there is a matching Passive Open at the remote socket or if the remote socket has issued a matching

Table 3.4.   TCP SERVICE PARAMETERS

Source Port	Identifier of the local TCP user
Timeout	The longest delay allowed for data delivery before automatic connection termination or error report. User specified
Timeout-action	In the event of a timeout, determines if the connection is terminated or an error is reported to the user
Precedence	Actual or requested precedence level for a connection. Takes on values zero (lowest) through seven (highest). Same parameter as defined in IP
Security-range	Security structure that specifies the allowed ranges in compartment, handling restrictions, transmission control codes, and security levels
Destination Port	Identifier of the remote TCP user
Destination Address	Internet address of the remote host
Security	Security information (including security level, compartment, handling restrictions, and transmission control code) for a connection. Same parameter as defined in IP
Data	Block of data sent by a TCP user or delivered to a TCP user
Data Length	Length of block of data sent or delivered
PUSH Flag	If set, this indicates that the associated data are to be provided with the data stream push service
URGENT Flag	If set, this indicates that the associated data are to be provided with the urgent data signaling service
Local Connection Name	The shorthand identifier of a connection defined by a (local socket, remote socket) pair. Provided by TCP
Description	Supplementary information in a Terminate or Error primitive
Source Address	Internet address of the local host
Connection State	State of referenced connection (CLOSED, ACTIVE OPEN, PASSIVE OPEN, ESTABLISHED, CLOSING)
Receive Window	Amount of data in octets the local TCP entity is willing to receive
Send Window	Amount of data in octets permitted to be sent to remote TCP entity
Amount Awaiting ACK	Amount of previously transmitted data awaiting acknowledgment
Amount Awaiting Receipt	Amount of data in octets buffered at local TCP and pending receipt by local TCP user
Urgent State	Indicates to the receiving TCP user whether there is urgent data available or whether all urgent data, if any, has been delivered to the user

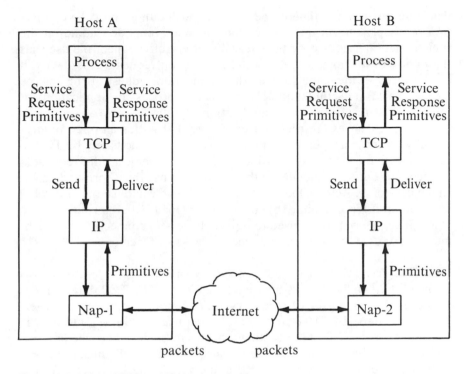

Figure 3.2.   Use of TCP and IP service primitives.

Table 3.5.   REQUIREMENTS FOR MATCHING OPEN PRIMITIVES

Active Open, Active Open
  Destination address in each primitive refers to the other socket
  Security parameters are identical

Active Open, Fully Specified Passive Open
  Destination address in each primitive refers to the other socket
  Security parameter in Active Open is within the range of the security-range
  parameter of the Passive Open

Active Open, Unspecified Passive Open
  Security parameter in Active Open is within the range of the security-range
  parameter of the Passive Open

Active Open. Table 3.5 summarizes the conditions for a match. If the two opens are matching and if the requested precedence levels differ, the higher level is used for the connection.

Several other points about the open request primitives should be noted. The requestor may specify a timeout for all data to be submitted to TCP on the connection. If data is not successfully delivered to the destination within the timeout period, TCP will either abort the connection or simply inform the user of the timeout event, depending on the timeout-action specified by the user. With the Active Open, the user has the option of including data with the connection request. This data will be delivered at the same time as the connection request at the remote socket. This is a useful feature for transaction processing applications or other request-response type of applications.

Two responses are received by a user that issues an open request primitive. First, an Open ID primitive is returned immediately by TCP to the requesting user to assign a local connection name to the requested connection. Future references to the connection use this shorthand name. In the case of an Active Open, if TCP is unable to establish the requested connection, it reports failure by means of an Open Failure primitive. The Open Success primitive is used to report successful connection establishment in the case of either Active Open or Passive Open.

Data Transfer.   Once a connection has been established between two sockets, the two TCP users may exchange data. The TCP data transfer service is viewed as a data stream service. As a practical matter, however, data is transferred to TCP from the sending user in blocks, and data is transferred from TCP to the destination user in blocks. The size of these blocks is variable and does not necessarily bear any relationship to segment size, nor is it necessary that the delivered data be blocked in the same fashion as it was blocked by the sending user.

A user sends data by means of the Send primitive. A block of data is passed to TCP, which buffers the data. If the PUSH flag is set, any outstanding data in the send buffer, including the data that has just been submitted, is immediately sent out in one or more segments and marked with a PUSH indicator. If the PUSH flag is not set, TCP may hold the data in the send buffer and send it out in one or more segments as convenient. For example, TCP may wait until more data is submitted to be able to send larger, more efficient segments.

Data arriving across a connection to a TCP entity is similarly buffered in a deliver buffer associated with that connection. If the arriving data is marked with a PUSH flag, that data, together with any data currently buffered, is immediately submitted to the destination user in a Deliver primitive. If incoming data is not marked with a PUSH flag, TCP delivers the data as convenient. For example, TCP may wait until more incoming data accumulate so as to minimize system interrupts. The nature of the delivery is implementation dependent. In general, we can say that the Deliver primitive signals the user that data have arrived, and that data must be processed by the user before it can be cleared by TCP.

An URGENT flag may also be associated with data submitted by a Send primitive. In this case, the associated data is marked with an URGENT indicator, and this indicator is delivered to the destination user along with the data. This is a signal to the destination user to accept and process the data as quickly as possible.

Finally, the Allocate primitive is used by a TCP user to issue TCP an incremental allocation for receive data. This quantity is the additional number of octets that the receiving user is willing to accept.

Connection Termination. A TCP user may terminate a connection in one of two ways: the Close primitive and the Abort primitive. The Close primitive requests that the connection be closed gracefully and indicates that the user has completed data transfer across the connection. Thus, a Close primitive also implies the push function. The issuance of a Close primitive triggers the following sequence of events:

1. The local TCP (where the Close was issued) transmits any buffered send data and then signals the remote TCP that it is closing the connection.
2. The remote TCP delivers all outstanding receive data to its user and informs the user of the remote Close request by means of a closing primitive.
3. The remote user may send any pending data and then issue a Close primitive.
4. The remote TCP transmits any outstanding send data and signals the other TCP that it is ready to terminate the connection.
5. The local TCP delivers any outstanding data to the local user and then issues a Terminate primitive. It also signals the remote TCP that it has terminated the connection.
6. The remote TCP issues a Terminate primitive to its user.

Once a TCP user has issued a Close primitive, it is obligated to continue to receive incoming data over the connection until TCP has informed the other side of the closing and delivered all outstanding data to the local user.

A user may close a connection abruptly by issuing an Abort primitive. The user accepts no more data over the connection and hence data may be lost in transit. The local TCP signals the remote TCP that the connection has been aborted; the remote TCP informs its user with a Terminate primitive.

A TCP connection can also be closed abruptly by TCP. If TCP is unable to maintain the connection for any reason, it issues a Terminate primitive.

Status and Error Reporting. The Status primitive allows a user to request the status of a particular connection. TCP supplies the information with a Status Response primitive. The parameters provided with this primitive are defined in Table 3.4. Most of these parameters relate to the protocol operation, which is described in the next section.

The Error primitive informs a TCP user of illegal service requests relating to the named connection or of errors relating to the environment.

State Machine Description

The service provided by TCP can conveniently be described by using a state machine description. At any time, the service that TCP provides a user with respect to a remote socket can be in one of five states:

- CLOSED: There is no connection.
- PASSIVE OPEN: The user has issued a Passive Open primitive; TCP can accept a matching connection request on behalf of the user.
- ACTIVE OPEN: The user has issued an Active Open primitive; TCP is attempting to establish the requested connection.
- ESTABLISHED: A connection has been established.
- CLOSING: The user has issued a Close primitive; TCP is attempting to close the connection gracefully.

Figure 3.3 illustrates the transitions that can occur between states, from the point of view of the service provided by TCP to a local user. Some of the transitions are labeled with service request primitives, and these are self-explanatory. The remaining transitions are labeled *segment exchange*. This indicates that the local TCP entity is exchanging segments with a remote TCP entity. For example, when a user issues an Active Open, TCP will exchange segments with a remote TCP entity in an attempt to establish the connection; the nature of this interaction is explored in Section 3.2.

Any connection involves services that are provided by two TCP entities. A composite state transition diagram, derived from the composition of two local state transition diagrams, is illustrated in Figure 3.4. The

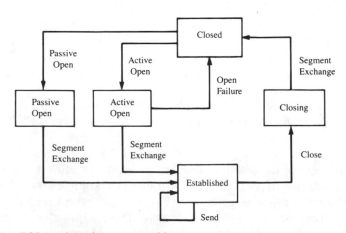

Figure 3.3. TCP local service state machine.

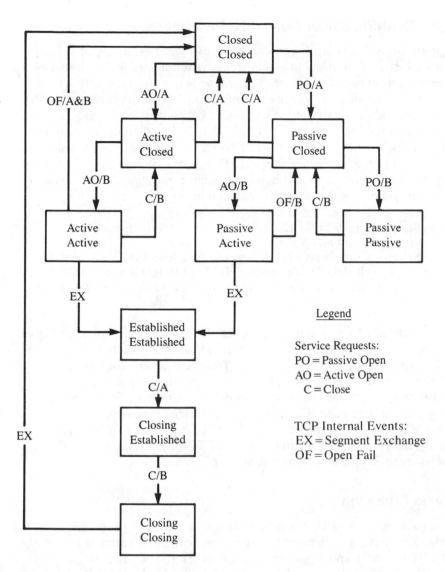

Figure 3.4. Composite TCP service state machine.

boxes represent the state of a pair of users, A and B; the actions on the transitions are labeled to indicate whether the corresponding action relates to A or B. The diagram indicates how a connection can be set up as a result of two Active Opens or an Active Open and a Passive Open.

These diagrams present only a subset of the possible actions. In particular, transitions relating to aborted connections are omitted for the sake of clarity.

3.2 TRANSMISSION CONTROL PROTOCOL

The transmission control protocol operates by the exchange of segments with other TCP entities. In establishing, maintaining, and terminating a connection on behalf of a user, TCP engages in a dialogue with a remote TCP entity, serving a remote user. Some of the segments exchanged carry user data; others serve only to transmit TCP control information.

Of course, TCP entities cannot exchange data directly. Instead, each segment is transmitted using the IP Send primitive and received using the IP Deliver primitive (see Figure 3.2). TCP is designed to assume that the underlying communications facility, available through IP, is unreliable. The worst-case assumptions that must be made are:

- Segments may be lost; a segment may be lost in transit or it may arrive with bit errors.
- Segments may arrive in a different order than they were sent.
- The transit delay from sending TCP entity to receiving TCP entity is unpredictable; it may be long and, what is worse, it may be variable.

TCP relies on a rather complex set of mechanisms to provide reliable service to users in the face of these difficulties. In this section, we provide a description of these mechanisms. Time and again, the same pattern emerges. Each necessary function must be implemented with mechanisms that overcome lost and misordered segments. Furthermore, the long and variable delay significantly complicates each task.

We begin with a brief description of TCP operation. This is followed by a detailed look at the three phases of TCP operation: connection establishment, data transfer, and connection termination.

Basic Operation

The basic purpose of TCP is to provide a means for two users to exchange data. This data is exchanged in segments, with each segment consisting of a TCP header and a portion of the user data. The segment header includes, of course, the destination port identifier so the receiving TCP entity can deliver the data to the appropriate user. But the header includes other control information needed for the proper functioning of TCP.

Figure 3.5 illustrates the basic operation of TCP. Data is passed to TCP by a user in a sequence of TCP Send primitives. These data are buffered in a *send buffer*. From time to time, TCP assembles data from the send buffer into a segment and transmits the segment. These data are transmitted by the IP service and delivered to the destination TCP entity, which strips off the segment header and places the data in a *receive buffer*. From time to time, the receiving TCP notifies its user that data are available for delivery by means of the TCP Deliver primitive.

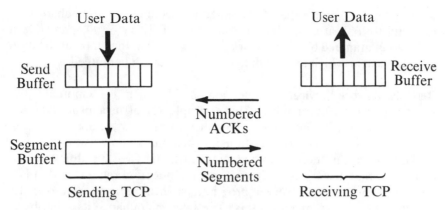

Figure 3.5. Basic TCP operation.

One difficulty that TCP faces is that segments may arrive out of order. To compensate, TCP numbers each transmitted segment sequentially, placing the sequence number in the TCP header. Because the segments are numbered sequentially, there is no ambiguity about the intended order, and the segments can be reordered appropriately before delivery of their data to the destination user.

A second difficulty is that TCP segments may be lost. The segment numbers help with this difficulty as well. The receiving TCP entity will acknowledge incoming segments by returning an ACK with a number that refers to the segment that is acknowledged. If a segment is lost, then its corresponding ACK cannot be issued. Accordingly, if the sending TCP entity does not receive an ACK to a particular segment, within a reasonable amount of time, it will retransmit the unacknowledged segment, using the same sequence number as before. To be able to do this, TCP must save a copy of each transmitted segment in a *segment buffer* until that segment is acknowledged.

With this brief look at the basic TCP operation, we turn now to the details.

Connection Establishment

The purpose of connection establishment is to set up a logical connection between two TCP users. This connection serves two purposes:

- It specifies the characteristics to be used for all data transfers on the connection, including precedence and security.
- It enables each TCP entity to maintain state information concerning the connection, such as last sequence number used, last sequence number acknowledged, and last sequence number received.

Before explaining the TCP connection establishment mechanism, it is useful to look at a simpler case in which delivery of all segments, in order, is guaranteed by the network service. We can then look at the more general case in which neither delivery nor order is guaranteed.

Reliable Network Service. Connection establishment is by mutual agreement and can be accomplished by a simple set of user primitives and control segments, as shown in the upper part of the state diagram of Figure 3.6. The states refer to the status of the connection between a pair of sockets. To begin, there is no connection (the CLOSED state). The user can signal that it will passively wait for a connection request with a Passive Open primitive. A server program, such as time sharing or a file transfer application, might do this. The user may change its mind by issuing a Close primitive. After the Passive Open is issued, TCP creates a connection object of some sort (e.g., a system control block) that maintains state information relating to the connection, and issues an Open ID primitive to the user. Initially, the connection is in the LISTEN state.

From the CLOSED state, the user may also issue an Active Open primitive, which instructs TCP to attempt connection establishment to a

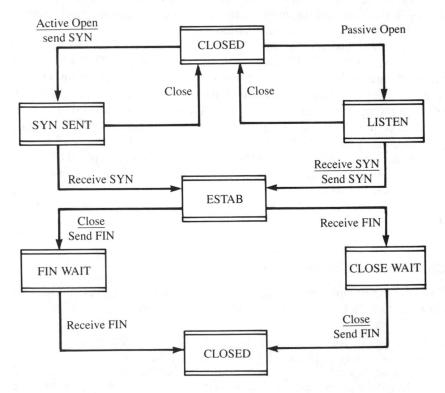

Figure 3.6. Simple connection state diagram.

designated user. In this case, TCP also sets up a connection object and issues an Open ID. In addition, TCP issues a connection request to the destination TCP entity in the form of a SYN (for synchronize) command. This command is carried by a TCP segment and interpreted as a request for connection to a particular port by the receiving TCP user. If the destination TCP entity is in the LISTEN state for that port, then a connection is established. To do this, the destination TCP entity:

- Signals the user that a connection is open in an Open Success primitive.
- Sends a SYN as confirmation to the remote TCP entity.
- Puts the connection object in the ESTABLISHED state.

When the responding SYN is received by the initiating TCP entity, it too can move the connection to an ESTABLISHED state. The connection is prematurely aborted if either user issues a Close primitive.

Figure 3.7 shows the robustness of this protocol. Either side can initiate a connection. Furthermore, if both sides initiate the connection at about the same time, it is established without confusion. This is because

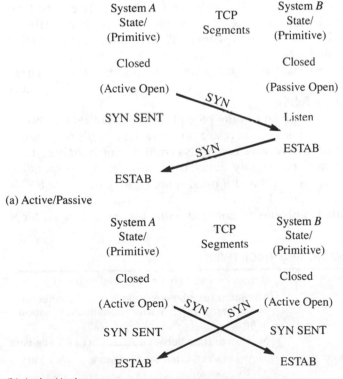

(a) Active/Passive

(b) Active/Active

Figure 3.7. The two-way handshake: connection establishment.

the SYN segment functions both as a connection request and a connection acceptance.

The reader may ask what happens if a SYN arrives while the requested user is CLOSED (not listening and not actively requesting a matching connection). Three courses are of action possible:

- TCP could reject the connection by sending a reset (RST) segment back to the other TCP.
- The request could be queued until a matching open is issued by the user.
- The user could be notified of the pending request.

The TCP specification dictates the first course of action: if an incoming connection request cannot be matched, it is refused.

Unreliable Network Service. Connection establishment, as described previously, calls for the exchange of SYNs, a procedure sometimes referred to as a *two-way handshake*. Now, let us assume an unreliable network service and suppose that TCP entity A issues a SYN to TCP entity B. A expects to get a SYN back, confirming the connection. Two things can go wrong: A's SYN can be lost or B's answering SYN can be lost. Both cases can be handled by use of a retransmit-SYN timer. After A issues a SYN, if its timer expires without receiving an acknowledging SYN, A reissues the SYN. (Note: the retransmit-SYN timer is only one of a number of timers needed for the proper functioning of TCP. These are listed in Table 3.6 together with a brief definition. The other timers are discussed in what follows.)

This technique may result in the receipt by B of duplicate SYNs. If A's initial SYN segment is lost, there are no duplicates. If B's response is lost, however, then B will receive two SYNs from A. Furthermore, if B's response was not lost, but simply delayed, A will get two responding SYNs. All of this means that A and B must simply ignore duplicate SYNs once a connection is established.

There are other problems to contend with. Just as a delayed SYN

Table 3.6. TRANSPORT PROTOCOL TIMERS

Retransmission timer	Retransmit an unacknowledged segment
Reconnection timer	Minimum time between closing one connection and opening another with the same destination address
Window timer	Maximum time between ACK/CREDIT segment
Retransmit-SYN timer	Time between attempts to open a connection
Give-up timer	Abort connection when no segments are acknowledged

or lost response can give rise to a duplicate SYN, a delayed data segment or lost acknowledgment can give rise to duplicate data segments. This situation will be examined more closely in the next subsection. For now, we simply assert that duplicate data segments are possible. Figure 3.8 illustrates this problem. Assume that with each new connection, each TCP module begins numbering its data segments with sequence number 0. In Figure 3.8, a duplicate copy of segment 2 from an old connection arrives during the lifetime of a new connection between the same two sockets, and is delivered to B before delivery of the legitimate data segment number 2. B accepts the old segment and discards the valid segment as a duplicate. One way of attacking this problem is to start each new connection with a different sequence number, far removed from the sequence number of the most recent connection. For this purpose, the connection request is of the form SYN i, where i is the sequence number of the SYN. For sequence number purposes, the SYN is considered to occur before the first actual octet of transmitted data. Thus, the data is sequence-numbered beginning with $i+1$.

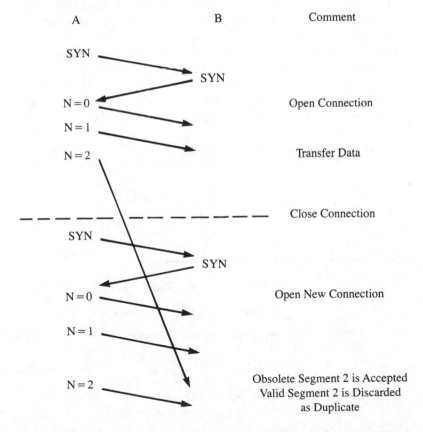

Figure 3.8.   The two-way handshake: problem with obsolete data segments.

Now, consider that a duplicate SYN i may survive past the termination of a connection. Figure 3.9 depicts the problem that may arise. An old, duplicate SYN i (request for connection, sequence number begins at i) arrives at B after the associated connection is terminated. B assumes that this is a fresh request and responds with SYN j. Meanwhile, A has decided to open a new connection with B and sends SYN k. B discards this as a duplicate. Now, both sides have transmitted and subsequently received a SYN segment, and therefore, think that a valid connection exists. However, when A initiates data transfer with a segment numbered $k+1$, B rejects the segment as being out of sequence.

The way out of this problem is for each side to acknowledge explicitly the other's SYN and sequence number. This procedure is known as a three-way handshake [TOML75, SUNS78, SUNS81]. The revised state diagram, which is the one employed by TCP, is shown in the upper part of Figure 3.10. A new state (SYN Received) is added (Table 3.7). In this state, the transport entity hesitates during connection opening to assure that the SYN segments sent by the two sides have both been acknowledged before the connection is declared established. In addition to the new state, there is a new control segment, RST, to reset the other side when an erroneous SYN is detected.

Figure 3.11 illustrates typical three-way handshake operations. As already discussed, an initiating SYN includes the sending sequence number (SYN i). The other side responds with a SYN/ACK segment, which includes the sending sequence number to be used by the TCP and also explicitly acknowledges the SYN and sequence number received from the initiating TCP; the actual convention is that the acknowledgment indicates the next expected sequence number (SYN j, ACK $i+1$). The initiating TCP must in turn acknowledge the SYN/ACK segment in its first

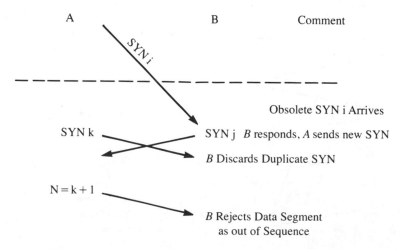

Figure 3.9. The two-way handshake: problem with obsolete SYN segments.

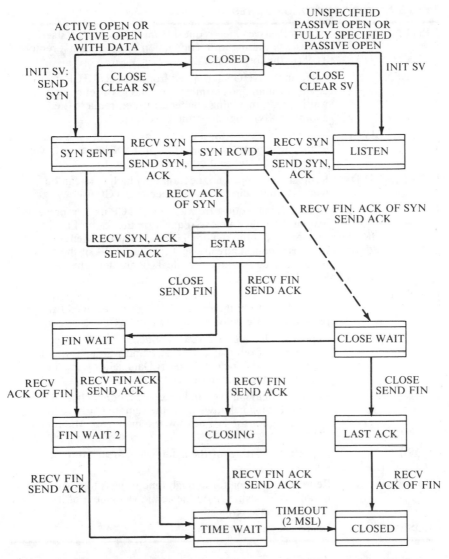

Figure 3.10. TCP entity state summary. MSL = max segment lifetime; SV = state vector; init = initialize; clear = nullify.

data segment (DATA $i+1$, ACK $j+1$). Next is shown a situation in which an old SYN i arrives at B after the close of the relevant connection. B assumes that this is a fresh request and responds with SYN j, ACK $i+1$. When A receives this segment, it realizes that it has not requested a connection, and therefore, sends a RST, ACK $j+1$. Note that the ACK $j+1$ portion of the segment is essential so that an old duplicate RST does not abort a legitimate connection establishment. The final example shows a

Table 3.7. **TCP CONNECTION STATES**

LISTEN	After a Passive Open request from the local TCP user, represents waiting for a connection request from a remote TCP (in the form of a SYN segment)
SYN SENT	After an Active Open request from the local TCP user and having sent an open request (i.e., a SYN), represents waiting for a matching connection open request (i.e., another SYN) from the remote TCP
SYN RECEIVED	Represents waiting for a confirming connection request acknowledgment (i.e., the ACK of the SYN) after having both received and sent connection requests
ESTABLISHED	Represents an open connection on which data can be passed in both directions between two TCP users
FIN WAIT1	After a Close request from the local TCP user, represents waiting for either a close request (in the form of a FIN segment) from the remote TCP, or an acknowledgment of the close request already sent (i.e., an ACK of the FIN). Data received from the remote TCP are delivered to the local TCP
FIN WAIT2	Represents waiting for a connection termination request (i.e., a FIN) from the remote TCP. Data received from the remote TCP are delivered to the local TCP
CLOSE WAIT	Represents having received a connection close request (i.e., a FIN) from the remote TCP and waiting for a close request from the local TCP user. Data sent by the local user are sent to the remote TCP
LAST ACK	Represents having sent and received a connection close request, having acknowledged the remote Close request, and waiting for the last acknowledgment from the remote TCP
CLOSING	Represents waiting for the acknowledgment from the remote TCP
TIME WAIT	Represents waiting for enough time to pass to ensure the remote TCP has received the acknowledgment of its conection close request
CLOSED	Represents no connection

case in which an old SYN/ACK arrives in the middle of a new connection establishment. Because of the use of sequence numbers in the acknowledgments, this event causes no mischief.

The upper part of Fig. 3.10 does not include transitions in which RST is sent. This was done for simplicity. The basic rule is: Send an RST if (1) the connection state is not yet ESTABLISHED, and (2) an invalid ACK (one that does not reference something that was sent) is received. The reader is invited to try various combinations of events to see that this connection establishment procedure works in spite of any combination of old and lost segments.

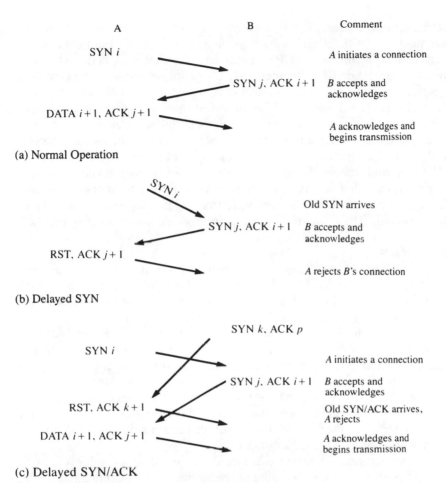

Figure 3.11. Examples of three-way handshake.

Data Transfer

Once a connection is established, data is transferred in data segments that contain sequence numbers. In the TCP view, every octet of data sent over a connection has a sequence number. The sequence number carried in the segment header is the sequence number of the first octet of data in the segment; the numbers of the remaining octets are implicit. Each data segment also includes, as an acknowledgment, the sequence number of the octet next expected from the other side. To expand on this description, three issues need to be examined:

- Retransmission strategy
- Duplicate detection
- Flow control

Retransmission Strategy.   Two events necessitate the retransmission of a segment. First, the segment may be damaged in transit but nevertheless arrive at its destination. TCP includes an error-detecting code in the segment header; therefore, the receiving TCP entity can detect the error and discard the segment. The second event is that a segment fails to arrive. In either case, the sending TCP does not know that the segment transmission was unsuccessful. To cover this contingency, a positive acknowledgment (ACK) scheme is used: The receiver must acknowledge successfully received segments. For efficiency, it is not required that there be an ACK for each received segment. Rather, a cumulative acknowledgment is permitted. That is, the receiver may wait until a number of segments have arrived and then send an ACK that acknowledges all the data so far received. Thus, an ACK $n+1$ is interpreted to mean that the TCP that issued the ACK has received all of the data up through sequence number n.

If a segment does not arrive successfully, no ACK will be issued and a retransmission is in order. To cope with this situation, there must be a timer associated with each segment as it is sent. If the timer expires before the segment is acknowledged, the sender must retransmit.

So the addition of a timer solves that problem. Next problem: At what value should the timer be set? If the value is too small, there will be many unnecessary retransmissions, wasting network capacity. If the value is too large, the protocol will be sluggish in responding to a lost segment. The timer should be set at a value a bit longer than the round trip delay (send segment, receive ACK). Of course this delay is variable even under constant network load. Worse, the statistics of the delay will vary with changing network conditions.

Two strategies suggest themselves. A fixed timer value could be used, based on an understanding of the network's typical behavior. This suffers from an inability to respond to changing network conditions. If the value is set too high, the service will always be sluggish. If it is set too low, a positive feedback condition can develop, in which network congestion leads to more retransmissions, which increase congestion. Accordingly, the TCP standard suggests the use of a dynamic timer, which adapts to changing delay characteristics in the network. Such a scheme requires that the TCP entity make an ongoing estimate of delay. There are problems with this approach [ZHAN86]. Suppose that TCP keeps track of the time taken to acknowledge data segments and sets its retransmission timer based on the average of the observed delays. This value cannot be trusted for three reasons:

- If a segment has been retransmitted, the sender cannot know whether the received ACK is a response to the initial transmission or the retransmission.

- The peer entity may not acknowledge a segment immediately. Recall that we gave it the privilege of cumulative acknowledgments. Furthermore, the amount of delay in sending an acknowledgment may vary in unpredictable ways.
- Internet traffic load and capacity conditions may change suddenly.

The first point above can be addressed by simply failing to include retransmitted segments in the calculation [KARN87]. If the estimate is based only on segments that are not retransmitted, then algorithms are available that do a good job of tracking delay changes [JACO88]. However, the second and third points above can still create difficulties.

Duplicate Detection.   If a segment is lost and then retransmitted, no confusion will result. If, however, an ACK is lost, one or more segments will be retransmitted and, if they arrive successfully, be duplicates of previously received segments. Thus, the receiver must be able to recognize duplicates. The fact that each segment carries a sequence number helps but, nevertheless, duplicate detection and handling is no easy thing. There are two cases:

- A duplicate is received before the close of the connection.
- A duplicate is received after the close of the connection.

Notice that we say "a" duplicate rather than "the" duplicate. From the sender's point of view, the retransmitted segment is the duplicate. However, the retransmitted segment may arrive before the original segment, in which case the receiver views the original segment as the duplicate. In any case, two tactics are needed to cope with a duplicate received before the close of a connection:

- The receiver must assume that its acknowledgment was lost, and therefore, must acknowledge the duplicate. Consequently, the sender must not get confused if it receives multiple ACKs to the same segment.
- The sequence number space must be long enough so as not to "cycle" in less than the maximum possible segment lifetime.

Figure 3.12 illustrates the reason for the latter requirement. In this example, the sequence space is of length 8. Suppose that A has transmitted numbers 0, 1, and 2 and receives no acknowledgments. Eventually, it times out and retransmits 0. B has received 1 and 2, but 0 is delayed in transit. Thus, B does not send any ACKs. When the duplicate number 0 arrives, B acknowledges 0, 1, and 2 with an ACK 3. Meanwhile, A has timed out again and retransmits 1, which B acknowledges with another ACK 3. Things now seem to have sorted themselves out and data transfer

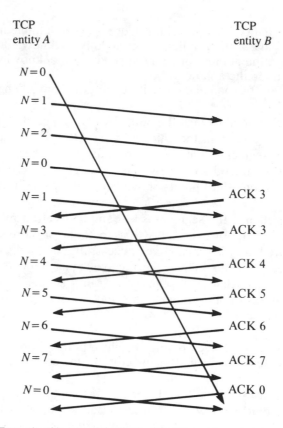

Figure 3.12. Example of incorrect duplicate detection.

continues. When the sequence space is exhausted, *A* cycles back to sequence number 0 and continues. Alas, the old 0 makes a belated appearance and is accepted by *B* before the new number 0 arrives.

It should be clear that the untimely emergence of the old number would have caused no difficulty if the sequence numbers had not yet wrapped around. The problem is: How big must the sequence space be? This depends on, among other things, whether the network enforces a maximum packet lifetime, and the rate at which numbers are being transmitted. Fortunately, each addition of a single bit to the sequence number field doubles the sequence space; therefore, it is rather easy to select a safe size. In the case of TCP, a 32-bit sequence-number field is used, which permits up to 2^{32} different sequence numbers.

A more subtle problem is posed by segments that continue to exist after the termination of the connection upon which they were spawned. If a new connection is set up between the same two sockets and the old segment reappears, it could be accepted on the new connection. To prevent this, the uniqueness of sequence numbers must be preserved not only within a connection but across connections.

One simple approach to this would be to extend the sequencing number scheme across connection lifetimes. This requires that a TCP entity remember the last sequence number used on a terminated connection. When a new connection is set up between the same pair of sockets, the initial sequence number is generated by incrementing the last sequence number used on the old connection.

This procedure works fine unless a system crash occurs. In that case, TCP may not remember what sequence number was last used between a given pair of sockets. To overcome this, TCP recommends the use of a combination of measures:

- *Clock-based initial sequence number:* When new connections are made, an initial 32-bit sequence number (ISN) is generated using the value of a 32-bit clock.
- *Quiet time:* If a system crash occurs and the system is brought back up, the TCP running on the system should refrain from emitting segments for a period of time equal to the maximum expected lifetime of a segment.

The clock-based ISN is designed to assure that ISNs from one connection to the next are unique. The clock, which may be a hardware or software clock, is assumed to increment once every 4 microseconds. Thus, the clock cycles once every 4.55 hours. Two comments are in order:

1. The only time that a new ISN will be in the neighborhood of an ISN from a prior connection is after a delay of over 4 hours. By then, any SYNs or data segments near that number should be long gone.
2. Because the clock is being incremented so rapidly, it is possible for it to "wrap around" and catch up with the actual sequence numbers being used on an existing connection. If the connection is then terminated and a new connection started, the obsolete-segment problem could occur. To avoid this, TCP should compare the new ISN with the last sequence number of a terminated connection and pause if necessary to allow the new ISN to be beyond the value of the last old sequence number.

The quiet-time strategy will work after a system crash if the maximum segment lifetime is known. In the absence of any other information, TCP recommends a value of 2 minutes. Although the standard does not mention it, the time-to-live parameter in the IP SEND primitive can be used to enforce a maximum segment lifetime.

Flow Control. The flow control mechanism is used in TCP to allow a receiving TCP to regulate the rate at which data arrives from a sending

TCP. This mechanism is complicated by the transit delay between the two TCP entities and by the fact that segments may be lost.

First, let us consider reasons why one TCP entity would want to restrain the rate of segment transmission over a connection from another TCP entity:

- The user of the receiving TCP cannot keep up with the flow of data.
- The receiving TCP itself cannot keep up with the flow of segments.

In either case, the problem manifests itself as a lack of receive buffer space (see Figure 3.5). Without some form of flow control, data may arrive faster than it can be processed. Eventually, the receive buffer is full and a new incoming segment must be discarded. This leads to inefficiency, as the sender must retransmit a segment that successfully made it through to the receiver.

To overcome this problem, TCP makes use of a credit allocation scheme. When a TCP entity acknowledges incoming data, it does so with a message of the form (ACK i, CREDIT j), with the following meaning:

- All sequence numbers through i-1 are acknowledged; the next expected sequence number is i.
- Permission is granted to send data corresponding to sequence numbers i through $i+j-1$.

Figure 3.13 illustrates the mechanism. For simplicity, we show data flow in one direction only and assume that segments (rather than octets) are numbered sequentially modulo 8. The circles indicate the range of sequence numbers, and the shaded portion indicates the window of sequence numbers that may be sent. Initially, A has a window of 7 sequence numbers (0 through 6). After sending data with sequence numbers corresponding to 0, 1, and 2, it has shrunk its window to a size of 4. Meanwhile, B acknowledges receipt of numbers 0, 1, and 2, and issues a credit of 5. This means that A can send 3, 4, 5, 6, and 7. However, by the time that this message has arrived at A, it has already sent 3 and 4; thus its remaining credit is only 3 (numbers 5, 6, and 7). As the exchange proceeds, A advances the trailing edge of its window each time that it transmits, and advances the leading edge only when it is granted credit.

Figure 3.14 shows the view of this mechanism from the sending and receiving sides; of course, both sides take both views because data may be exchanged in both directions. From the sending point of view, sequence numbers fall into four regions:

- *Data sent and acknowledged:* Beginning with the initial sequence number used on this connection through the last acknowledged number.

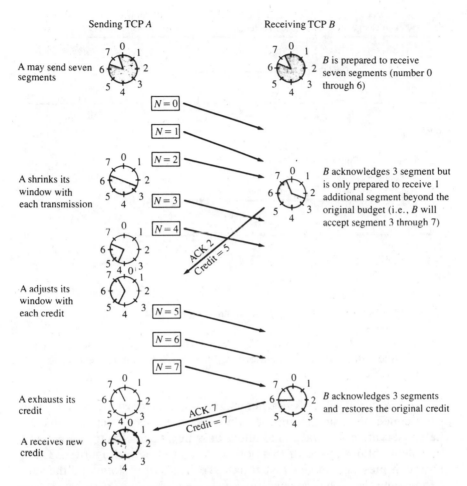

Figure 3.13. Example of TCP credit allocation protocol.

- *Data sent but not yet acknowledged:* Represents data that has already been transmitted and the sender is awaiting an acknowledgment.
- *Permitted data transmission:* The window of allowable transmission, based on credit allocated from the other side.
- *Unused and unusable numbers:* Numbers beyond the window.

From the receiving point of view, the concern is for received data and for the window of credit that has been allocated (Figure 3.14b).

This mechanism is quite powerful. Consider that the last message issued by *B* was (ACK *i*, CREDIT *j*). Then:

- To increase or decrease credit to an amount *k* when no additional data has arrived, *B* can issue (ACK *i*, CREDIT *k*).

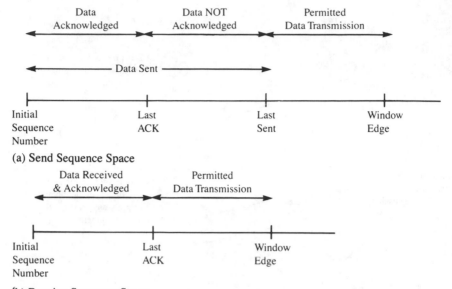

Figure 3.14. Sending and receiving flow control perspectives.

- To acknowledge incoming data corresponding to m additional sequence numbers without increasing credit, B can issue (ACK $i + m$, CREDIT $j - m$).

In the credit allocation scheme, the receiver needs to adopt some policy concerning the amount of data it permits the sender to transmit. The conservative approach is to allow only new segments up to the limit of available buffer space. If this policy were in effect in Figure 3.13, the first credit message implies that B has five free buffer slots, and the second message that B has seven free slots.

A conservative flow control scheme may limit the throughput of the TCP connection in long-delay situations. The receiver could potentially increase throughput by optimistically granting credit for space it does not have. For example, if a receiver's buffer is full but it anticipates that it can release space for two segments within a round-trip propagation time, it could immediately send a credit of 2. If the receiver can keep up with the sender, this scheme may increase throughput and can do no harm. If the sender is faster than the receiver, however, some segments may be discarded. This necessitates the retransmission of segments that have successfully traversed the internet, and is inefficient of both host and network resources.

One problem with the ACK/CREDIT approach is that segments may arrive out of order; this includes segments with credit allocation. Consider that a TCP entity may sometimes find it desirable to decrease outstanding offered credit on a connection, because expected resources did not become available, or because resources had to be reallocated to serve another connection. If sequencing is not guaranteed, a situation such as that shown in Figure 3.15 might arise. After TCP entity A has sent segment 1, B responds with a new credit allocation of 6. A short time later, and before additional segments arrive, B discovers a potential shortfall and sends a reduced credit allocation of 4. However, this allocation overtakes the earlier one and arrives first. It appears to A that B has initially granted an allocation of 4 and then obtained additional resources, and increased the allocation to 6. Thus, while B is not prepared to receive any more segments at this point, A feels entitled to send two additional segments. To avoid this problem, the standard strongly recommends that windows are not reduced.

A second problem to consider is that an ACK/CREDIT segment may be lost. This is easily handled by TCP: Future acknowledgments will resynchronize the protocol. Furthermore, if no new acknowledgments are forthcoming, the sender times out and retransmits a data segment, which triggers a new acknowledgment. However, it is still possible for deadlock to occur. Consider a situation in which B sends (ACK N, CREDIT 0), temporarily closing the window. Subsequently, B sends (ACK N, CREDIT M), but this segment is lost. A is awaiting the opportunity to send data and B thinks that it has granted that opportunity. To overcome this problem, a window timer can be used. This timer is reset with each outgoing ACK/CREDIT segment. If the timer ever expires, the protocol entity is required to send an ACK/CREDIT segment, even if it duplicates a previous one. This breaks the deadlock and also assures the other end that the protocol entity is still alive.

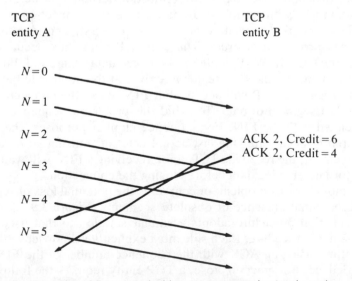

Figure 3.15. Examples of flow control with a nonsequenced network service.

Connection Termination

The state diagram of Figure 3.6 defines the use of a simple two-way hand-shake for connection establishment, which was found to be unsatisfactory in the face of an unreliable network service. Similarly, the diagram defines a simple procedure for graceful connection termination. First, consider the side that initiates the termination procedure:

1. In response to a user's close primitive, a FIN segment is sent to the other side of the connection, requesting termination.
2. Having sent the FIN, the TCP entity places the connection in the FIN WAIT state. In this state, TCP must continue to accept data from the other side and deliver that data to its user.
3. When a FIN is received in response, TCP informs its user and closes the connection.

From the point of view of the side that does not initiate a termination:

1. When a FIN segment is received, TCP informs its user of the termination request (close primitive) and places the connection in the CLOSE WAIT state. In this state, TCP must continue to accept data from its user and transmit it in data segments to the other side.
2. When the user issues a Close primitive, TCP sends a responding FIN segment to the other side and closes the connection.

This procedure ensures that both sides have received all outstanding data and that both sides agree to connection termination before actual termination. As with the two-way handshake for connection establishment, however, this procedure is inadequate. First, consider that segments may arrive out of order. Thus, the following may occur. A TCP entity in the CLOSE WAIT state sends its last data segment, followed by a FIN segment, but the FIN segment arrives at the other side before the last data segment. TCP will accept that FIN, close the connection, and lose the last segment of data. To avoid this problem a sequence number is associated with the FIN. For sequence number purposes, the FIN is considered to occur after the last actual octet of transmitted data. With this refinement, the receiving TCP, upon receiving a FIN, will wait if necessary for late-arriving data before closing the connection.

A more serious problem, of course, is the potential loss of segments and the potential presence of obsolete segments. Figure 3.9 shows that the termination procedure adopts a similar solution to that used in the establishment procedure. Each side must explicitly acknowledge the FIN of the other, using an ACK with the sequence number of the FIN to be acknowledged. For graceful close, a TCP entity requires the following:

- It must send a FIN i and receive an ACK i
- It must receive a FIN j and send an ACK j
- It must wait an interval equal to the twice the maximum expected segment lifetime

The first two events may occur in either order. Furthermore, a FIN and ACK may be transmitted in one segment. The TIME WAIT state is not strictly necessary but does allow enough time for the remote TCP to receive the ACK of the FIN.

Crash Recovery

When the system upon which a TCP entity is running fails and subsequently restarts, the state information of all active connections is lost. The affected connections become *half-open* because the side that did not fail does not yet realize the problem.

The still active side of a half-open connection can close the connection using a give-up timer. This timer measures the time the transport machine will continue to await an acknowledgment (or other appropriate reply) of a transmitted segment after the segment has been retransmitted the maximum number of times. When the timer expires, the transport entity assumes that the other transport entity or the intervening network has failed, closes the connection, and signals an abnormal close to the transport user.

In the event that a transport entity fails and quickly restarts, half-open connections can be terminated more quickly by the use of the RST segment. The failed side returns a RST segment to every segment that it receives. When the RST reaches the other side, it must be checked for validity based on the sequence number segment, because the RST could be in response to an old segment. If the reset is valid, the transport entity performs an abnormal termination.

These measures clean up the situation at the TCP level. The decision as to whether to reopen the connection is up to the TCP users. The problem is one of synchronization. At the time of failure, there may have been one or more outstanding segments in either direction. The TCP user on the side that did not fail knows how much data it has received, but the other may not, if state information were lost. Thus, there is the danger that some user data will be lost or duplicated.

3.3   TRANSMISSION CONTROL PROTOCOL SEGMENT FORMAT

A single header format is used for all TCP segments. This allows a single segment to be used to carry both user data and control messages, such as

SYN, FIN, and ACK. The disadvantage of this approach is that because one header must support all protocol mechanisms, it is rather large (Figure 3.16). The fields are:

- *Source port (16 bits):* Identifies source port
- *Destination port (16 bits):* Identifies destination port
- *Sequence number (32 bits):* Sequence number of the first data octet in this segment, except when SYN is present. If SYN is present, it is the initial sequence number (ISN) and the first data octet is ISN + 1
- *Acknowledgment number (32 bits):* A piggybacked acknowledgment. Contains the sequence number of the next octet that the TCP entity expects to receive
- *Data offset (4 bits):* Number of 32-bit words in the header
- *Reserved (6 bits):* Reserved for future use
- *Flags (6 bits):*
  URG: Urgent pointer field significant
  ACK: Acknowledgment field significant
  PHS: Push function
  RST: Reset the connection
  SYN: Synchronize the sequence numbers
  FIN: No more data from sender
- *Window (16 bits):* Flow control credit allocation, in octets. Contains the number of data octets beginning with the one indicated in the acknowledgment field that the sender is willing to accept
- *Checksum (16 bits):* The one's complement of the sum modulo 2^{16} − 1 of all the 16-bit words in the segment plus a pseudoheader (described later)
- *Urgent Pointer (16 bits):* Points to the octet following the urgent

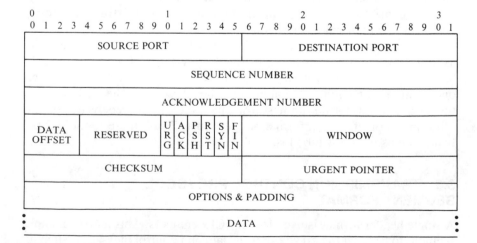

Figure 3.16. TCP header format.

data. This allows the receiver to know how much urgent data are coming
* *Options (Variable):* At present, only one option is defined, which specifies the maximum segment size that will be accepted

Several of the fields in the TCP header warrant further elaboration. The *source port* and *destination port* specify the sending and receiving users of TCP. As was the case with IP, there are a number of common users of TCP that have been assigned numbers (Table 3.8). These numbers should be reserved for that purpose in any implementation. Other port numbers must be arranged by agreement between communicating parties.

The *sequence number* and *acknowledgment number* are bound to octets rather than to entire segments. For example, if a segment contains sequence number 1000 and includes 600 octets of data, the sequence number refers to the first octet in the data field; the next segment in logical order will have sequence number 1600. Thus, TCP is stream oriented. That is, TCP accepts a stream of octets from the user, groups them into segments as it sees fit, and numbers each octet in the stream.

Table 3.8. ASSIGNED PORT NUMBERS

5	Remote Job Entry	68	Bootstrap Protocol Client
7	Echo	69	Trivial File Transfer Protocol
9	Discard	75	any private dial out service
11	Active Users	77	any private RJE service
13	Daytime	79	Who is on system
15	Who is up?	101	NIC Host Name Server
17	Quote of the day	102	ISO-TSAP
19	Character Generator	103	X.400
20	FTP (Default Data)	104	X.400-SND
21	FTP (Control)	105	CSNet Name Server
23	TELNET	109	Post Office Protocol, Version 2
25	SMTP	113	Authentication Service
37	Time	115	Simple File Transfer Protocol
39	Resource Location Protocol	119	Network News Trans. Protocol
42	Host Name Server	123	Network Time Protocol
43	NICNAME (who is)	129	Password Generator Protocol
53	Domain Name Server	161	SNMP Agent Port
67	Bootstrap Protocol Server	162	SNMP Management Station Port

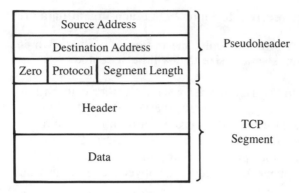

Figure 3.17. Scope of TCP checksum.

The *checksum* field is used for error detection, as described in Appendix B. The TCP checksum covers the entire segment (header plus data) plus a 96-bit pseudoheader prefixed to the TCP header at the time of calculation (at both transmission and reception). The pseudoheader contains the source internet address, destination internet address, protocol, and TCP segment length (Figure 3.17). On transmission, these parameters are the same ones that are passed to IP in the Send primitive; on reception, these parameters are available from the IP Deliver primitive (see Table 2.4). By including the pseudoheader in the checksum, TCP protects itself from misdelivery by IP. That is, if IP delivers a segment to the wrong host, even if the segment contains no bit errors, the receiving TCP entity will detect the delivery error.

3.4 IMPLEMENTATION POLICY OPTIONS

The TCP standard provides a precise specification of the protocol to be used between TCP entities. However, certain aspects of the protocol admit several possible implementation options. Although two implementations that choose alternative options will be interoperable, there may be performance implications. The design areas for which options are available are the following:

- Send policy
- Deliver policy
- Accept policy
- Retransmit policy
- Acknowledge policy

Send Policy. In the absence of pushed data and a closed transmission window (see Figure 3.14a), a sending TCP is free to transmit data at its own convenience. As data are issued by the user, they are buffered in the transmit buffer. TCP may construct a segment for each batch of data provided by its user or it may wait until a certain amount of data accumulates before constructing and sending a segment. The actual policy will depend on performance considerations. If transmissions are infrequent and large, there is low overhead in terms of segment generation. On the other hand, if transmissions are frequent and small, then the system is providing quick response.

Deliver Policy.   In the absence of a Push, a receiving TCP is free to deliver data to the user at its own convenience. It may deliver data as each in-order segment is received, or it may buffer data from a number of segments in the receive buffer before delivery. The actual policy will depend on performance considerations. If deliveries are infrequent and large, the user is not receiving data as promptly as may be desirable. On the other hand, if deliveries are frequent and small, there may be unnecessary processing both in TCP and in the user software.

Accept Policy.   When all data segments arrive in order over a TCP connection, TCP places the data in a receive buffer for delivery to the user. It is possible, however, for segments to arrive out of order. In this case the receiving TCP entity has two options. First, TCP can elect to accept only segments that are in order. Any segment that arrives out of order is discarded. This makes for a simple implementation, but places a burden on the networking facility, as the sending TCP must time out and retransmit segments that were successfully received but rejected because of misordering. Furthermore, if a single segment is lost in transit, then all subsequent segments must be retransmitted once the sending TCP times out on the lost segment.

Second, the receiving TCP can accept all segments that are within the receive window (see Figure 3.14b). This may reduce retransmissions but requires a more complex acceptance test and a more sophisticated data storage scheme to buffer and keep track of data accepted out of order.

Retransmit Policy.   TCP maintains a queue of segments that have been sent but not yet acknowledged. The TCP specification states that TCP will retransmit a segment if it fails to receive an acknowledgment within a given time. A TCP implementation may employ one of three retransmission strategies:

- *First-only:* Maintains one retransmission timer for the entire queue. If an acknowledgment is received, removes the appropriate segment or segments from the queue and resets the timer. If the timer expires, retransmits the segment at the front of the queue and resets the timer.

- *Batch:* Maintains one retransmission timer for the entire queue. If an acknowledgment is received, removes the appropriate segment or segments from the queue and resets the timer. If the timer expires, retransmits all segments in the queue and resets the timer.
- *Individual:* Maintains one timer for each segment in the queue. If an acknowledgment is received, removes the appropriate segment or segments from the queue and destroys the corresponding timer or timers. If timers expire, retransmits the segments individually and resets their timers.

The first-only policy is efficient in terms of traffic generated as only lost segments (or segments whose ACK was lost) are retransmitted. Because the timer for the second segment in the queue is not set until the first segment is acknowledged, however, there can be considerable delays. The individual policy solves this problem at the expense of a more complex implementation. The batch policy also reduces the likelihood of long delays but may result in unnecessary retransmissions.

The actual effectiveness of these policies depends in part on the accept policy of the receiver. If the receiver is using an in-order accept policy, then it will discard segments received after a lost segment. This fits best with batch retransmission. If the receiver is using an in-window accept policy, then a first-only or individual retransmission policy is best. Of course, in a mixed network of computers, both accept policies may be in use.

Acknowledge Policy.   When in-order data is accepted, the receiving TCP has two options concerning the timing of acknowledgment:

- When data is accepted, immediately transmit an empty (no data) segment containing current acknowledgment information.
- When data is accepted, record the need for acknowledgment, but wait for an outbound segment with data on which to piggyback the ACK. To avoid a long delay, set window timer (see Table 3.6); if the timer expires before acknowledgment, transmit an empty segment.

The *automatic ACK* approach is simple and keeps the remote TCP fully informed, which limits unnecessary retransmissions. However, it results in extra segment transmissions, namely the segments that contain only the ACK. Furthermore, the policy can cause a further load on the network. Consider that one side receives a segment and immediately sends an ACK. Then, the data in the segment is released to the application, which expands the receive window, triggering another ACK (to provide additional credit to the other side). Finally, the application may send an acknowledgement to the data that it received, which is sent as a TCP data segment.

Because of the potential overhead of the automatic ACK, the *delayed ACK* is typically used. Recognize, however, that the use of the delayed ACK requires more processing at the receiving end and complicates the task of estimating round-trip transmission delay on the sending end.

3.5   USER DATAGRAM PROTOCOL

In addition to TCP, there is one other transport-level protocol that is in common use as part of the DOD protocol suite: the user datagram protocol (UDP) specified in RFC 768 [POST80].

The UDP provides a connectionless service for application-level procedures. It enables a procedure to send messages to other procedures with a minimum of protocol mechanism. An example of the use of UDP is in the context of network management.

UDP sits on top of IP. Because it is connectionless, UDP has very little to do. Essentially, it adds a port addressing capability to IP. This is best seen by examining the UDP header, shown in Figure 3.18. The header includes a source port and destination port. As in the case of TCP, the well-known ports defined in Table 3.8 may be used. The length field contains the length of the entire UDP segment, including header and data. The checksum is the same algorithm used for TCP and IP and described in Appendix B. For UDP, the checksum applies to the entire UDP segment plus a pseudo-header prefixed to the UDP header at the time of calculation, and is the same one used for TCP (Figure 3.17). If an error is detected, the segment is discarded and no further action is taken.

The checksum field in UDP is optional. If it is not used, it is set to zero. However, it should be pointed out that the IP checksum applies only to the IP header and not to the data field, which in this case consists of the UDP header and the user data. Therefore, if no checksum calculation is performed by UDP, then no check is made on the user data.

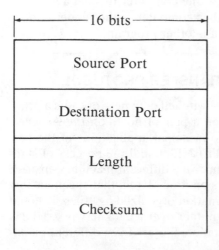

Figure 3.18.   UDP header.

4

File Transfer Protocol

Tony Michel

The ability to exchange information among computers is important in many modern information systems. It is not easy to provide a general means of information exchange, as the way that information is organized and stored differs greatly among different systems. Because it has been proven difficult to establish standards for how information is treated within systems, standards have focused on the process of exchange, and this is the province of the file transfer protocol (FTP). FTP provides a way for one computer to send a file to (push) or get (pull) a file from another computer, either under control of a human user, or on behalf of another program.

4.1   INTRODUCTION TO FILE TRANSFER PROTOCOL

The first application of the first packet switched data network was a primitive FTP that sent test traffic between a pair of hosts on the Arpanet. This quickly grew into one of the two principal applications of the network, called the FTP (the other was TELNET), and the process of standardization and implementation on numerous different machines ensued. FTP is a protocol, or set of agreements on procedures, that specifies how a particular kind of information, information organized as "files," should be transferred from one computer to another over a data network. FTP is intended to support implementations on computers from different manufacturers, and makes few assumptions about the details of the operating systems. FTP is a specification for the behavior of a computer, as seen by another computer, and does not deal (too much) with the details of the implementation on a particular machine.

From the beginning it was clear that FTP would be complex, because the problem is complex. The way that files are stored, accessed, and protected differs greatly among different types of computers. In fact, it is difficult even to find a single definition of a file that would satisfy all systems. Instead, FTP presumes some basic properties, such as data type, file organization, and file ownership, that are common to files on most systems, and provides a means by which one computer can manipulate these properties of files on another computer without knowing in detail much about that other system. Files on a remote system are manipulated by means of a set of commands and responses that are defined by FTP, and that are exchanged by the two machines. Examples of manipulation are: get a file from, or send a file to, a remote system.

FTP does not attempt to translate files from one computer type to another, or establish a single *network virtual file*. Rather, it provides three dimensions, data types, file types, and transmission modes, that can be used by the two computers to establish a common ground. For example, when an IBM machine, which normally stores data as file of EBCDIC (Extended Binary Coded Decimal Interchange Code) records, sends data to a UNIX machine, which stores data as a simple string of ASCII bytes, the IBM machine will normally first convert into the Internet standard data type for text files, which is ASCII. FTP is not concerned with how this conversion is done, only that it be done before the data are sent across the network connection. The IBM machine would send the file as a nonrecord-structure file in stream transmission mode.

FTP is a fairly "low level" standard and is not involved with the higher level structure of a file, beyond the defined data types. For example, the revisable-form type of text files used by most text processing programs and editors can be transferred verbatim by FTP, but will be intelligible only to systems that support the specific formats used at the source. FTP will obligingly transfer an ASCII file to an EBCDIC machine without complaint. Some sophisticated FTP applications may issue a warning if the data "looks funny," for example, if an ASCII text file has a large number of control characters, but other than warnings, will proceed without intervention.

Figure 4.1 shows the elements involved in a file transfer. The object is to move a file from wherever it is (the Source File) to somewhere else (the Destination File). The files are stored in the file systems, normally on random access disk file systems, in general-purpose host computers. The host computers will have hardware for connection to a data network, and network protocol software that includes FTP application-level software.

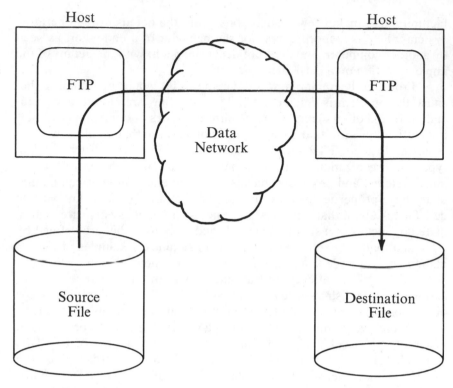

Figure 4.1. FTP overview.

FTP is normally used to support immediate, or real-time file movement. The file transfer begins immediately upon initiation of the FTP application program, and the initiating user or program must suspend other action and await the completion before proceeding. Because many things affect the speed of the transfer, such as the size of the file and the capacity of the network, FTP is generally not time sensitive. A transfer can sometimes take a long time (many hours) to complete.

The Initiator

The initiator of a transfer can be either a human or a computer program. The human will normally use an application program called the *User FTP Program* that is one of the common network utilities. User FTP provides access to all the capability of the protocol and requires that the user make only sensible transfers of like to like file and data types.

Some machines also provide an interface so that an applications program can itself call the User FTP to initiate a transfer. In this case, the user program must supply all the information needed, including the account identifier, access codes, and file name, as well as option specifications. This is a common technique used by many systems to periodically fetch the network Host Name table from a central database.

Architectural Underpinning

FTP is designed to be implemented on any size host, and effective implementations are found on small personal computers such as MSDOS machines as well as the largest mainframes.

FTP is at the application level and relies on an underlying layer, specifically transmission control protocol (TCP), to provide reliable transfer and data pacing and to manage the set-up and disconnection of the underlying network connections. The Department of Defense architecture has no Presentation Layer to specify information formats, and therefore, this job falls to FTP, which contains specifications for data and control formats. Below TCP, IP (Arpanet Internetwork Protocol) and lower-level network access protocols must be provided. FTP relies on an essentially error- and trouble-free environment provided by these lower-level mechanisms and provides no such mechanism itself.

The Three Dimensions for Options

The first dimension is *data type*. Text data may be represented as either ASCII or EBCDIC characters, whereas all other data (binary data) are treated as a bit stream (image) or as groups of bits (logical bytes). The second and third dimension are concerned with the internal problem of representing files and the external problem of moving the file data across the TCP connection, respectively. The second dimension of *file structure* is provided for the convenience of the specific implementations. For example, some file systems require that data be written into a file one record at a time. FTP provides a way of marking the transmitted data stream so that the receiver can accumulate data into a buffer until an End of Record is encountered, whereupon the entire buffer can be written as a single record into the destination file. The third dimension of *transmission mode* allows the transfer to support data compression and transfer checkpoint and restart.

The TCP connection, which underlies the FTP transfer, provides a *stream* service. Individual 8-bit bytes may be sent in whatever way is convenient for the controlling FTP. Individual transmissions are not required to employ any interrecord markers or other block separators. FTP does provide, however, a mechanism for marking the end of a Block and this marking can be used by record-oriented file system interfaces or for checkpoint/restart of failed transfers (Figure 4.2). Use of these capabilities is at the option of and controlled by the FTP application.

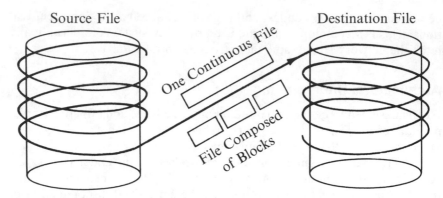

Figure 4.2. Continuous and blocked files.

Table 4.1. FTP USERS AND SERVERS

User	Server
Initiates connection	Responds
Must log in	Enforces protection
Specifies file type and name	Manages transfer

Users and Servers

Normally, two different computers, called *hosts* are involved. Although the two hosts are essentially equals or *peers,* each side of the transfer is specialized (Table 4.1). The host that initiates the transfer is called the *User* or *Client.* The User chooses the name of the file, and the options to be used in the transfer. The Server accepts (or rejects) the requested transfer based on its file system protection criteria, and on the options requested. If the transfer is accepted, the Server is responsible for actually establishing and managing the transfer.

Getting and Fetching

The User FTP may specify either direction of transfer as shown in Figure 4.3. Transfer from the User to the Server is called *sending* or writing the file. From Server to User the operation is called *getting* or reading. In both cases, it is a matter of the specific implementation to avoid file name conflicts and ensure that the user has the authority to extract information or deposit it as the case may be. Some implementations (such as most UNIX systems) overwrite a file of the same name, whereas others (like TOPS-20) create a new file version number and save an old file of the same name.

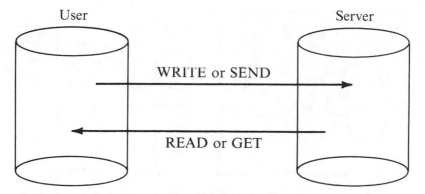

Figure 4.3. Reading and writing.

Overview of a Transfer

The following example shows a simple transfer progressing through all the stages. No errors are encountered and the details of the option specification are not explored. The complexities of detail are treated in a later section. The transfer proceeds through six phases, each of which is diagrammed and briefly discussed in one of the numbered steps of the transfer. This is an idealized, simplified example in which each step is distinct. In real applications, some of these steps might not be apparent to a user or might fail due to an error.

In Figure 4.4a, a user program invokes the user or client FTP program of the local system. The user supplies the address of the remote system to which access is desired. The FTP User Program, in turn, opens a TCP connection, called the Control Connection, to the remote host. All commands and responses will pass across this control connection.

Figure 4.4b depicts the access control process. The user supplies an account name and password to the local system, which in turn forms the FTP commands and sends them to the Server. In this case the account and password are valid, and are accepted. FTP takes no part in the actual user authorization process. It simply provides a conduit by which the information can be passed to whatever mechanism is used with the Server to control access. In most systems this is the main user login mechanism. If you can log in to a system, then you can FTP to (from) it. The access control mechanism does not establish the direction of the transfer.

In Figure 4.4c, the specific details of the transfer are given: file name, direction of transfer (get or put), and details of data and file type, as well as mode of transfer. As with access control, the user (or user program) might not see all the details of this step. It is the User FTP Program that interprets the user's intention and sends a series of FTP commands across the control connection. When all commands are re-

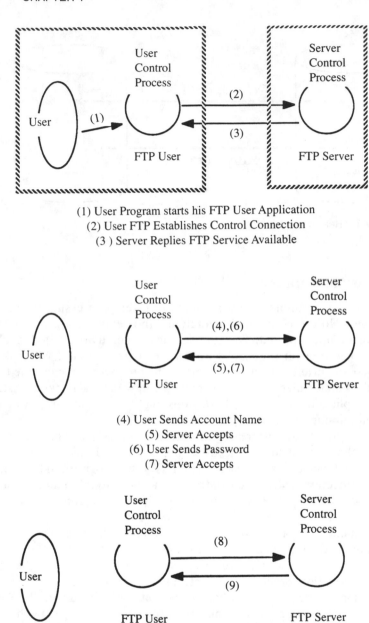

(1) User Program starts his FTP User Application
(2) User FTP Establishes Control Connection
(3) Server Replies FTP Service Available

(a)

(4) User Sends Account Name
(5) Server Accepts
(6) User Sends Password
(7) Server Accepts

(b)

(8) User Specifies File Name and Options
(9) Server Accepts

(c)

Figure 4.4. Overview of a transfer.

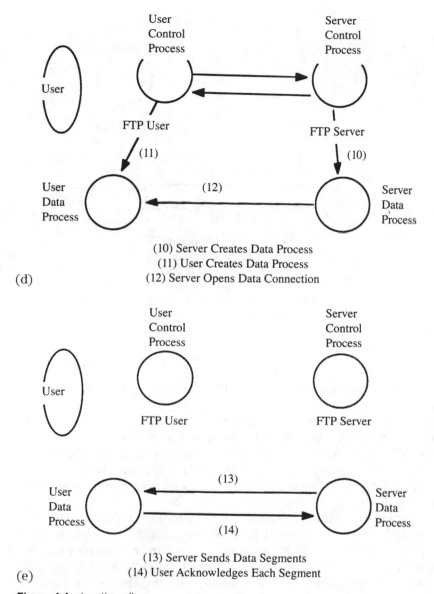

(10) Server Creates Data Process
(11) User Creates Data Process
(12) Server Opens Data Connection

(d)

(13) Server Sends Data Segments
(14) User Acknowledges Each Segment

(e)

Figure 4.4   (continued)

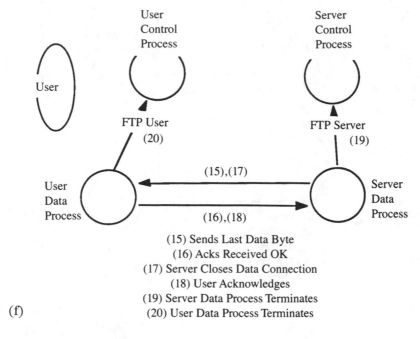

(15) Sends Last Data Byte
(16) Acks Received OK
(17) Server Closes Data Connection
(18) User Acknowledges
(19) Server Data Process Terminates
(f)   (20) User Data Process Terminates

Figure 4.4 (continued)

ceived and acknowledged, then the FTP User may presume that the transfer will proceed.

In Figure 4.4d, the first step of the actual data transfer begins. The FTP Server opens a second TCP connection, the data connection, back to the FTP User, with each end using the appropriate local parameters. Both ends are by now in agreement that the file may be transferred in the specified direction, using the data type, file type, and transfer mode given by the FTP User.

Figure 4.4e shows the actual data transfer as it proceeds. The user, the User FTP and the Server FTP processes all await the completion of the data transfer connection. The data transfer can be a complex process. As shown, this transfer is a *retrieve* operation in which a file is moved from the Server to the User. The Server and the User work together, using the TCP error and flow control mechanisms of the data connection to read data out of the source file, encapsulate an appropriate number of bytes in TCP segments, and write the received segments into the destination file at the user host. TCP is responsible for retransmission of segments when errors are detected, and for metering the flow out of the source and onto the TCP connection.

When the Server finds it has fetched the last data byte from the source file, it sends off the last TCP segment and then initiates a CLOSE of the data connection (Figure 4.4f). The User FTP data process takes this normal close as a signal that the transfer is completed, and then both user and server terminate the data connection. The control connection remains open, and can be used to control another data transfer, over a new data connection, or it may close at this point.

The considerable detail of the option specification process, and of the command/response and error handling are discussed in the next section.

4.2 OPTIONS

The design of FTP, as in all engineering products, is a result of many compromises between capability and complexity. As more features, such as supported data types and transmission modes, are included in the specification, the implementations necessarily will become more complex. If FTP explicitly provided support for each data and file type, on each kind of the common computers, it would require a daunting specification. On the other hand, if FTP defined a single *Network Virtual File* type into which a file must be converted before transfer, it would probably not be possible to serve enough different computer types to achieve consensus. FTP therefore, attempts neither of these extremes. Instead, it is presumed that files are objects in a computer's mass storage memory that share a few properties regardless of the machine type. Files have symbolic names that allow them to be uniquely identified within a particular file system or directory. A file has an owner and has protection against unauthorized access or modification by others. Finally, a file may be read from (copied from) or written into. Within this fairly simple framework, FTP contrives to support the movement of files among diverse computers over various data networks. To support the needs of specific computers and operating systems, FTP provides a mechanism for negotiating a transfer's options in three dimensions: data type, file type, and transfer mode. The range of choices is complex enough that normally a transfer must be thought out in advance, and programmed by a human, at least the first time. It is the problem of the system programmer to determine how a particular file on the system can be mapped into one of the standard file types, using one of the standard data types, and transferred using a standard mode, such that it is useful at the destination. Because FTP must support exchange of files among otherwise incompatible systems, this is no mean task.

Data Types

There are four defined data types. Of these, two are most suitable for representing text files: the ASCII and EBCDIC types. Text files might be computer program sources, word processing documents, or any sort of information that is ultimately destined to be displayed to a human on a terminal or printer. Text files are normally stored as strings of sequential characters, and Figure 4.5 shows a fragment of the file containing "...HELLO..." as it might appear first in a 16-bit machine, such as the DEC PDP-11, and then as in a 36-bit machine such as the DEC PDP-10.

The second principal category is nontext files and there are two of these types: the IMAGE and the LOGICAL BYTE SIZE. Nontext types are normally employed for binary program images, most types of encoded data, and tabular data that cannot be strictly handled as text.

ASCII.   Type ASCII is the most common representation for FTP text files. Type ASCII is almost what it seems except that the ASCII codes, which require 7 bits, are contained in 8-bit fields as shown in Figure 4.6. This representation is called NVT-ASCII. It seems to be a good match to the internal structures of most modern machines that have word lengths at multiples of 8 bits and use a similar internal representation. Machines with 20 bits and 36 bits have a bigger computational job with this representation, however.

EBCDIC.   Although NVT-ASCII is the preferred text data type for FTP, it is more convenient in some cases (for example, when one IBM host sends to another IBM host) to keep the data in the native form for IBM machines, which is type EBCDIC (Figure 4.7). In this case, the transfer will operate just as for type ASCII, but the receiving and sending system need not do the fruitless conversion into ASCII and then back again to

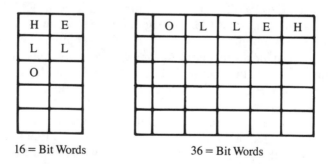

16 = Bit Words   36 = Bit Words

Figure 4.5.   Text file representation in memory.

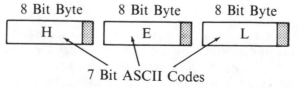

Figure 4.6.   NVT ASCII.

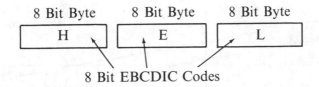

Figure 4.7.   EBCDIC text files.

EBCDIC. It also avoids dealing with the problem of EBCDIC characters that have no representation in ASCII.

Files of either type ASCII or type EBCDIC may have a further specification of how they are to be presented to a line or page printer. Because some systems find it convenient to include printer control characters within the text to be printed, three choices are offered: nonprint, TELNET formatting, and Carriage control formatting.

The nonprint option is suitable for files that are not destined to a line printer. The other two options allow the transfer to preserve information about the vertical carriage control that might be used by a printing process. With TELNET formatting, it is requested that embedded characters (⟨carriage return⟩, ⟨line feed⟩, ⟨new line⟩, ⟨vertical tab⟩, and ⟨form feed⟩) be extracted from the data stream and used in the page formatting. With carriage control formatting, the FORTRAN convention is used. The first character of each line is carriage control for that line, and four defined values allow for single spacing, double spacing, top of page, and "no line feed" for overprinting.

Image.   To exchange data between machines of the same type, the IMAGE data type is provided. With IMAGE files, no attempt is made to make them generally intelligible, as in types ASCII or EBCDIC, which are universally defined. An IMAGE transfer causes the first bit in the source to appear in the first destination bit, the second to the second, and so forth. No bits are skipped, preset, or otherwise modified (Figure 4.8). During the transfer, the data are packed into 8-bit bytes and passed across the TCP connection. The last byte of the transfer will be padded out to an integral 8-bit byte, but the receiving FTP data process removes this 8-bit organization and deletes any padding. The Image type is most often used with files that are executable programs, function libraries, and other sorts of files that have been translated or compiled, and will be of use only to a known processor type.

Type IMAGE could be used to transfer ASCII or EBCDIC files between machines of the same type, as IMAGE preserves all the information in the file. Between machines of different type, however, it is not generally successful to use IMAGE for anything.

Individual Bits are Copied...   To Their Respective
Positions

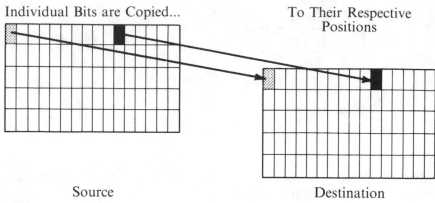

Source   Destination

Figure 4.8.   Image file transfer.

Logical Byte Size.   The final data type is the Logical Byte Size type, which is used when there is a data unit size that must be preserved. The Logical Byte type takes an argument, which is the size of the byte. The source and destination machines are at liberty to deal with the logical bytes in whatever way they must. In this context, the notion of a byte is more general than the usual contemporary meaning. A logical byte may be of any number of bits in length, and may or may not be aligned with the computer's memory word size. This type is most often used to ensure that executable program images compiled on one machine but sent to and stored on a second machine, can be correctly interpreted and manipulated on the second machine. For example, if a memory image of a 32-bit machine is to be sent to a 36-bit machine, and manipulated there, Logical Byte Size provides a way to specify that successive 32-bit values be forced into successive 36-bit memory words. Even among different types of machines of the same word length, there are differences in how the bytes that compose a word are addressed. Logical Byte Size can be used to force successive full words of bits to remain ordered across the transfer.

File Types

The purpose of offering several file types is to promote a convenient and efficient interface to the file system of the source and destination computers. Because there are only three defined file types, it is not possible to address the idiosyncrasies of all existing operating systems. But this set of options seems well suited to the majority of machines that are common in the contemporary Darpa Internet.

File Structure.   This simplest of structures presumes that the file is simply a string of bytes (which will be specified by the *data type* of the transfer). The string is presumed to be terminated by an End Of File marker.

Most transfers use this type. Figure 4.9 illustrates a *file structured* file as it might appear in a file system.

Record Structure.   It is not always desirable to consider a file as a string of bytes. In some operating systems files must be handled or, at least, are more efficiently handled as *records* (Figure 4.10). A record might be the

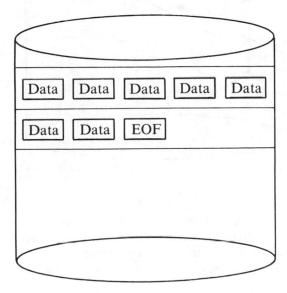

Figure 4.9.   File structure.

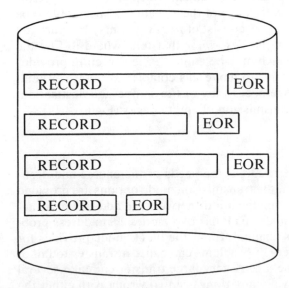

Figure 4.10.   Record structure.

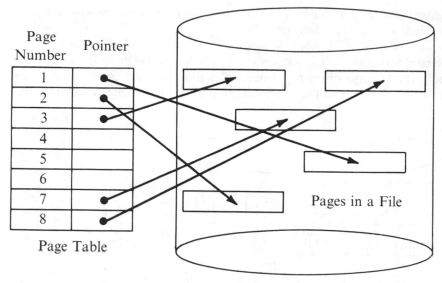

Figure 4.11. Paged structure.

natural size used by the file system disk interface hardware controller. When it is desirable to preserve a record marking across the file transfer, a record structure may be used. Record Structure causes transmission of individual records, separated by the standard End of Record marker, for the specified data type.

Page Structure. Because Digital Equipment Corp TOPS-20 systems were very prominent in the early days of the Arpanet, a special file type is defined for them. TOPS-20 files consist of *pages* that may be scattered across the file system, and a *file descriptor* that tells where to find the individual pages, some of which may be empty. Page Structure provides a way for two TOPS-20 systems to move this complex structure around, resolving conflicts in the page occupancy of the source and destination, and avoiding the (useless) transmission of empty pages (Figure 4.11).

Transmission Modes

While the data and file types address the needs of the source and destination host operating system, the transmission mode options are provided to optimize the use of the communications network. In addition to a simple, unembellished stream mode, FTP has two modes that address problems in the communications channel. First, the block mode provides for restarting a transfer. A variety of problems can cause a transfer to fail or be interrupted before completion. A very large transfer can take several hours, and during this interval many things can go wrong with either the network or the hosts. The restart capability allows data sent in a failed transfer to be *salvaged* at the destination. A new transfer can pick up where the old left one off, which obviates the need to resend data already correctly received. The second enhanced mode allows for data compression. In some cases, such as text files, there are enormous amounts of repetition and redundancy, such as long strings of the same character, or of the *space* character that often is used to fill out *white space* in a file. In these cases, a simple data compression technique can sometimes reduce dramatically the number of bits transferred. The compressed mode allows for this option.

Stream. Stream mode is the simplest, and is the default for all transfers. In stream mode, the unmodified, raw data are sent over the data connection. Because there is no specialized processing of the data at either end, this is simplest from the implementation standpoint, and imposes the least computation burden on the user and server systems.

There is no restriction on the file type used with stream mode. For record-structure files, a two-byte control code is used to indicate end of record (EOR) or end of file (EOF). The first byte is all ones, the escape character. The second byte has a value of 1, 2, or 3 to indicate EOR, EOF, or both, respectively. If a byte of all ones is to be sent as data, this is represented by two bytes of all ones. The unnecessary second byte is stripped by the receiving FTP. For file-structure files, EOF is indicated by the sending FTP closing the data connection; all transferred bytes on the data connection are data bytes.

Block. Block mode is provided to allow for restarting of failed transfers. When this mode is accepted, the source encapsulates the data for transfer into blocks of a stylized format shown in Figure 4.12. The transfer then consists of a sequence of these blocks. The source and the destination may record the progress of the transfer, and if interrupted, restart the transfer from the last correctly received block. The specification does not say how long the blocks may be, or establish any policy for how the checkpointing and restart operations should be conducted.

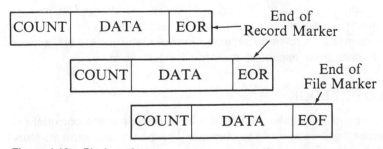

Figure 4.12. Block mode.

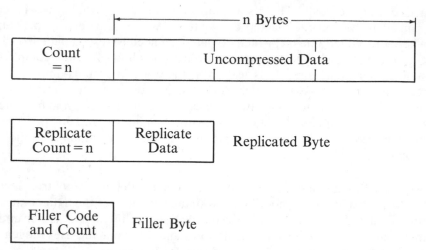

Figure 4.13. Compressed data mode.

Compressed. Compressed mode provides a way to improve efficiency of the transfer by allowing the source to squeeze sequences of the same character into a coded sequence. Uncompressed text is sent unmodified, as shown in Figure 4.13. A block of data begins with a code byte that says how many uncompressed data bytes follow. When the source file contains a section with the same data value repeated a number of times, the repeated bytes are extracted and a second type of coded block is sent. The 2-byte sequence allows repetitions of up to 63 of the specified bytes to be signaled. The destination FTP data connection must expand the repetition code, and reinsert the specified number of specified data character. A further compression is provided for the special character ⟨space⟩ that appears frequently in all sorts of text files and can be signaled by the single character Filler String byte.

Protection

The protection feature provides simple access control at connection setup time, based usually on a login criteria. The user needs read access to fetch, and write access plus directory write access to write or delete. Most operating systems have no separate mechanism for network access and so must adapt some aspect of their local mechanism.

4.3   A CLOSER LOOK

Two important aspects of the design of FTP will be further considered: the two-connection model and the command/response mechanism. During most of the transfer operation, there are two TCP connections simul-

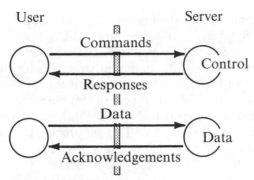

Figure 4.14. Connection management.

taneously active between the user and the server (Figure 4.14). One connection, the control connection, handles commands and responses, whereas the other, the data connection, handles the data and the acknowledgments. The virtue of this design is that with control and data paths separated, some additional flexibility is possible. The management, especially the flow control, of the control and data processes can be separate. Also, third-party transfers are possible.

Connection Management Considerations

Flow control management is complex because of the power of the underlying TCP connection. TCP imposes no particular data block size on its users. Therefore, commands and responses, which will be fairly short bursts of characters, can be handled as appropriate for transactions: individual commands must be immediately parsed and interpreted, and appropriate responses generated quickly, as the transfer is presumably hung awaiting the reply. Commands and responses are fairly (hopefully, exactly) balanced on the control connection. As a result of these characteristics, an optimum implementation for the control connection would run at high priority, in a character-oriented mode, with little or no pipelining expected. The underlying TCP would not expect to have to reassemble out-of-sequence segments, as all commands and responses would be completely contained in single segments.

The data connection, on the other hand, is the opposite of the control connection in several respects. Most of the time, FTP is dealing with files that are large compared with the size of a practical IP datagram. The data connection, therefore, would try to send large TCP segments, and perhaps would try to pipeline, by sending a number of segments ahead of the received segment acknowledgments. The flow of data will be greater than the reverse flow of acknowledgments. Furthermore, neither the data sender nor the data receiver needs to look at or process the data in any way. Data can be passed directly from the TCP connection into the receiving file system. Finally, the urgency of returning acknowledgments is much less than for the control connection. The data recipient can afford to wait and combine ACKS for multiple data segments, if that is helpful. These considerations make the optimum strategies for the data connection rather different from those for the control connection. However, not all implementations take full advantage of this potential.

A rather different consideration is the third-party capability. Figure 4.15 shows such an operation. An FTP user process on host A can establish two control connections, one to host B and one to host C. In this case, both hosts B and C are in the role of Server. The host A User can command host B to passively wait, and then command host C to initiate a data connection. This provides a means to move a file from B to C without giving a user on either B or C access to the file system on either host. This technique can help solve some aspects of privacy and information security, provided that somewhere a trusted host A can be found to supervise.

All of this power and flexibility is not without cost. Synchronizing

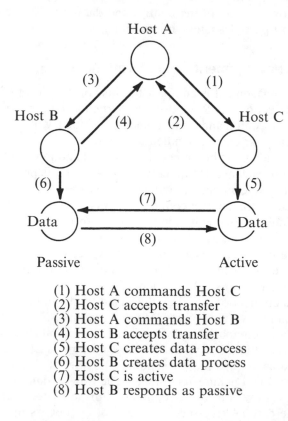

(1) Host A commands Host C
(2) Host C accepts transfer
(3) Host A commands Host B
(4) Host B accepts transfer
(5) Host C creates data process
(6) Host B creates data process
(7) Host C is active
(8) Host B responds as passive

Figure 4.15. Third-party transfer.

the control and data processes is important and, in some operating systems, difficult. Systems that have a high cost to establish or maintain a TCP connection are doubly burdened by FTP. Failure recovery can be complex because either the data or the control connection, or both, can presumably fail and require some sort of intervention.

Commands and Responses

Figure 4.16 shows the relationship of the FTP control and data connections. Commands are sent by the User (Client) encoded as NVT-ASCII strings, which are 4-character sequences. Responses by the server are 3-digit codes, plus an optional string of text that may be used by the recipient to help explain things to a human user, or to construct a log file entry. A complete list of the FTP commands and the interpretation of the reply codes can be found in the military standard, and an overview of several example operations is given here.

The control connection in FTP makes use of conventions from the TELNET protocol. This can be achieved in two ways: either by implementing the rules of the TELNET protocol directly in the FTP module, or by invoking a separate TELNET module in the same system. Ease of implementation, sharing code, and modular programming argue for the second approach. Efficiency and independence argue for the first approach. In practice, FTP relies on very little of the TELNET protocol; therefore the first approach does not necessarily involve a large amount of code.

Establishing the Control Connection

The control connection is established by the User, or Client system, by opening a TCP connection to the desired Server and specifying TCP destination port 21 (decimal). The TCP processing program on all servers

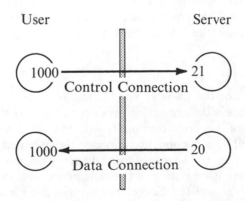

Figure 4.16.   Control and data ports.

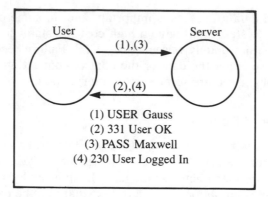

Figure 4.17. Access commands and responses.

(which operate according to convention) will pass such an inbound request to the FTP server program, which generates the appropriate replies.

When the control connection is open, but before the data connection is established, the user authentication process may be required by the server. The User must supply an account name and may be challenged for a password, depending on local practice and policy at the Server. Figure 4.17 shows the exchange of symbolic commands and numeric responses that are part of the access procedure. The User commands and the Server responses may or may not be visible to the human user or user program at the User end of the connection. The user program may create its own strings for local display to the user.

Specifying the Configuration

After the control connection is open and the FTP session has proceeded beyond access control, it is necessary to establish the parameters of the transfer. Figure 4.18 shows the User requesting data type EBCDIC with record structure and stream transfer mode. This might be suitable, for instance, for sending files into an IBM host.

The Data Transfer

Upon acceptance of the transfer specifications, both the User and the Server must initiate a data handling process to support the data connection. The details of this operation differ with the operating systems (Figure 4.19). In UNIX, a second user process is spawned by the control process, which is then the *parent* of the data process. In a simpler system, like MS-DOS, there is no notion of multiple processes. In all cases, however, both the User and the Server control function must inform their respective data functions of the chosen file name, transfer direction, and

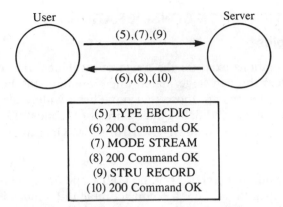

Figure 4.18. Transfer specification.

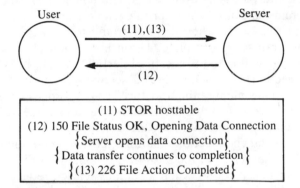

Figure 4.19. Data transfer phase.

specifications. When these internal details are worked out, each end is ready for the data connection. In the case under discussion, the STOR function will send the file "hosttable" from the User to the Server, at the initiative of the Server, which does a *pull* of the file into its own file system. In stream mode there is no punctuation of the transfer data stream, and therefore, the data transfer proceeds without intervention until the User discovers the last data byte in the file and signals an End of File. Upon receipt of the EOF, the Server closes the data connection and terminates the data process. In a system such as UNIX, the termination would signal "completion with no errors" and from this the control process would deduce that all went well. Not all operating systems provide adequate interprocess communication for this sort of signaling, and this can sometimes make difficult the orderly recovery from problems in some operating systems.

4.4   IMPLEMENTATION CONSIDERATIONS

Host Examples

FTP implementations exist for the range of machines from desktop personal computers through large mainframes. Some of the best and most
useful implementations are those that have been widely distributed and
have seen a lot of use and debugging. Three of the most ubiquitous FTP
implementations are those of UNIX, IBM's VM Operating System, and
for MS-DOS.

UNIX.   Many different versions of the UNIX operating sytem have been
fielded and among these there are considerable differences in the details
of the network support software. In most modern systems, however, the
architecture of the user FTP is as shown in Figure 4.20. The operating
system kernel contains the TCP, IP, and usually a variety of choices for
local network interface. The user FTP function is performed by an applications program that runs as an unprivileged user process. The user FTP
program is invoked only when there is traffic to be sent, and operates
only until the transfer is complete. Upon invocation (1), the user FTP
opens a TCP connection to the specified destination (2), that will become
the data connection, and then creates a second user process (3) that as-
sists with the management of the transfer. The first process deals with the
data transfer, whereas the other process receives and processes responses
(4) from the control connection. At the conclusion of the transfer, the
server closes the data connection, and this signals completion to the user.
    For UNIX server FTP, the structure is somewhat different (Figure
4.21). A server never knows when a remote service request will arrive
from the network, and therefore, the usual approach is to provide an applications process that is initiated at system startup and that remains

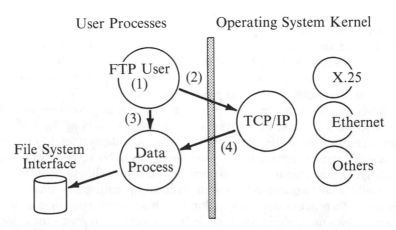

Figure 4.20.   UNIX user FTP structure.

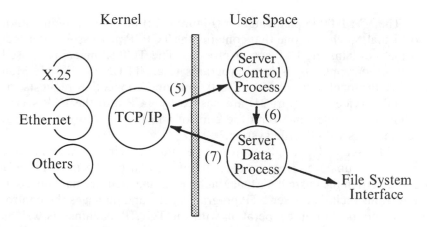

Kernel   User Space

Figure 4.21.   UNIX server FTP structure.

runnable at all times thereafter. This server process is given control, by the underlying TCP processor, of inbound connection requests (5) that specify TCP destination port 21 (decimal), which is the FTP request port. Immediately upon receipt of such a request, the FTP server creates a new process specifically dedicated to the most recent FTP request, and passes control to that new process. The principal server then returns to listen for further FTP requests. In this way any number of simultaneous transfers may be set up, limited only by the maximum number of processes the system is able to manage and the number of TCP connections it can handle. When the control processes have worked out preliminaries as to file name, transfer mode, and so forth, then another process is created (6) to establish (7) and manage the data connection, and this persists until the completion of the data transfer.

IBM VM.   VM is a popular operating system on medium- and large-sized IBM mainframes. It provides a multiuser, multiprocess capability in a different way from UNIX. The machine's resources of CPU cycles, memory, and input/output devices are managed by the VM supervisor that arranges a complete Virtual Machine for each of the users. Within a Virtual Machine either a user program or a system utility may reside, each alone, and from its own point of view independent and in control of a complete machine. Within a Virtual Machine, a program may create and manage multiple processes and may manage memory and those input/output devices that have been assigned to it. Individual Virtual Machines are protected from one another by the VM memory management, and are given controlled access to the file system, subject to file ownership policies, and there is a mechanism for communications between Virtual Machines.

The VM FTP implementation (Figure 4.22) involves a minimum of two Virtual Machines: one that contains the TCP/IP processor and a second that contains the FTP server process. The TCP/IP machine is used by the other applications level programs (e.g., TELNET, Simple Mail Transfer Protocol, and others) as well. Inbound connection requests for the FTP service port (port 21) are passed by TCP into the FTP server machine that implements both the control and the data processes, and that interfaces with the file system.

VM User FTP is implemented in yet another Virtual Machine, one per user. A human or program user may load and invoke the FTP user program within the current Virtual Machine. Using the intermachine communications facility, a User FTP program opens and manages the control and data connection in cooperation with the TCP/IP machine, as well as the file system interface. By confining all aspects of TCP/IP as well as higher level protocols within Virtual Machines, it is possible for the VM implementation to run in unmodified VM systems without any special code in the operating system itself. This is an important difference from the UNIX architecture, which contains the network software in the system kernel, where configuration management and vendor support is sometimes harder to arrange. One drawback of the VM implementation is that running communications software in a user machine, rather than in the operating system, is inefficient.

MS-DOS.   The most popular hardware and software architecture is probably that of the IBM Personal Computer, and its compatible competitors, which use the MS-DOS operating system. MS-DOS is the essence of simplicity, compared with systems like UNIX or IBM VM. MS-DOS provides a single threaded, single-process environment with few restrictions on program behavior. Programs are free to provide their own input/output device drivers, and manipulate the file system at will. An FTP implemen-

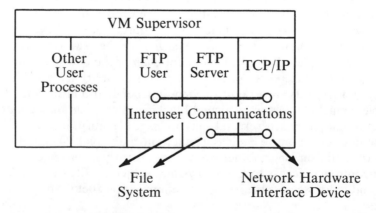

Figure 4.22.   IBM VM FTP implementation.

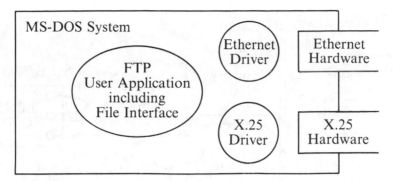

Figure 4.23.   MS-DOS FTP user implementation.

tation has been produced for this system (Figure 4.23) which bundles the entire repertoire, from device driver through FTP user application functions, and including TCP and IP as well, into a single program that runs as a more or less indivisible unit, taking over the entire PC. This program has a rather considerable advantage over some other techniques for PC file exchange, such as those that rely on various sorts of terminal emulation. In general, performance and reliability, and the ability to handle a wide range of data types without regard to particular reserved characters, make FTP an attractive option for linking PCs with mainframes.

Performance of FTP

The system planner often needs to know what throughput, usually in terms of bits moved per second, can be achieved by FTP. Many things influence throughput in real networks. Traffic load serving other network users, transmission capacity of the raw network links, and competing users on the server and user host system are important factors. Other important factors, and ones that are harder to analyze, are determined by the details of the implementation. The quality of the underlying TCP implementation is particularly important in the internetwork environment. Poor management of TCP flow control can be very costly for FTP performance. Although it is difficult to make general statements, it is useful to have an example of what FTP can achieve in a specific network environment. Figure 4.24 shows the configuration used for a series of tests on the BBN Communications Corp. internetwork. The BBNNet has several major segments, including a large wide area network supporting X.25 and 1822 host interfaces, 50 Kb trunks, and using BBNCC C/30 packet switches. The hardware and software is the same as in the Defense Data Network (DDN). Into this wide area network are gatewayed several 10 Mb Ethernet Networks. Hosts may attach either to the Ethernets or to the wide area network, as is convenient. Using the ASCII text file "/usr/dict/words" a set of four transfer experiments are performed. The hosts are lightly loaded at the time, and the networks and gateways are

10 Mb Ethernet

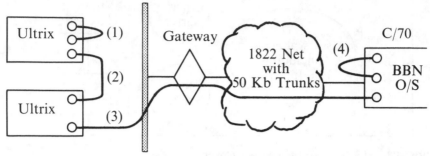

(1) Ultrix to self via Ethernet—168,000 bits/second
(2) Ultrix to Ultrix via Ethernet—272,000 bits/second
(3) Ultrix to C/70 via 50 Kb net—28,800 bits/second
(4) C/70 to self via 1822 net—55,000 bits/second

Figure 4.24.   Typical FTP throughput performance.

uncongested. Throughputs obtained are outlined in Figure 4.24 and are fairly repeatable.

Summary

FTP has matured into a reliable, widely available standard on many of the types of computers that are used in modern communications-oriented systems. Essentially all of the machines accessible on the TCP/IP inter-network, and similar networks, have working FTPs. As with all complex standards, however, implementations of FTP vary in supported features. Most implementations support those data types and transfer modes of use in communicating with like systems, and all systems support basic NVT-ASCII in stream mode. Moving simple text files, and some kinds of numerical data, works fairly well. More complicated applications, involving moving executable program images, and perhaps storing such images in intermediate systems as distribution points, can be troublesome.

From another point of view, FTP provides a fairly low-level of functionality. The user process must interact with a lot of the details of establishing the transfer path and managing the transfer. Another, perhaps more modern, approach can be seen in the network-oriented distributed file systems. These network file systems can shield the user process from most knowledge of the intermachine transfer, and this can help to greatly reduce application systems complexity. On the other hand, network file systems must presume considerable knowledge about their correspondent systems, and this can limit their power to offer interoperation among different types of systems. It is likely that both approaches will exist, side by side, for the foreseeable future, as each has advantages.

5

Simple Mail Transfer Protocol

Paul Mockapetris

5.1 ELECTRONIC MAIL

One of the deadliest wasters of time in the office is a phenomenon known as *telephone tag*. Mr. X calls Ms. Y, who is away from her desk. Some time later Y returns the call but X is out or on another line. X is now "it" and must return Y's return to X's call. And so on. . . Independent studies have shown that over 70 percent of all business telephone calls do not reach the intended recipient on the first try [MARI79]. The problem is that the caller and callee must both be at their phones and available to answer at the same time. If the caller could simply write a note and leave it on the callee's desk, the problem could be avoided. Electronic mail provides a way to do this.

Electronic mail addresses another problem as well: the office paper explosion. Offices generate a tremendous amount of paperwork, most of it in the form of internal memos and reports; over 80 percent of all business documents are textual and/or numeric (no graphs), and originate and remain within the same organization [POTT77].

Electronic mail, also known as a computer-based message system (CBMS), is a facility that allows users at terminals to compose and exchange messages. The messages need never exist on paper unless the user (sender or recipient) desires a paper copy of the message. Some electronic mail systems serve only users on a single computer; others provide service across a network of computers. In this section, we briefly look at the functionality of single-system electronic mail, then turn our attention to the more interesting case (for this book) of network electronic mail. In the remainder of this chapter, the simple mail transfer protocol (SMTP) standard is described.

Single-System Electronic Mail

The simplest, and by far the most common, form of electronic mail is the single-system facility. This facility allows all the users of a shared computer system to exchange messages. Each user is registered on the system and has a unique identifier, usually the person's last name. Associated with each user is a mailbox. The electronic mail facility is an application program available to any user logged onto the system. A user may invoke the electronic mail facility, prepare a message, and *send* it to any other user on the system. The act of sending simply involves putting the message in the recipient's mailbox. The mailbox is actually an entity maintained by the file management system, and is in the nature of a file directory. One mailbox is associated with each user. Any *incoming* mail is simply stored as a file under that user's mailbox directory. The user may later go and fetch that file to read the message. The user reads messages by invoking the mail facility and *reading* rather than *sending*. In most systems, when the user logs on, he or she is informed if there is any new mail in the user's mailbox.

A basic electronic mail system performs four functions:

- *Creation:* A user creates and edits a message, generally using a rudimentary editing capability. Most systems also allow the user to create a message using the system editor or a word processor, and then incorporate the resulting file as the body of the message.
- *Sending:* The user designates the recipient (or recipients) of the message, and the facility stores the message in the appropriate mailbox(es).
- *Reception:* The intended recipient may invoke the electronic mail facility to access and read the delivered mail.
- *Storage:* Both sender and recipient may choose to save the message in a file for more permanent storage.

Because we are interested in the networking aspects of electronic mail, the topic of basic user services will not be pursued further. More detail can be found in [HIRS85] and [BARC81].

Network Electronic Mail

With a single-system electronic mail facility, messages can only be exchanged among users of that particular system. Clearly, this is too limited.

In a distributed environment, we would like to be able to exchange messages with users attached to other systems. Thus, we would like to treat electronic mail as an application-layer protocol that makes use of lower layer protocols to transmit messages [DEUT86].

Figure 5.1 suggests the internal system architecture required. Let us refer to a single-system mail facility as a *native mail* facility. For native mail, three major modules are needed. Users will interact with native mail via terminals; hence, terminal-handling software is needed. Mail is stored as files in the file system; therefore, file-handling software is needed. Finally, there must be a native mail package that contains all the logic for providing mail-related services to users.

To extend this system to *network mail,* two more modules are needed. Because we are going to communicate across some sort of network or transmission system, communication input/output logic is needed; in the most general case, this would encompass layers 1 through 6 of the OSI model. Mail transfer logic, which knows how to invoke the communications function, is also needed to specify the network address of the recipient, and to request whatever communication services are needed (e.g., priority). Note in Figure 5.1 that the user does not directly interact with the mail transfer module. Ideally, the user interface for local or remote mail should be the same. If the user designates a local recipient, the message is stored in a local mailbox. If a remote recipient is designated, the native mail module passes the message to the mail transfer module for transmission across the network. Incoming mail from the net-

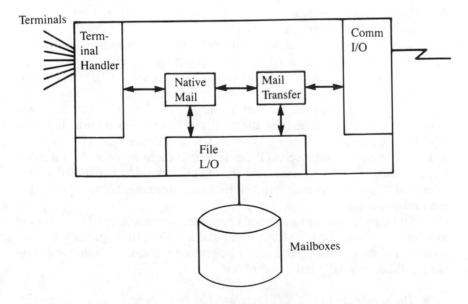

Figure 5.1.   Conceptual structure of electronic mail system.

work is routed to the appropriate mailbox and, henceforth, treated the same as other messages in the mailbox.

Many vendors now offer a network version of their basic electronic mail facility. However, this will only allow the user to send mail to users on systems of the same vendor. As in other areas, standards are needed. It is to such a standard that we now turn our attention.

5.2   INTRODUCTION TO SIMPLE MAIL TRANSFER PROTOCOL

What the Protocol Does

The Simple Mail Transfer Protocol, or SMTP, is the standard protocol for transferring mail between hosts. The protocol was defined in RFC 821, and later formalized as MIL-STD-1781. The differences between the two are in the style of presentation, rather than content.

Although messages transferred by SMTP usually follow the format defined in RFC 822 [CROC82], SMTP is not concerned with the format or content of messages themselves, with two minor exceptions. This idea is often expressed by saying that SMTP uses information written on the *envelope* of the mail, but does not look at the contents of the envelope. The two exceptions are that SMTP does standardize the message character set as 7 bit ASCII (with a high order 0 bit for 8 bit transmission channels), and SMTP does add log information to the start of the delivered message that indicates the path the message took.

The overall flow of mail in a typical system is illustrated in Figure 5.2. The top part of the figure illustrates outgoing mail, the bottom part illustrates incoming mail.

Mail is created by a user agent program in response to user input. The queued message is placed on an outgoing mail queue of some form, along with other messages from this user and other users of the local host. The queue is serviced by an SMTP sender, which typically is an always-present server process on the host. The SMTP sender takes messages from this queue and transmits them to the proper destination host via SMTP transactions over one or more TCP connections on TCP port 25. A host may have multiple SMTP senders active simultaneously if it has a large volume of outgoing mail, and should also have the capability of creating SMTP receivers on demand so that mail from one host cannot delay mail from another.

The input required by the SMTP sender is contained in the outgoing mail queue. Although the structure of the outgoing mail queue will vary a great deal depending on the host's operating system, each queued message will conceptually have two parts:

- The message text
- A list of mail destinations

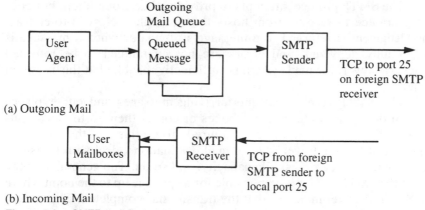

(a) Outgoing Mail

(b) Incoming Mail

Figure 5.2.   SMTP mail flow.

The message text includes the RFC 822 header and the body of the message composed by the user.

The list of all mail destinations for the message is typically derived by the user agent program from the 822 message header, but often differs as mail group lists may be expanded, mnemonic names replaced with actual mailbox names, duplicates removed, destinations may have been specified as blind carbon copies (BCCs), and so on. The basic idea is that the multiple formats and styles preferred by humans in the user interface are replaced by a standardized list suitable for the SMTP sender process.

The SMTP sender scans the outgoing queue, and opens outgoing TCP connections to deliver the mail. Whenever the SMTP sender is able to complete delivery of a particular message to one or more users on a specific host, it deletes the corresponding destinations from the message's destination list. When all destinations for a particular message are processed, the message text and destination list for that message may be deleted from the queue. The SMTP sender can perform a variety of optimizations. If a particular message is sent to multiple users on a single host, the message text need only be sent once. The SMTP sender can also transfer multiple messages over a single TCP connection.

The SMTP sender must deal with a variety of errors. The destination host may be unreachable, out of operation, or the TCP connection may fail while mail is being transferred. The sender should requeue the mail for later delivery, but give up after some period rather than queue the message indefinitely. This is a policy decision, but most systems will retry for several days. Another sort of error occurs with faulty destination addresses. This condition is fairly common: the sender may have mistyped or misguessed a mail destination, or the intended destination user may have moved on to a new machine. The SMTP sender must deal with these problems and either forward the message or return an error notification to the message's originator.

The SMTP protocol attempts to provide reliable operation, but does not guarantee to recover from hosts that lose files. No end-to-end acknowledgment is returned to a message's originator when a message is successfully delivered, and errors are not guaranteed to be returned either. However, the mail system is sufficiently reliable that this is not an issue.

The SMTP receiver accepts arriving messages and either places them in the appropriate user mailboxes or copies them to the local outgoing mail queue if forwarding is required. To do this job, the SMTP receiver must be able to verify local mail destinations, deal with transmission problems, lack of disk file capacity, and so on. The general strategy is that the SMTP sender is responsible for a message up to the point where the SMTP receiver indicates that the transfer has completed. This means that the sender has most of the error recovery responsibility and that errors during completion indication may cause duplicate, but not lost, messages. The SMTP receiver's error recovery responsibilities are limited to giving up on TCP connections that fail or are inactive for very long periods.

In most cases, messages go directly from the mail originator's machine to the destination machine. However, mail will occasionally go through intermediate systems. One way for this to happen is for the sender to specify a route to the destination in the form of a sequence of servers. A more common event is forwarding caused by the fact that a user has moved.

Although this overall structure was in the designer's mind when SMTP was defined and influences its specification, the SMTP protocol is limited to the conversation that takes place between the SMTP sender and SMTP receiver. The main function is the transfer of messages, although there are some ancillary functions dealing with mail destination verification and handling.

Basic Elements

Conventions. There are a number of conventions that apply to SMTP, and often mail in general. All mail software should obey the robustness principle, which says "Be conservative in what you do, be liberal in what you accept from others." In effect this means that an implementation of SMTP should follow the standard exactly in what it transmits, but may often want to accept input that is not permitted under strict interpretation of the standard. Mail is perhaps the clearest case where interoperability with the maximum number of counterparts can be more important than purity to the standard.

Character case should be preserved, but should not be significant.

In particular, commands and replies are not case sensitive. That is, a command or reply word may be upper case, lower case, or any mixture of upper and lower case. Note that this is not true of mailbox user names. For some hosts the user name is case sensitive, and SMTP implementations must take care to preserve the case of user names as they appear in mailbox arguments. Host names are not case sensitive.

Commands and replies are composed of characters from the ASCII character set. When the transport service provides an 8-bit byte (octet) transmission channel, each 7-bit character is transmitted right justified in an octet with the high order bit cleared to zero. In some systems it may be necessary to transform the data as it is received and stored. This may be necessary for hosts that use a different character set than ASCII as their local character set, or that store data in records rather than strings. If such transforms are necessary, they must be reversible—especially if such transforms are applied to mail being relayed.

In the SMTP standard as well as this discussion, when specifying the general form of a command or reply, an argument (or special symbol) will be denoted by a meta-linguistic variable (or constant), for example, ⟨string⟩ or ⟨reverse-path⟩. Here the angle brackets indicate that these are meta-linguistic variables. However, some arguments use the angle brackets literally. For example, an actual reverse-path is enclosed in angle brackets, i.e., ⟨John.Smith@ISI.EDU⟩ is an instance of ⟨reverse-path⟩ (the angle brackets are actually transmitted in the command or reply).

In explaining dialogue between SMTP senders and receivers this discussion annotates transmissions with a S: if the transmission was sent by the SMTP sender, and R: if by the receiver. These strings are not part of real transmissions.

Mailbox Specifications.   When mail is sent, the sender and recipients of the message are identified using character strings. These strings have the format of user@domain, where domain identifies a particular organization or host that receives mail, and user identifies a specific account or mailbox in that domain. For example, Mockapetris@ISI.EDU identifies user Mockapetris in mail domain ISI.EDU. The use of host names in the domain part is becoming archaic as mail systems adopt more of a distributed system organization as opposed to the large timesharing systems of the past [COME85]. The domain naming system is still evolving, and is the subject of several RFCs [RFC 882, RFC 883, RFC 973, RFC 974].

Paths.   It is occasionally necessary to augment the mailbox specification with routing information that describes a path to the mailbox. In SMTP, the intermediate hops are specified in the form of a list of domains in front of the mailbox specification. Each of the intermediates is prefaced with an @. Multiple intermediates are separated by ",",s, whereas the last intermediate is separated from the mailbox by a ":". For example:

> Smith@ISI.EDU
> @SRI-NIC.ARPA:Smith@ISI.EDU
> @MIT.EDU,@UCI.EDU,@SRI-NIC.ARPA:Smith@ISI.EDU

The first line is a simple mailbox; the others are paths leading to the same mailbox. In the second line the mail is to pass through SRI-NIC.ARPA before going to Smith's mailbox in the ISI.EDU domain. In the last example, the mail is to pass through MIT.EDU, then UCI.EDU, then SRI-NIC.ARPA before its final destination in the ISI.EDU domain.

Simple mailboxes suffice for most mail; paths are useful for debugging, and are occasionally used to reach *difficult* destinations. When a message is delivered to its ultimate destination it contains a list of intermediates that forwarded the message; this list can be used to construct a return path for return mail.

Commands.   The SMTP sender manages the activities on the TCP connection by issuing a series of commands to the receiver. SMTP commands take the form of a single line of text. The command begins with a four-letter code. Arguments depend on the command code, and if present, are separated from the command code by a space. The command concludes with a carriage return/line feed. The following are the SMTP commands:

> HELO ⟨SP⟩ ⟨domain⟩ ⟨CRLF⟩
> MAIL ⟨SP⟩ FROM:⟨reverse-path⟩ ⟨CRLF⟩
> RCPT ⟨SP⟩ TO:⟨forward-path⟩ ⟨CRLF⟩
> DATA ⟨CRLF⟩
> RSET ⟨CRLF⟩
> SEND ⟨SP⟩ FROM:⟨reverse-path⟩ ⟨CRLF⟩
> SOML ⟨SP⟩ FROM:⟨reverse-path⟩ ⟨CRLF⟩
> SAML ⟨SP⟩ FROM:⟨reverse-path⟩ ⟨CRLF⟩
> VRFY ⟨SP⟩ ⟨string⟩ ⟨CRLF⟩
> EXPN ⟨SP⟩ ⟨string⟩ ⟨CRLF⟩
> HELP [⟨SP⟩ ⟨string⟩] ⟨CRLF⟩
> NOOP ⟨CRLF⟩
> QUIT ⟨CRLF⟩
> TURN ⟨XRLF⟩

Some example commands with arguments are:

> MAIL FROM:⟨Postel@BEL.ISI.EDU⟩
> QUIT

The MAIL command has an argument that specifies a path; the QUIT command takes no arguments.

SMTP contains optional commands. That is, SMTP receivers are not required to implement all commands, but all SMTP senders are required to deal with SMTP receivers that implement only the minimum implementation. The minimum implementation includes: HELO, MAIL, RCPT, DATA, RSET, NOOP, and QUIT.

Replies. The SMTP receiver returns a reply to the SMTP sender in response to each command sent by the SMTP sender to the SMTP receiver; each command generates exactly one reply. Like the command, the reply is ASCII text. Most replies use one line, although multiline replies are occasionally used.

The reply consists of a three-digit number followed by some text. The number is intended to be an easily decoded signal that can drive transitions in a state-machine style implementation of the SMTP sender. The text is often just a string explaining the number and is intended for consumption by humans monitoring the progress of a SMTP transaction and can be ignored by the SMTP sender; usually the SMTP transaction would proceed without human supervision, and the text would only be passed back to the user in automatic mail describing fatal errors.

In some cases a reply contains text used by the SMTP sender. For example:

```
250 OK
250 Horrible error
251 User not local; will forward to ⟨Jones@ISI.EDU⟩
```

The first example is the standard success reply; the 250 is significant, the OK is just for readability. The second reply might confuse a human, but should have the same effect as the first on a SMTP sender. The last reply has a 251 code and happens to be followed by text for humans and a real argument in ⟨⟩ for the SMTP sender. Note that the existence of such an argument depends on the command that provoked the reply; most commands do not get replies with arguments. If the 251 reply were returned for a command that did not expect an argument in the reply, the text would simply be ignored (e.g., VRFY, discussed below).

Multiple line replies are occasionally needed. For example, a SMTP sender can ask the SMTP receiver to expand a mailing list name into its membership list. Such a reply might need to include dozens or hundreds of mailboxes. In such a case, each argument (mailbox) is sent on a separate reply line, but the multiple reply lines are joined into what is conceptually a single reply. Each line of a multiline reply begins with the reply code, and all but the last line of the reply have the space separator after the number replaced by a "-". For example:

```
250-O
250 K
```

```
250-A1 Calico ⟨ABC@MIT.EDU⟩
250-⟨XYZ@NASA.GOV⟩
250 ⟨XYZZY@ADVENTURE.COM⟩
```

The first reply illustrates a silly, but legal use, of multiline replies for a simple success reply with no real arguments. The second example illustrates a reply that might be returned in response to a mailing list expansion command.

The reply codes themselves are carefully constructed to make programming of the SMTP sender straightforward. Each digit has a unique purpose:

- The first digit of the three-digit code is a summary response and indicates whether the response is good, bad, or incomplete. An unsophisticated SMTP sender is able to select a correct next action (e.g., abort, retry later, success) based solely on this leading digit.
- The second digit informs the SMTP sender approximately what kind of error occurred (e.g., syntax error). A clever SMTP can use this information to choose nearly optimal next actions.
- The last digit is used for fine gradations between the cases specified by the first two digits.

At present, five values are defined for the first digit of the reply code:

1yz   Positive Preliminary reply
> The command has been accepted, but the requested action is being held in abeyance, pending confirmation of the information in this reply. The SMTP sender should send another command specifying whether to continue or abort the action.
> [*Note:* SMTP does not have any commands that allow this type of reply, and therefore, does not have the continue or abort commands. This type is defined for compatibility with other protocols.]

2yz   Positive Completion reply
> The requested action has been successfully completed. A new request may be initiated.

3yz   Positive Intermediate reply
> The command has been accepted, but the requested action is being held in abeyance, pending re-

ceipt of further information. The SMTP sender should send another command specifying this information. This reply is used in command sequence groups.

4yz   Transient Negative Completion reply
        The command was not accepted and the requested action did not occur. However, the error condition is temporary and the action may be requested again. The sender should return to the beginning of the command sequence (if any). It is difficult to assign a meaning to *transient* when two different sites (SMTP receiver and sender) must agree on the interpretation. Each reply in this category might have a different time value, but the SMTP sender is encouraged to try again. A rule of thumb to determine if a reply fits into the 4yz or the 5yz category (see below) is that replies are 4yz if they can be repeated without any change in command form or in properties of the sender or receiver (e.g., the command is repeated identically and the receiver does not put up a new implementation).

5yz   Permanent Negative Completion reply
        The command was not accepted and the requested action did not occur. The SMTP sender is discouraged from repeating the exact request (in the same sequence). Even some *permanent* error conditions can be corrected, so the human user may want to direct the SMTP sender to reinitiate the command sequence by direct action at some point in the future (e.g., after the spelling has been changed, or the user has altered the account status).

The second digit encodes responses in specific categories:

x0z   Syntax: These replies refer to syntax errors, syntactically correct commands that do not fit any functional category, and unimplemented or superfluous commands.

x1z   Information: These are replies to requests for information such as status or help.

x2z   Connections: These are replies referring to the transmission channel.

x3z   Unspecified as yet.

x4z   Unspecified as yet.

x5z   Mail system: These replies indicate the status of the receiver mail system vis-a-vis the requested transfer or other mail system action.

5.3   BASIC MAIL TRANSFER

The unit of SMTP activity is a TCP connection between a SMTP sender and a SMTP receiver. The SMTP protocol resembles prior protocols, such as FTP, in that it consists of a one-for-one exchange of commands from the sender and responses by the receiver. Commands and replies are usually in the form of single lines of ASCII, with the exception of the message body, which consists of multiple lines, and occasional multiple line replies. The activity over a single TCP connection can be broken down into three phases:

>   Connection setup that readies the connection for use
>
>   Mail transfer that consists of one or more transactions. Each transaction moves a single piece of mail to one or more destinations
>
>   Connection closing that gracefully closes the connection

Connection Setup

The purpose of the connection setup phase is to initiate the TCP connection and perform some elementary checks to insure that the sender and receiver are willing to cooperate. This phase has the following sequence:

1. The sender opens a TCP connection to the receiver
2. The receiver identifies itself
3. The sender identifies itself
4. The receiver accepts the sender's identification

The TCP connection setup uses port 25 on the receiver, and an arbitrary sender port. As soon as the receiver is able to send, it *replies* to the connection initiation and identifies itself with a greetings message. The greetings message gives the primary name of the receiving host and signifies whether the SMTP receiver is able to accept mail. A 220 reply is positive, and a 421 reply indicates that mail service is not available. The host name should be the first word following the reply code. For example:

>   R:220 C.ISI.EDU SMTP service ready
>   R:421 C.ISI.EDU System going down

The sender waits for the greetings message before sending any data. Once a positive greetings message is received, the sender identifies itself in a HELO command. The HELO command has the name of the sender as an argument. The receiver sends a reply that indicates whether it is willing to believe the indicated identity. Once this reply is received by the

SMTP sender, the connection is ready for use. If host C.ISI.EDU were to open a SMTP connection to SRI-NIC.ARPA, the connection might look like the following:

```
R: 220 SRI-NIC.ARPA SMTP service ready
S: HELO C.ISI.EDU
R: 250 OK
```

Mail Transfer

The mail transfer phase of the SMTP connection may be used to transmit an unlimited number of messages, but each transfer is a logically separate transaction. Each mail transaction has three logical parts:

1. A MAIL command that identifies the originator of the message.
2. One or more RCPT commands that identify recipients of the message.
3. A DATA command that transfers the message text.

The MAIL command names the source of the message. In a single-hop mail delivery, this will be the originating mailbox. If a message traverses multiple hops, the path in the MAIL command will name the hops that have been taken so far on the path specified by the original sender of the message. The SMTP receiver sends a reply that indicates whether it believes in the domain(s) found in the MAIL command. The SMTP receiver may reject a MAIL command on the grounds that the domain specified in the FROM: argument is unknown to it, and hence the receiver cannot reply to it. Some SMTP receivers act in this way, others do not.

All SMTP programs must deal with the special case of a null FROM: field in a MAIL command. This is used for sending automatically generated mail error messages. The rationale is that we never want such mail to generate a reply because we might then set off infinite mail loops between SMTPs sending an infinite sequence of error messages. The interpretation we use is that if the FROM: argument is null, we never send errors back, and error messages are always sent with a null FROM:.

Some example mail commands:

```
S: MAIL FROM: ⟨Postel@ISI.EDU⟩
R: 250 OK

S: MAIL FROM:⟨⟩
R: 250 OK
```

The second part of the mail transfer gives a path for each destination of the mail. Each path is given in a separate RCPT command from the SMTP sender, and the SMTP receiver sends a separate reply for each proposed mail destination. Outside of rare errors caused by lack of resources, the SMTP receiver responds in one of four ways:

1. Accept the destination with a 250 reply
2. Reject the destination with a 550 reply
3. Signal that the destination will require forwarding, AND agree to do the forwarding with a 251 reply
4. Signal that the destination will require forwarding, BUT refuse to do the forwarding with a 551 reply

In the last two cases, SMTP receiver knows that the mailbox specified in the RCPT has changed. Note that either the user or the domain, or both, may have changed. The SMTP receiver includes the new mailbox in the reply, enclosed in ⟨⟩. For example:

S: RCPT TO:⟨Postmaster@ISI.EDU⟩
R: 250 OK

S: RCPT to:⟨Unknown@ISI.EDU⟩
R: 550 No such user

S: RCPT TO:⟨Postel@C.ISI.EDU⟩
R: 251 User not local; will forward to ⟨Postel@bel.ISI.EDU⟩

S: RCPT TO: ⟨Mockapetris@C.ISI.EDU⟩
R: 551 User not local, please try ⟨Mockapetris@Venera.ISI.EDU⟩

The model we have is one in which the SMTP sender offers a series of names and the SMTP receiver either rejects each name or enters it (or the forwarding name) on a list. If a message follows, it will go to all names on the list. The SMTP sender will typically notify the message's originator of problem destinations via automatically generated mail (unless a null FROM: was used).

If the path specified in the RCPT is not a simple mailbox, i.e., if this is just one hop in a path, then special processing may be required. If the path in the RCPT has a first hop that is the same as the host of the SMTP receiver, then the first hop is deleted from the RCPT path and added to the path from the MAIL command. Conceptually, when a message leaves an originating host for a multiple hop path to some destination, the path in the RCPT lists all hosts to be visited, and the path in the MAIL command lists all hosts that the message has visited. As the message traverses the network, the list of visited hosts grows longer and the list of hosts yet to be visited grows shorter. In any case, an audit trail or return path is maintained. The cleverness of the SMTP software varies; some SMTPs will automatically delete consecutive hops to the same hosts, other will not.

After all recipients have been sent, the body of the message is sent with a DATA command. The DATA command sequence is more complicated than other commands. It begins with the DATA command itself, which signifies that a message body is about to follow. The SMTP receiver acknowledges the DATA command and agrees to accept the mail via an intermediate reply. The sender then sends the body of the message. The message body consumes as many lines as required, and is terminated by a line consisting of only a dot, or to be more precise, the five character sequence ⟨CR⟩ ⟨LF⟩.⟨CR⟩⟨LF⟩, where ⟨CR⟩ and ⟨LF⟩ correspond to the carriage return and line feed characters. Because a line with just a dot might occur naturally in a message, the SMTP sender adds a second dot to the front of message lines that start with a dot, and the SMTP receiver strips off the added dots. Using this transparency mechanism, arbitrary text may be included in the message body.

For example, suppose we have a message by Smith at host Alpha.ARPA, to Jones, Green, and Brown at host Beta.ARPA. Here we assume that host Alpha contacts host Beta directly.

```
S: MAIL FROM:⟨Smith@Alpha.ARPA⟩
R: 250 OK
S: RCPT TO:⟨Jones@Beta.ARPA⟩
R: 250 OK
S: RCPT TO:⟨Green@Beta.ARPA⟩
R: 550 No such user here
S: RCPT TO:⟨Brown@Beta.ARPA⟩
R: 250 OK
S: DATA
R: 354 Start mail input; end with ⟨CRLF⟩.⟨CRLF⟩
S: Date: 23 Oct 86 11:22:33
S: From: John Smith
S: To: Jones@Beta.ARPA,Green@Beta.ARPA
S: CC: Brown@Beta
S:
S: I agree to your terms.
S:
S: John
S: ⟨CRLF⟩.⟨CRLF⟩
R: 250 OK
```

The mail has now been accepted for Jones and Brown. Note that the content of the message does not effect the operation of either the SMTP sender or receiver. In this case, this principle is illustrated in that SMTP sees no distinction between the To: and CC: recipients, and SMTP is not concerned with the use of the abbreviation Beta for Beta.ARPA in the CC: field of the 822 header. If the SMTP sender wished to send another message it could start at this point with another MAIL command. Otherwise, the SMTP sender would proceed to close the TCP connection.

One way to think of the transaction is from the point of view of the SMTP receiver. When called upon to provide mail service, it initializes three buffers: one for the name of the sender, one for a list of recipients, and one for the message text. A successful MAIL command fills the sender buffer; successful RCPT commands add to the recipient buffer; the DATA command fills the text buffer. The return address comes first so errors can always be returned. Recipients are verified before the text of the message is sent as it would make no sense to send the text over the TCP connection if no recipients were successful. The SMTP receiver accepts no responsibility for delivery until all three buffers have been satisfactorily loaded, then completes the transaction via the 250 OK response to the DATA command.

In spite of retries in the event of transient errors, a mail delivery may fail due to a hard error, such as a bad destination or intermediate hop, or by persistent transient errors beyond the tolerance of the retry mechanism. In such cases, the SMTP sender will give up, compose an error notification message, and send the message back to the originator of the mail that failed. If the error was detected in a reply, the text of the reply is usually included in the message. The error notification will also include at least enough of the original message to allow the originator to identify which message failed.

Connection Closing

The SMTP sender closes the connection in two steps. The first step is to send a QUIT command and wait for a reply. The second step is to initiate a TCP close operation for the connection. The receiver initiates its TCP close after sending its reply to the QUIT command. For example:

```
S: QUIT
R: 250 Ciao
R: ⟨TCP close⟩
S: ⟨TCP close⟩
```

Note that the two TCP close operations do not send actual characters, but are typically control functions.

Logging Information

SMTP adds two types of logging information to the mail text that eventually gets put in the user mailbox. The first are timestamp or *Received* lines and the second is the return path.

Each time a SMTP receiver copies in mail following a DATA command, it first puts a timestamp line at the start of the mail. The line is supposed to follow a rigid syntax from the SMTP specification and contains the names of the hosts for the SMTP sender and receiver, a time, and so forth. Although this information is often found, many systems do not exactly conform to the specification. This is not a major problem, as the information is primarily used by humans for debugging. Because SMTP receivers add this information any time a message is copied, mail that is forwarded or contains a path that is not a simple mailbox specification will include multiple timestamp lines.

The return path is added to the mail text when the message reaches the SMTP receiver that will place it in the user mailbox. This line contains the reverse path back to the originator of the message that was constructed from the paths in the RCPT and MAIL commands.

The following illustrates this information from one message:

```
Return-Path: @C.ISI.EDU:gross@gateway.mitre.org
Received-Date: Fri, 17 Apr 87 06:36:27 PDT
Received: from C.ISI.EDU by venera.isi.edu (5.54/5.51)
        id AA24919; Fri, 17 Apr 87 06:36:27 PDT
Received: FROM VENERA.ISI.EDU BY C.ISI.EDU WITH TCP; 17
Apr 87 06:26:58 PDT
Posted-Date: Fri, 17 Apr 87 09:29:07 EDT
Received: from GATEWAY.MITRE.ORG by venera.isi.edu (5.54/
5.51)
        id AA24763; Fri, 17 Apr 87 06:26:59 PDT
Return-Path: ⟨gross@gateway.mitre.org⟩
```

The message in question was forwarded, which accounts for the multiple return path lines. This message also illustrates some of the liberties taken with the standard.

5.4 OTHER SMTP COMMANDS

Reset

The RSET command specifies that the current transaction is to be aborted. Any stored sender, recipients, or other state must be discarded, and the SMTP receiver must send a 250 OK reply.

The SMTP receiver should not regard this as anything extraordinary. Some SMTP senders use this following a 251 "will forward" response to a RCPT command, because they are programmed to do the forwarding themselves.

Sending

The main use of SMTP is to deliver mail to users' mailboxes. Some hosts provide features that can display messages directly on a user's terminal (usually requiring that the user be online at the time). SMTP provides optional support for this type of activity, called sending. The support takes the form of three commands, which otherwise take the same arguments as MAIL, and are used in place of the MAIL command in transactions:

SEND   This command requires that the message go to the user's terminal. If the user is not active or not accepting terminal messages, a 450 reply should be returned for the corresponding RCPT command. The transaction is successful if it is delivered on the terminal.

SOML   The send or mail command asks that the message be sent to the user's terminal if possible, and the user's mailbox if not. The transaction is successful if the message is delivered to either.

SAML   The send and mail command asks that the message be sent to both the user's terminal the user's mailbox. The transaction is successful if the message is delivered to the mailbox.

These commands get the same reply codes as the MAIL command.

Help

This optional command allows the SMTP receiver to send helpful information to the sender of the HELP command. This command is optional. The HELP command may use its argument to select more specific information in a response. The reply will often include a software version number and a list of optional commands that are supported. This command has no effect on the state of any transaction in progress.

An example:

```
S: HELP
R: 214-Commands:
R: 214-  HELO  MAIL  RCPT  DATA  RSET
R: 214-  NOOP  QUIT  HELP  VRFY  EXPN
R: 214-For more info use "HELP ⟨topic⟩".
R: 214-To report bugs in the implementation contact
eric@Berkeley.ARPA
```

R: 214-or eric@UCB-ARPA.ARPA.
R: 214-For local information contact postmaster at this site.
R: 214 End of HELP info

Because the text in the HELP command does not have a set format, its usefulness is limited to cases where a human is attempting to debug a SMTP problem by mimicking the operation of the SMTP sender using TELNET. This is possible as all of the SMTP dialogue is done using ASCII text and no binary information is exchanged.

NOOP

This optional command has no function other than to generate a 250 OK reply. This command has no particular use outside of debugging.

Verifying and Expanding

SMTP provides optional commands to verify a user (VRFY) and to expand a mailing list (EXPN). Both of these take a character string as an argument. For VRFY, the string is a user name, and the response must include the user's mailbox and may include the full name of the user. For EXPN, the argument names a mailing list, and the reply must list all mailboxes in the list, and may include the corresponding full user names.

The purpose of these commands is to give a sophisticated mail system more information for providing improved service. With VRFY, a partial destination specification can be refined. With EXPN, a mailer might eliminate duplicate destinations when a message is sent to more than one mailing list.

The term user name is meant to include whatever is used locally for unique mailbox names, but can also include whatever less specific strings the system cares to support.

Systems frequently have difficulty in distinguishing between a mailing list with one user and a user name. Systems that choose to do so can use 550 replies to signal an error when verifying a mailing list (550 verify users, not mailing lists) or expanding a unique user name (550 expand mailing lists, not users).

The following example illustrates two uses of VRFY:

S: VRFY js
R: 250 John Smith ⟨js@HOSTX.ARPA⟩

S: VRFY sssss
R: 550 sssss . . . User Unknown

In the first case, the user John Smith has a userid of "js." In the second case, the user is unknown to the receiver.

The following example illustrates two uses of EXPN:

```
S: EXPN James-bros
R: 250-Jesse James ⟨JJ@HOSTX.ARPA⟩
R: 250 Frank James ⟨J@HOSTX.ARPA⟩

S: EXPN Executive-Washroom-List
R: 550 Access Denied to you.
```

In the first case the mailing list was expanded, in the second, the list contents were protected from outside access and an error was returned.

TURN

TURN is a command that reverses the roles of an SMTP sender and SMTP receiver, which have already established a SMTP connection. The idea behind TURN is that there are circumstances under which it makes sense to minimize the number of connections or circumstances where creating a connection is expensive.

TURN is optional. The SMTP receiver may refuse it as not implemented. Most existing SMTP implementations do this. A 502 reply is used to refuse TURN.

If the SMTP receiver honors TURN, it replies with a 250 OK reply, and then waits for a connection opening reply from its opposite number. For example:

```
S:TURN
R:250 OK
S:220 Simple mail transfer service ready
```

Note that the S label on the last line is deceptive as that end of the connection has become a SMTP receiver.

5.5   DETAILS

Standard Reply Codes

At present, the following reply codes are defined:

211 System status, or system help reply
214 Help message
[Information on how to use the receiver or the meaning of a particular non-standard command; this reply is useful only to the human user]

220 ⟨domain⟩ Service ready
221 ⟨domain⟩ Service closing transmission channel
250 Requested mail action okay, completed
251 User not local; will forward to ⟨forward-path⟩

354 Start mail input; end with ⟨CRLF⟩.⟨CRLF⟩

421 ⟨domain⟩ Service not available, closing transmission channel

[This may be a reply to any command if the service knows it must shut down]
450 Requested mail action not taken: mailbox unavailable
[E.g., mailbox busy]
451 Requested action aborted: local error in processing
452 Requested action not taken: insufficient system storage

500 Syntax error, command unrecognized
[This may include errors such as command line too long]
501 Syntax error in parameters or arguments
502 Command not implemented
503 Bad sequence of commands
504 Command parameter not implemented
550 Requested action not taken: mailbox unavailable
[E.g., mailbox not found, no access]
551 User not local; please try ⟨forward-path⟩
552 Requested mail action aborted: exceeded storage allocation
553 Requested action not taken: mailbox name not allowed
[E.g., mailbox syntax incorrect]
554 Transaction failed

Note that the text is suggested, not mandatory.

Standard Relationship Between Commands and Replies

The following state diagrams illustrate the operation of a simple-minded SMTP implementation. The numbers on the arcs are the first digit of the reply codes. For each command there are three possible outcomes: *success* (S), *failure* (F), and *error* (E). In the following state diagrams we use the symbol B for *begin,* and the symbol W for *wait for reply.*

Figure 5.3a represents most of the SMTP commands, i.e., HELO, MAIL, RCPT, RSET, SEND, SOML, SAML, VRFY, EXPN, HELP, NOOP, QUIT, and TURN.

The DATA command is more complex (Figure 5.3b). *Data* is a series of lines sent from the sender to the receiver with no response expected until the last line (containing only a ".") is sent.

To guarantee interoperability, new SMTP implementations should restrict the reply codes they use to already defined command/reply pairs.

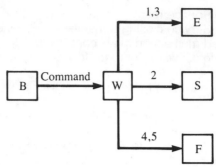

(a) Most SMTP Commands

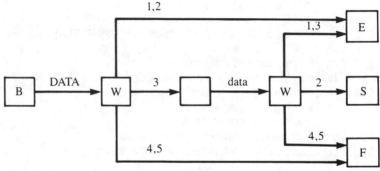

(b) The DATA Command

Legend

B = Begin   S = Success
W = Wait for Reply   F = Failure
E = Error   1,2,3,4,5 = First digit of reply code

Figure 5.3. State diagram representation of SMTP commands.

Table 5.1 lists alternative success and failure replies for each command. These must be strictly adhered to; a receiver may substitute text in the replies, but the meaning and action implied by the code numbers and by the specific command/reply sequence cannot be altered.

Each command is listed with its possible replies. The prefixes used before the possible replies are *P* for preliminary (not used in SMTP), *I* for intermediate, *S* for success, *F* for failure, and *E* for error. The 421 reply (service not available, closing transmission channel) may be given to any command if the SMTP receiver knows it must shut down.

Sizes

There are several objects that have required minimum maximum sizes. That is, every implementation must be able to receive objects of at least

Table 5.1.   POSSIBLE REPLIES TO SMTP COMMANDS

CONNECTION SETUP	S: 220
	F: 421
HELO	S: 250
	E: 500, 501, 504, 421
MAIL	S: 250
	F: 552, 451, 452
	E: 500, 501, 421
RCPT	S: 250, 251
	F: 550, 551, 552, 553, 450, 451, 452
	E: 500, 501, 503, 421
DATA	I: 354 → data → S: 250
	F: 552, 554, 451, 452
RSET	S: 250
	E: 500, 501, 504, 421
SEND	S: 250
	F: 552, 451, 452
	E: 500, 501, 502, 421
SOML	S: 250
	F: 552, 451, 452
	E: 500, 501, 502, 421
SAML	S: 250
	F: 552, 451, 452
	E: 500, 501, 502, 421
VRFY	S: 250, 251
	F: 550, 551, 553
EXPN	S: 250
	F: 550
	E: 500, 501, 502, 504, 421
HELP	S: 211, 214
	E: 500, 501, 502, 504, 421
NOOP	S: 250
	E: 500, 421
QUIT	S: 221
	E: 500
TURN	S: 250
	F: 502
	E: 500, 503

S, Success; F, Failure; E, Error.

these sizes, but must not send objects larger than these sizes. By the robustness principle, each implementation should, to the maximum extent possible, use techniques that impose no limits on the size that can be received.

User: The maximum total length of a user name is 63 characters.

Domain: The maximum total length of a domain name or number is 64 characters.

Path: The maximum total length of a reverse-path or forward-path is 256 characters (including the punctuation and element separators).

Command line: The maximum total length of a command line including the command word and the ⟨CRLF⟩ is 512 characters.

Reply line: The maximum total length of a reply line including the reply code and the ⟨CRLF⟩ is 512 characters.

Text line: The maximum total length of a text line including the ⟨CRLF⟩ is 1000 characters (but not counting the leading dot duplicated for transparency).

Recipients buffer: The maximum total number of recipients that must be buffered is 100 recipients.

Errors due to exceeding these limits may be reported by using the reply codes, for example:

```
500 Line too long.
501 Path too long
552 Too many recipients.
552 Too much mail data.
```

5.6 RFC 822

822 Format

Messages carried by SMTP use the so-called 822 format, after RFC 822, which defines a format for the message that SMTP carries. The 822 format is really a set of usually observed conventions rather than a strict definition. There are several reasons why strict adherence is not enforceable:

- Much of the information is consumed by human message readers, not programs, and humans are tolerant of diversity.
- Most people write their message software to be as accepting as possible, because it is often easier to change local software to be more accepting rather than to convince a foreign sender to adjust a format.
- RFC 822 allows for extensions to the header format it defines.

The overall structure of an 822 message is very simple. A message consists of some number of header lines *(the header)* followed by unrestricted text *(the body)*. The header is separated from the body by a blank line. Put differently, a message is ASCII text, and all lines up to the first blank line are assumed to be header lines used by the user agent part of the mail system.

A header line usually consists of a keyword, a ":", and the keyword's arguments, but the format does allow a long line to be broken up into several lines. The most frequently used keywords are *From, To, Subject,* and *Date,* which give the name of the originator of the message, message destinations, message subject, and time of posting. The user agent program typically prompts for the To: and Subject: fields, automatically builds a legal header, and lets the user type arbitrary text in the body. For example, user Jim Jones might compose the following message:

From: Jim Jones ⟨JONES@SRI-NIC.ARPA⟩
Subject: Deadlines
To: pvm@VENERA.ISI.EDU

Paul, its me again, I'd be overjoyed if you could produce that overview by next Friday, May 23rd. Think you can make that?

Jim

The message header contains from, to, and subject specifications. Everything after the To: line is message body. The From: field in this message illustrates some of the versatility possible within the 822 specification; the "Jim Jones" string is a comment overridden by the machine readable text inside the ⟨⟩. The user does not have to remember all of the details of the syntax; these lines are constructed by the user agent program in response to the user input, and the user agent will typically allow shorthands, user or host directories, and so on. For example, user Jones might have his preferred From: line stored in a configuration file.

The user agent takes the message and queues it for the local SMTP sender. Note that while the user agent uses the 822 header From: and To: fields to build the list of destinations for SMTP, these From: and To: fields are not otherwise related to the similar fields used in SMTP.

When delivered to the destination user, the message might look like:

Return-Path: JONES@SRI-NIC.ARPA
Posted-Date: Mon 11 May 87 08:47:09-PDT
Received-Date: Mon, 11 May 87 08:47:43 PDT
Received: from SRI-NIC.ARPA by venera.isi.edu (5.54/5.51)
        id AA07235; Mon, 11 May 87 08:47:43 PDT
Date: Mon 11 May 87 08:47:09-PDT
From: Jim Jones ⟨JONES@SRI-NIC.ARPA⟩
Subject: Deadlines
To: pvm@VENERA.ISI.EDU

message	=	fields *(CRLF *text)	; everything after first null line is ; message body

fields	=	dates source 1*destination *optional-field	; creation time ; author id & one address required ; others optional

dates	=	orig-date [resent-date]	; original ; forwarded
orig-date	=	"Date" ":" date-time	
resent-date	=	"Resent-Date" ":" date-time	

source	=	[trace] originator [resent]	; network traversals ; original mail ; forwarded
trace	=	return 1*received	; path to sender ; receipt tags
return	=	"Return-path" ":" route-addr	; return address
received	=	"Received" ":" 　["from" domain] 　["by" domain] 　["via" atom] 　*("with" atom) 　["id" msg-id] 　["for" addr-spec]	 ; one per relay ; sending host ; receiving host ; physical path ; link/mail protocol ; receiver message identifier ; initial form
originator	=	authentic ["Reply-To" ":" 1#address]	; authenticated address
authentic	=	"From" ":" mailbox ("Sender" ":" mailbox 　"From" ":" 1#mailbox)	; single author ; actual submittor ; Multiple authors or not sender
resent	=	resent-authentic ["Resent-Reply-To" ":" 1#address]	
resent-authentic	=	"Resent-From" ":" mailbox / ("Resent-Sender" ":" mailbox 　"Resent-From" ":" 1#mailbox)	

destination	=	"To" ":" 1#address / "Resent-To" ":" 1#address / "cc" ":" 1#address / "Resent-cc" ":" 1#address / "bcc" ":" #address / "Resent-bcc" ":" #address	; primary ; secondary ; blind carbon

Figure 5.4. Formal specification of RFC 822 format.

optional-field	=	/ "Message-ID" ":" msg-id	
		/ "Resent-Message-ID" ":" msg-id	
		/ "In-Reply-To" ":" *(phrase / msg-id)	
		/ "References" ":" *(phrase / msg-id)	
		/ "Keywords" ":" #phrase	
		/ "Subject" ":" *text	
		/ "Comments" ":" *text	
		/ "Encrypted: ":" 1#2word	
		/ extension-field	/ to be defined
		/ user-defined-field	/ may be pre-empted

msg-id   =   "<" addr-spec ">"   ; unique message identifier

extension-field =   <Any field which is defined in a document published as a formal extension
                    to RFC 822; none will have names beginning with the string "X-">

user-defined-field =
                    <Any field which has not been defined in RFC 822 or published as an
                    extension to RFC 822; names for such fields must be unique and may be
                    pre-empted by published extensions>

---

date-time   =   [day ","] date time   ; dd mm yy hh:mm:ss zzz

day   =   "Mon" / "Tue" / "Wed" / "Thu"
                    / "Fri" / "Sat" / "Sun"

date   =   1*2DIGIT month 2DIGIT   ' day month year

month   =   "Jan" / "Feb" / "Mar" / "Apr"
                    / "May" / "Jun" / "Jul" / "Aug"
                    / "Sep" / "Oct" / "Nov" / "Dec"

time   =   hour zone

hour   =   2DIGIT ":" 2DIGIT [":" 2DIGIT]   ; 00:00:00 — 23:59:59

zone   =   "UT" / "GMT" / "EST" / "EDT"
                    / "CST" / "CDT" / "MST" / "MDT"
                    / "PST" / "PDT" / 1ALPHA
                    / (("+" / "-") 4DIGIT)   ; local differential hours+minutes

---

address   =   mailbox / group   ; one addressee or named list

group   =   phrase ":" [#mailbox] ";"

mailbox   =   addr-spec / phrase route-addr   ; simple address or name & addr-spec

route-addr   =   "<" [route] addr-spec ">"

route   =   1#("@" domain) ":"   ; path-relative

addr-spec   =   local-part "@" domain   ; global address

local-part   =   word *("." word)   ; uninterpreted case-preserved

domain   =   sub-domain *("." sub-domain)

sub-domain   =   domain-ref / domain-literal

domain-ref   =   atom   ; symbolic reference

Figure 5.4   (continued)

Trollheim: + 1 (415) 325-9427 ACE: + 1 (408) 996-2042
Message-Id: ⟨12301541766.31.JONES@SRI-NIC.ARPA⟩

Paul, its me again, I'd be overjoyed if you could produce that domain overview by next Friday, May 23rd. Think you can make that?

Jim

This message includes the original input plus other lines added by the sender's software and logging information added by the SMTP processes that handled the message.

Formal Specification

Figure 5.4 contains the formal specification of the RFC 822 message format, in a modified Backus-Naur form. The notational conventions are:

- Words in lower case represent variables or rules.
- DIGIT is any decimal digit; CRLF is carriage return, line feed.
- Quotation marks enclose literal text.
- Elements separated by slash ("/") are alternatives.
- Ordinary parentheses are used simply for grouping.
- The character "*" preceding an element indicates repetition. The full form is:

  <I>*<J>element

  indicating at least I and at most J occurences of element. *element allows any number, including 0; 1*element requires at least one element; and 1*2element allows 1 or 2 elements; <N>element means exactly N elements.
- Square brackets, "[""]", enclose optional elements.
- The construct "#" is used to define repetition, with the following form:

  <I>#<J>element

  indicating at least I and at most J elements, each separated by a comma.
- A semicolon at the right of a rule starts a comment that continues to the end of the line.

6

TELNET

Sue McLeod

6.1 REQUIREMENT FOR REMOTE TERMINAL ACCESS

An early motivation for data networks like the ARPANET was to provide remote access to interactive systems across the network, that is, to allow a terminal user at site *A* to interact with a process at host *B* as if it were a local user [DAV177]. The user's local host makes a connection to the remote, target host where the user logs on and is treated like a local user. Because of the requirement that remote users log on to the target host, remote terminal access is often called remote log on.

Remote terminal access continues to be a useful network service. It is particularly useful within an organization where users require access to many hosts. For example, a technical department has hosts and terminals for doing software development. The finance department has another host for doing payroll. The finance host has an interactive program for collecting time reporting information and the finance department prefers that the technical departments do this data entry. Instead of having a separate terminal directly connected to the finance host, the technical department could use a remote terminal access protocol from its host over a network to the finance host. This reduces the number of physical terminals required to access host resources in the organization, and provides the benefits of a network (lower cost, higher reliability) between sites that are geographically separate.

Remote terminal access tries to simulate direct access from a terminal to a host; however, hosts generally handle only directly connected terminals with a particular set of terminal characteristics, such as the mapping between special keys and functions like Break or Transmit. Methods to allow a host to accept terminal traffic from the network or an application include (1) defining a pseudoterminal that the operating system treats like a terminal but can be used by another program to communicate with the terminal handling functions of the host or (2) defining generalized Input/Output (I/O) routines so that the operating system treats all I/O the same regardless of the device. As networking becomes more commonplace, operating systems are being developed that do not assume directly connected terminals and provide more generalized I/O. However, to add remote terminal access capabilities to an operating system that handles only directly connected terminals, some modifications may be required to provide a pseudoterminal capability. The details of that capability depend on the type of remote access protocol used; it is described for the TELNET protocol later in this chapter.

Hosts generally support only a small number of terminal types, each with a specific set of terminal characteristics. For networks with only those known terminals wanting to access the hosts, remote terminal access is straightforward. The terminal specifies its type or set of characteristics to the host and all communication is in the terminal's native mode. This type of access protocol is very efficient and provides adequate service for small networks where device types are known and do not change often. Many LAN environments fall into this category. However, for a network such as ARPANET, the number of terminal types may be very large, and sites cannot control the terminal types used at other sites; therefore, the characteristics of a terminal requesting access to a host may not be known or supported by the host. Remote terminal access should still be allowed; however, a more complex protocol is required. In addition to providing data transfer between the terminal and the host, this protocol must also provide mechanisms for the terminal and the host to agree on the *language* they will use for that data transfer, and must perform translantions between native mode and this agreed upon language. This can be done with a Virtual Terminal Protocol.

6.2 VIRTUAL TERMINAL PROTOCOLS

A virtual terminal protocol provides this common *language* to be used on a connection by defining a virtual terminal and a protocol for transferring data and control information across the network. A virtual terminal is an imaginary device with a well-defined set of characteristics. These characteristics are defined in general terms, specifying functions, so that implementers can choose the most efficient way to handle them. Both sides generate data in their native language. The virtual terminal protocol implementation then translates into the virtual terminal language for transmission to the other side of the network connection. The receiving virtual terminal protocol implementation then does a reverse translation from the virtual terminal language to the native language. This is shown in Figure 6.1.

The transfer protocol defines:

1. The form in which data will be passed, for example, as a stream of bytes or in formatted messages.
2. How the virtual terminal's control signals will be passed and how to distinguish them from data.
3. The mode of the data transfer, that is, half- or full-duplex, synchronous or asynchronous, and how data transfer is controlled.
4. How out-of-band signals and special priority interrupts are transferred and how they should be interpreted.
5. How data delivery to the peer user is controlled.

Virtual terminal implementations must understand the virtual terminal and transfer protocol, must send and receive data on the network according to that protocol, and must translate from the virtual terminal to the native mode for terminals or processes using the virtual terminal protocol.

A useful, but not necessary, feature of a virtual terminal protocol is the ability to negotiate about the characteristics of the virtual terminal or

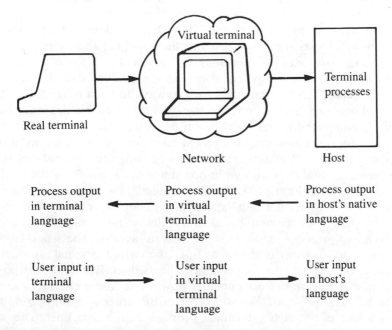

Figure 6.1.   Virtual terminal concept.

the details of the transfer protocol. This allows users and processes to define a remote terminal access service that provides service as close as possible to native mode. For example, if the virtual terminal is defined to look like a scroll-mode terminal, but both the host and the terminal can support page-mode, full-screen editors, the virtual terminal protocol should allow them to agree on a new virtual terminal and transfer protocol that provides that type of service.

Although virtual terminal protocols are often described as supporting terminal-to-process communication, they are often general enough to also support process-to-process and terminal-to-terminal communication over a network. However, they are always used for interactive, terminal-type traffic.

All virtual terminal protocols provide the capabilities described previously. They differ in how the virtual terminal characteristics are defined and agreed upon, the services provided by the transfer protocol, and the transfer protocol itself.

The rest of this chapter describes the details of the Department of Defense (DOD) standard virtual terminal protocol, TELNET.

6.3   DEPARTMENT OF DEFENSE STANDARD TELNET

The TELNET virtual terminal protocol was originally defined in 1972 for use on the ARPANET [DAV177]. It was updated and was widely used on the ARPANET by 1977, and became a military standard in 1984 [DCA84c].

The network environment that TELNET was designed for is shown in Figure 6.2. Hosts were connected to the network, and users accessed the network using backend terminals. All protocols were implemented in the hosts. The internetwork environment has evolved over the past 10 years to include LANs connected by gateways to each other and to the long-haul network. There are fewer backend *dumb* terminals; users have terminals connected to the LAN by an interface unit with the protocols necessary for communicating with local hosts, or they have workstations that can be looked at as single user hosts running the full protocol suite or as terminal emulators with an in-board interface unit. This site configuration is shown in Figure 6.3. For the terminals, the access protocol will usually be one of the terminal-specific protocols described previously. This is sufficient to communicate locally; the terminal may access a virtual terminal protocol in the host for remote access. The workstations may also work this way or they may have the virtual terminal protocol as well, and thus, be able to access remote hosts directly. For the purposes of this discussion we will not consider how the terminal interfaces to the virtual terminal protocol. We will refer to the processor supporting the terminal side of the virtual terminal protocol as the user host. The processor supporting the process side is called the process host. The TEL-

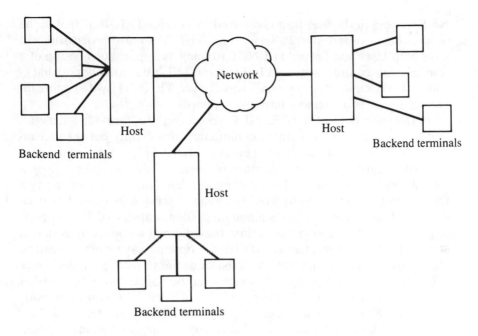

Figure 6.2.   Original ARPANET environment.

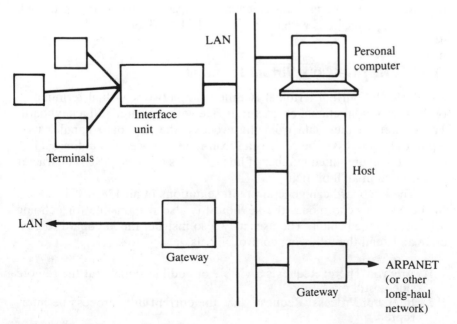

Figure 6.3.   LAN site configuration.

NET process in the user host is referred to as User TELNET; that in the process host is referred to as Server TELNET. Most host processors will have both User and Server TELNET running as applications on top of a transmission control protocol (TCP). User TELNET will support back-end or LAN connected terminals and Server TELNET will support incoming requests for remote terminal support.

The objectives of the TELNET design were to "provide a general, bi-directional character-oriented communications facility between terminal devices and terminal-oriented process" [DAV177]. To define a protocol that could be used on a number of systems, the designers chose a virtual terminal that was a lowest common denominator of existing systems [POST85]. This was to provide a general service that could be used by even simple systems. To accomodate systems capable of more sophisticated terminal-type communication, they defined an option negotiation and subnegotiation mechanism. TELNET options have been defined to change the virtual terminal characteristics or the transfer protocol. Once a TELNET session has started, options can be negotiated until the User and Server TELNET agree on the minimum service they want to support.

The following sections describe the TELNET virtual terminal characteristics, the transfer protocol, and the option negotiation mechanism. A TELNET implementation does not exist by itself on a processor and some of the most important design and implementation decisions are based on the interfaces between the TELNET processes and other related processes. The general requirements for these interfaces are described. The chapter concludes with examples of TELNET options.

The TELNET Network Virtual Terminal

The TELNET virtual terminal is called the network virtual terminal or NVT. It is a bidirectional character device with a printer and a keyboard. The printer handles data from the process; the keyboard handles user input to the process. The NVT is a scroll-mode device with unlimited line length and an unlimited number of lines. It uses the 7-bit ASCII character set encoded in an 8-bit field.

The keyboard can generate representations of all 128 ASCII codes. In the default echo mode, the keyboard is also responsible for echoing user data to the printer. The user may also instruct the keyboard to generate and send the following control signals.

1. Are You There: Requests a visible or audible signal that the remote side is still operating.
2. Interrupt Process: Requests that the current user process be interrupted.
3. Abort Output: Requests that the current user process be allowed to run to completion, but that no more output be sent to the printer.

4. Erase Character: Requests that the previous character be erased from the data stream.
5. Erase Line: Requests that the previous line (from the current character back to the last newsline) be erased from the data stream.
6. Break: This code is to provide a signal outside the ASCII character set to indicate the Break or Attention signal available on many systems.

For directly connected terminals, there are signals the user can send to which the host responds immediately. Replicating this is difficult in a network where flow control mechanisms may queue these signals behind regular data, thereby delaying their transmission. The TELNET Sync signal is defined to provide this out-of-band signaling. It tells the underlying network protocols to deliver the special signal as quickly as possible and the receiving TELNET to process it before other data that may be waiting in the queue.

The NVT printer has an unspecified line width and page length. It can produce the 95 ASCII graphic characters (codes 32 through 126), and responds to the following control codes:

1. NUL: No operation
2. Line Feed (LF): Move to next print line
3. Carriage Return (CR): Move to beginning of print line

The effects of the BELL (BEL), Backspace (BS), Horizontal Tab (HT), Vertical Tab (VT), and Form Feed (FF) characters are defined, but the standard does not require that they be supported. Table 6.1 summarizes these printer codes and their interpretation. Notice that the NVT also does not support control codes related to screens such as Home or clear screen.

Table 6.1. PRINTER CODES AND THEIR INTERPRETATION

Name	Code	Meaning
NULL (NUL)	0	No Operation
Line Feed (LF)	10	Move to next print line
Carriage Return (CR)	13	Move to beginning of print line
Bell (BEL)	7	Produce audible or visible signal
Back Space (BS)	8	Move print head one position to the left
Horizontal Tab (HT)	9	Move print head to next horizontal tab stop*
Vertical Tab (VT)	10	Move print head to next vertical tab stop*
Form Feed (FF)	12	Move printer to the top of the next page

*TELNET does not define a mechanism for establishing where such tabs stops are located. There are options defined for this.

Because the interpretations of Carriage Return, Line Feed, and newline vary between systems, TELNET provides precise definitions of how they should be used. The NVT newline character is the combination ⟨CR LF⟩. The TELNET process must translate the local newline character(s) into this character sequence. These characters can also be sent separately. To avoid confusion, a CR that is sent by itself to move the curser back to the beginning of the current line is followed by a NUL character.

The TELNET Transfer Protocol

TELNET data transmission is done over a full-duplex network connection provided by the lower layer protocols. However, TELNET data is actually sent in half-duplex mode, that is, in one direction at a time. In the terminal-to-process direction, the newline character signifies the end of user input. In the process-to-terminal direction, the TELNET Go Ahead command is used to turn the line around. When these signals occur in the data stream, the receiver may begin sending data. Because the underlying connection is full-duplex, control signals can be sent in both directions regardless of the data transmission direction. This allows the terminal user, for example, to send an Abort Output when the process is sending data to the printer.

Data is sent as a stream of 8-bit bytes. There is no other formatting to the data. Control signals and other nondata information are sent as TELNET commands. These commands occur as strings of bytes embedded in the data byte stream. There are commands corresponding to the user control signals described previously. There are also commands used between the TELNET processes as part of the transfer protocol and for option negotiation and subnegotiation. These are

1. Go Ahead: The line turn-around signal for half-duplex data transfer
2. Data Mark: A stream synchronizing character for use with the Sync signal
3. WILL: A negotiation command
4. WONT: A negotiation command
5. DO: A negotiation command
6. DONT: A negotiation command
7. Subnegotiation Begin: Begin subnegotiation command
8. Subnegotiation End: End subnegotiation command

The command identifier is encoded as an 8-bit byte as shown in Table 6.2. The Interpret As Command or IAC character (encoded as 255) precedes all TELNET commands in the data stream to distinguish them from user or process data. (If a 255 is part of the data stream, it must also be preceded by an IAC.) Thus, regular TELNET commands are 2 bytes long.

Table 6.2.   TELNET COMMAND ENCODING

Definition	Abbreviation	Code
End of subnegotiation	SE	240
No operation	NOP	241
Data Mark	DM	242
Break	BRK	243
Interrrupt Process	IP	244
Abort Output	AO	245
Are You There	AYT	246
Erase Character	EC	247
Erase Line	EL	248
Go Ahead	GA	249
Begin subnegotiation	SB	250
WILL		251
WONT		252
DO		253
DONT		254
Interpret As Command	IAC	255

Option negotiation commands are 3 bytes long. The third byte is the option identifier. Option subnegotiation commands will vary in length, but they always begin with the 3-byte sequence ⟨IAC SB option-id⟩ and end with the 2-byte sequence ⟨IAC SE⟩.

When processing the data stream from the network, TELNET scans every character. The appropriate translation is made between the NVT ASCII and the host's data representation. If TELNET finds an IAC, it should not send it on as data but must treat the next character as a TELNET command. If this next character is a 255, it is forwarded as data. If it is a negotiation command, TELNET gets the next byte to determine which option is being negotiated before starting the negotiation process. If the character following the IAC is a subnegotiation command, TELNET must buffer all characters up to the ⟨IAC SE⟩ sequence before processing the subnegotiation command.

Data from the host to the network must also be processed one character at a time. The host to NVT translation must be done and host control characters must be translated into the TELNET command sequence. User or process requests for option negotiation must be formatted into the appropriate character sequence and put in the data stream.

The TELNET data transfer protocol minimizes transmission overhead because it does not require extra bytes for message headers. However, processing overhead is high because both User and Server TEL-

NET must process data a character at a time to perform the data translation and scan for TELNET commands. This is the classic trade-off between message and stream protocols.

The final feature of the transfer protocol is the TELNET Sync signal. This allows out-of-band signaling between the terminal and the process. It is not an explicit TELNET command but consists of a TELNET command sequence followed by an IAC Data Mark (DM) sequence sent in head-of-queue fashion over the network connection. This allows it to bypass flow control in the network and be processed at the receiving end ahead of other data. How this is sent depends on the transport layer services available. For TCP networks, the data mark sequence is sent as TCP Urgent data. This is the stream synchronizing mark that tells the receiver to return to normal processing.

To send an out-of-band signal, TELNET should send the appropriate TELNET command followed by the Data Mark sequence ⟨IAC DM⟩ as TCP Urgent data. When TELNET receives a TCP Urgent notification, it should scan the data stream for TELNET commands as normal, but throw away any data. TELNET commands are handled normally. This continues until the Data Mark is found when processing returns to normal.

TELNET Option Negotiation

The TELNET designers provided option negotiation as part of the TELNET specification because they realized some terminals and processes may be able to support capabilities beyond those provided by the NVT. Option negotiation allows one side of a TELNET connection to request an option and the other side may accept or reject that request. If both sides agree on an option, it is put into effect immediately after negotiation is complete. Negotiation can take place at any time after the connection is established; however, most implementations negotiate options immediately after the connection is opened. This way they get the best possible service throughout the connection.

TELNET options are not part of the TELNET protocol specification. They are published as RFCs and assigned identifiers in those RFCs. Options currently defined are shown in Table 6.3. Those that are most widely used are described later in this chapter. The options can be divided into three major categories as shown in Table 6.3. The first category includes options that change, enhance, or refine the characteristics of the NVT. For example, options 8 through 16 allow further definition of the NVT printer characteristics. This also includes options that define a new virtual terminal to replace the NVT. Option 20, the Data Entry Terminal option, defines a network virtual data entry terminal that can be used to support this class of terminals on a TELNET connection. Options in the second category change the transfer protocol. For example, the Suppress

Table 6.3.   ASSIGNED TELNET OPTIONS

Option ID	Name	RFC #	Category
0	Binary Transmission	856	2
1	Echo	857	1
2	Reconnection	*	3
3	Suppress Go Ahead	858	2
4	Approx Message Size Negotiation	*	2
5	Status	859	3
6	Timing Mark	860	2
7	Remote Controlled Trans and Echo	726	1
8	Output Line Width	*	1
9	Output Page Size	*	1
10	Output Carriage-Return Disposition	652	1
11	Output Horizontal Tab Stops	653	1
12	Output Horizontal Tab Disposition	654	1
13	Output Formfeed Disposition	655	1
14	Output Vertical Tabstops	656	1
15	Output Vertical Tab Disposition	657	1
16	Output Linefeed Disposition	658	1
17	Extended ASCII	698	2
18	Logout	727	3
19	Byte Macro	732	2
20	Data Entry Terminal	735	1,2
21	SUPDUP	736,734	3
22	SUPDUP Output	749	3
23	Send Location	779	3
24	Terminal Type	930	3
25	End of Record	885	2
26	TACACS User Identification	927	3
27	Output Marking	933	3
28	Terminal Location Number	947	3
29	3270 Regime	1041	1,2
30	X.3 PAD	1053	1,2
31	Negotiate about window size	1073	1
32	Send terminal speed information	1079	1
33	Remote flow control	1080	2
255	Extended-Options-List	861	3

*Published in the DDN Protocol Handbook, NIC 50005, December 1985 [DCA85].

Go Ahead option requests that Go Ahead commands not be used. This would make the data transfer protocol full-duplex instead of half-duplex. Options that define new commands or control features of the transfer protocol are also included in this category. The End of Record option, for example, defines a TELNET command to indicate an end of user input to the process [POST83a]. The third category of options allows other information that is not part of the user data or the transfer protocol to be defined and passed over the connection. This category includes the Status option that requests the remote side to send the status of all options that have been negotiated on the connection.

Most TELNET options can be put into effect on one side of the connection or for one direction of the data transfer without affecting the operation of the other side. For these options, two separate negotiations must take place if the option is desired on both sides of the connection. For example, the End of Record option may be negotiated for the terminal-to-process direction of data transfer. This would define an end of record TELNET command (IAC EOR) to indicate the end of user input to the process. It could be separately negotiated in the other direction to define a similar character to signal the end of process data being sent to the printer.

The option negotiation protocol was designed to be symmetric. Either side may initiate negotiation for an option to be put into effect on either side of the connection. The User TELNET side may initiate negotiation about its own preference for Echoing, for example, or Server TELNET may make the request. Negotiation can ask that a new option be enabled for the connection or that a currently enabled option be disabled. The protocol was also designed so that there is no ambiguity if both sides make the same request and the messages pass each other on the network. The specific examples given below will show how this works.

There are a few rules that implementations must follow to provide correct option negotiation.

1. You may always reject a request to enable an option.
2. You must always accept a request to disable an option.
3. Options are not enabled until the negotiation is complete.
4. Never negotiate (either request or respond) about something that is already true; that is, do not initiate or respond to a request to initiate an option that is already in effect.

There are four option negotiation commands. Their meanings are given below, but their interpretation depends on the context of the negotiation.

1. WILL: Sender would like to enable the option.
2. DO: Sender would like the other side to enable the option.

3. WONT: Sender would not like to enable this option.
4. DONT: Sender would not like the other side to enable this option.

There are six possible negotiation sequences that can occur with the TELNET option negotiation protocol. The first four assume the option is not in effect when negotiation begins. The last two assume that the option is already in effect.

Case 1:

Side *A* would like to enable the option. Side *B* agrees.

Side *A* sends: ⟨IAC WILL option-id⟩

Side *B* sends: ⟨IAC DO option-id⟩

In this case the WILL is a request and the DO an affirmative response.

Case 2:

Side *A* would like to enable the option. Side *B* does not agree.

Side *A* sends: ⟨IAC WILL option-id⟩

Side *B* sends: ⟨IAC DONT option-id⟩

The DONT is a negative response in this case.

Case 3:

Side *A* would like side *B* to enable the option. Side *B* agrees.

Side *A* sends: ⟨IAC DO option-id⟩

Side *B* sends: ⟨IAC WILL option-id⟩

Here the DO is the request and the WILL the affirmative response.

Case 4:

Side *A* would like side *B* to enable the option. Side *B* does not agree.

Side *A* sends: ⟨IAC DO option-id⟩

Side *B* sends: ⟨IAC WONT option-id⟩

The WONT is a negative response in this case.

The first and third cases show that the commands can be either requests or responses depending on the context of the negotiation. It is also easy to see that if Side *A* and *B* both initiated negotiation for case 1 or 3 there would be no ambiguity. Side *A* would believe that Side *B*'s message was a response to its request and vice versa. The negotiation would end successfully. Cases 2 and 4 show why options should not be enabled until the negotiation is complete; the receiver of a request to enable an option may always refuse to do so.

An option may be disabled by one of the following sequences:

Case 5:

Side *A* would like to disable the option. Side *B* must agree.

Side *A* sends: ⟨IAC WONT option-id⟩

Side *B* sends: ⟨IAC DONT option-id⟩

Here the WONT is a request and the DONT the affirmative response.

Case 6:

Side *A* would like side *B* to disable an option. Side *B* must agree.

Side *A* sends: ⟨IAC DONT option-id⟩

Side *B* sends: ⟨IAC WONT option-id⟩

For this case, the DONT is the request and the WONT the affirmative response.

These commands sequences are summarized in Table 6.4.

Because the protocol is symmetric and dependent on the context of ongoing negotiation, implementations must handle negotiation carefully. In general, each side must keep track of which options are in effect and which are currently under negotiation. The functions that send and receive data from the network must communicate about ongoing negotiation to ensure that the current status is known to both functions. General algorithms for handling incoming option commands are given below.

```
If command is WILL
    If remote side has the option enabled already
        Do Nothing
    Else If I am waiting for a response to a DO for this option
        Remember that remote side has enabled the option
    Else (this is a new request)
        If I want the remote side to enable this option
            Send ⟨IAC DO option-id⟩
            Remember that remote side has enabled the option
        Else
            Send ⟨DONT option-id⟩
```

Table 6.4.   OPTION NEGOTIATION PROTOCOL

Request	Meaning	Response	Negotiation Result
WILL	Sender wants to enable the option	DO	Receiver agrees—option is enabled at sender side
WILL	Sender wants to enable the option	DONT	Receiver disagrees—option is not enabled at sender side
DO	Sender wants receiver to enable the option	WILL	Receiver agrees—option is enabled at receiver side
DO	Sender wants receiver to enable the option	WONT	Receiver disagrees—option is not enabled at receiver side
DONT	Sender wants to disable option	WONT	Receiver agrees—option is disabled at receiver side
WONT	Sender wants receiver to disable the option	DONT	Receiver agrees—option is disabled at sender side

```
If command is DO
    If I have the option enabled already
        Do Nothing
    Else If I am waiting for a response to a WILL for this option
        Enable the option
    Else (this is a new request)
        If I want to enable this option
            Send ⟨WILL option-id⟩
            Enable the option
        Else
            Send ⟨WONT option-id⟩
If command is DONT
    If I am waiting for a reply to a WILL
        Forget I asked—receiver refused my request
    Else If I have the option enabled already
        Disable it
    Else
        Do Nothing
If command is WONT
    If I am waiting for a reply to a DO
        Forget I asked—receiver refused my request
    Else If remote side has the option enabled already
        Remember that it is disabled
    Else
        Do Nothing
```

The actions taken to enable or disable an option depend on the definition of the option. Some options are defined so that option negotiation determines if both sides can support that option. Then further negotiation, using TELNET subnegotiation commands, is done to exchange more information. The Terminal Type option works this way. Option negotiation only establishes that each side can handle the more detailed negotiation. Then subnegotiation is used to exchange the information about the terminal types each side can support. The subnegotiation protocol, that is, the format, sequencing, and interpretation of the subnegotiation messages, is defined as part of the option specification. In some cases, more than one option must be negotiated before a particular service is enabled.

The TELNET Echo Option

Although TELNET options are defined for a wide variety of functions, very few are implemented in more than a handful of implementations. Most options are difficult to implement because they introduce complexity into the translation required at one or both ends of the connection, the pseudoterminal interface, or the interface between User and Server TELNET.

The Echo option [POST83b] is one of the most widely used TELNET option. As discussed earlier, the echoing of user input is an important part of remote access. The Echo option is itself relatively simple. It impacts, however, the interfaces between User TELNET and the terminal handler, and Server TELNET and the process. This option illustrates that it is sometimes difficult to correctly implement even a simple option if these interfaces do not provide the capabilities described previously.

The echoing of user input to user's display is an important part of interactive access as it allows the user to see the input to the process. In most cases, users should see their input before the process receives it. This is not always true, however. For example, user passwords are often not displayed on the screen for security reasons and other characters, such as backspace, have an effect on the screen but the actual character is not displayed.

Echoing over a network is a little more complex than in the local access case. The default TELNET echo mode is to have user input echoed locally. In most cases, this is the best way to handle echoing. The user sees the input immediately; errors can be corrected locally; and the terminal handler or User TELNET can buffer a full line of data before sending it across the network, saving the high overhead associated with sending single characters over the network. If the host process needs to control echoing, as with user logon, however, the TELNET Echo option allows Server TELNET to take control of echoing user input. The negotiation sequence would be:

> Server TELNET sends: IAC WILL Echo
>
> User TELNET sends: IAC DO Echo

User TELNET would then turn off the local terminal's echoing capability. When Server TELNET controls echoing, User TELNET should send each character of user input as it receives it so that it may be echoed as quickly as possible. This allows the user to see the input before entering the end-of-line character that signals that the data may be sent to the host process. If the user makes a typing error or wishes to change the input, the backspacing (TELNET Erase Character command) and corrected input must also be sent over the network. When Server TELNET receives a character it should buffer it for sending to the process and send it back over the network to be displayed on the printer as the echo. Server TELNET should buffer a full line of input and perform any editing before forwarding it to the process. This remote echo operation is shown in Figure 6.4.

A major disadvantage of remote echoing is this character-at-a-time operation. Every character is sent as a single character packet over the network twice, first as the user input and then as the echo. This is a lot of transmission overhead when TCP and IP add header, for every character and TCP must generate acknowledgments for each character. The advantage is, however, that the host process can control echoing.

To make the most efficient use of the network and provide host control when necessary, the Echo option should be negotiated only for those specific cases when host control is necessary. For example, Server TELNET could volunteer to Echo (send an ⟨IAC WILL Echo⟩) while the logon process is executing, then disable Echo (send an ⟨IAC WONT Echo⟩) when the process is complete.

The Echo option specification indicates that Echo can also be negotiated for the process to terminal traffic. However, echoing process output back to the process is not usually a meaningful concept. It may be useful for terminal-to-terminal traffic. The specification also shows that each side may want to control echoing for the other. This situation, if used, must be implemented carefully to avoid infinite echoing. If Server TELNET echoes all data from the network back to User TELNET and vice versa, unless new data can be differentiated from echoes, the data will loop through the network indefinitely.

The correct implementation of the Echo option places strict requirements on the interfaces between Server TELNET and the process and User TELNET and the terminal handler. On the User TELNET side, the interface must provide the capability for User TELNET to control whether characters are echoed locally. Because most systems provide mechanisms for an application program to control the terminal handling function, this capability is often easy to provide. When negotiation for Server TELNET to control echoing is complete, User TELNET must

User types but does not see on the printer

user inpo<bs>ut<nl>

User TELNET sends to Server TELNET

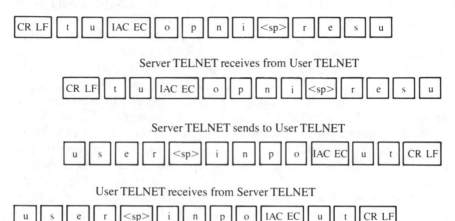

Server TELNET receives from User TELNET

Server TELNET sends to User TELNET

User TELNET receives from Server TELNET

Server TELNET sends to application process

user input <nl>

User TELNET sends to printer

user inpo<bs>ut<nl>

☐ x - represent data packets or buffers

Figure 6.4. Remote echo operation.

turn off local echo. Otherwise, the user will see double echoes, one from the local system and one from Server TELNET. (In fact, this is often the first "bug" found in new TELNET implementations.) A similar capability is required on the Server side. The process must be able to control the echoing of user input, just as it can with directly connected terminals. However, Server TELNET is actually another process that is trying to imitate a terminal. Most systems do not provide a mechanism for processes to communicate about terminal control. Therefore, the TELNET-to-process or pseudoterminal interface must provide this capability. Otherwise, Server TELNET will echo all user input including such things as passwords that should not be echoed.

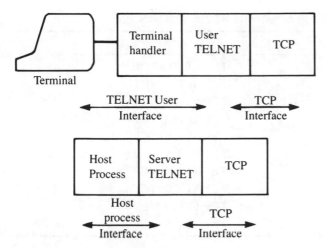

Figure 6.5. Implementation interfaces.

6.4 TELNET INTERFACES

The TELNET specification, like most protocol specifications, defines the protocol between User and Server TELNET and the processing that takes place within the TELNET processes. The specification says very little about how the TELNET processes interface to TCP, the user, and the terminal-oriented processes in the host. Figure 6.5 shows a more complete picture of the interfaces required in a full TELNET implementation. In some implementations, these interfaces may be simple subroutine calls; in others, they may be across board or processor boundaries. For example, many commercially available TCP implementations for personal computers have a separate processor board that runs TCP and the lower protocol layers. TELNET runs as an application in the personal computer operating system. The TCP interface must, therefore, cross this board boundary. In all cases, interfaces play an important role in the current implementation of the TELNET protocol. Although their implementations will vary, these interfaces have some general requirements. These are discussed in what follows.

TELNET to TCP Interface

TELNET, in its current form, is a presentation/application layer protocol that runs on top of TCP. TCP and the lower layer protocols provide a reliable network connection between the user and the server TELNET processes. Like all upper layer protocols in the MIL-STD protocol suite, the server host uses a well-known port, in this case number 23, to accept incoming requests for TELNET service. Server TELNET requests that

Table 6.5. **TELNET-TO-TCP INTERFACE REQUIREMENTS**

General Interface	Direction
TCP-open	TELNET to TCP
Connection is open	TCP to TELNET
Connection refused	TCP to TELNET
Connection aborted	TCP to TELNET
TCP-Close	TELNET to TCP
TCP-Write	TELNET to TCP
TCP-Read	TELNET to TCP
TCP-Write-Urgent	TELNET to TCP
Urgent Notification	TCP to TELNET
TCP Write-Push	TELNET to TCP

TCP do a listen on port 23. TELNET should close the TCP connection when the user logs off the server host or otherwise indicates that the session with that host is complete. Once the connection is established between User and Server TELNET, TCP is used to send the data and TELNET commands. For the correct operation of the Sync signal, the TELNET process must be able to request that data be sent as TCP Urgent data, and receive TCP Urgent Notifications from TELNET. TELNET may optionally use the TCP Push capability to indicate when data should be sent to the destination. This is helpful if TCP tries to send fixed size segments and will delay transmission until enough data is received to fill a segment. Because user input may be of varying lengths and is usually short, the TCP Push can be used after a ⟨CR LF⟩ to ensure that the user data is sent immediately. The general requirements for the TELNET interface to TCP are shown in Table 6.5. The details of this interface depend on the protocol implementations. This table shows the type of communication required between the two protocols, not the actual interface messages.

The TELNET to Host Process Interface

For a Server TELNET implementation, a mechanism must be available for the TELNET process to communicate with the host's terminal handling process. We will call this the pseudoterminal interface. How this interface is implemented depends on the host environment, the type of network communications support available, and how Server TELNET is implemented. In addition to passing data in both directions, this interface must provide the following general features:

1. Terminal Control

In some situations, the host process needs to control how TELNET handles user input. A good example of this is echoing during the user logon process. To keep the user's password from being echoed, the logon process would turn off echoing at the terminal after requesting the password, and turn it back on after the password is received. For the user to see the correct operation of terminal-oriented processes in the TELNET environment, the pseudoterminal interface must allow the host process to request control over the terminal or to notify TELNET about how user input should be handled. TELNET can then negotiate options or take other appropriate actions to make sure the terminal input is handled correctly.

2. Special Signaling

The pseudoterminal interface must transfer data and *regular* control signals between the process and TELNET. It must also provide an out-of-band or head-of-queue signaling capability. This is often difficult to provide on an interface that handles data transfer in only one direction at a time, or one that crosses processor boundaries. This signaling capability allows Server TELNET to forward TELNET Sync signals and the host's translation of the TELNET Break command to the process, or receive special signals from the process to be forwarded to User TELNET.

The TELNET User Interface

A User TELNET implementation needs a mechanism for accepting data from the user both for local processing and for sending to the remote process. This TELNET user interface is not part of the TELNET specification; implementers are free to provide any type of user interface that best suits their users. However, this interface should have the following minimum features:

1. Remote and Local Mode

Before the connection to the remote host is established, users can interface directly to the User TELNET process. Local commands should be available (1) to request a connection to a remote host, (2) to set local terminal characteristics, and (3) to set TELNET-related parameters. Once the connection to a remote host is established, users should be in remote mode, that is, all data input by the user is translated and sent to the Server TELNET as input for the process. While in remote mode, users need a mechanism for *escaping* back to local mode to communicate with User TELNET. This would be necessary, for example, if the user wanted to change terminal characteristics and negotiate options during the connection. This escape mechanism can be implemented many ways, but it should be *advertised* to the user when User TELNET is first executed. When the user escapes to local mode, some indication should be received (a special prompt character, for example) that the user is talking to User TELNET rather than the host process.

2. Local Commands

Some local commands that are helpful to the user are:

1. Help: A listing of local commands and their meaning, how to initiate control signals, and what the escape mechanism is.
2. Change local terminal characteristics
3. Open: Open a connection to a remote host
4. Close: Close a connection to a remote host
5. Status: Includes peer one is connected to, escape character, and enabled options

Some implementations may also allow the users to initiate option negotiation. If so, commands should be defined to specify (1) the option, (2) which side of the connection negotiation is for, and (3) whether the option should be enabled or disabled.

3. Local Representation of Control Signals

The TELNET specification defines the control signals that can be sent between User and Server TELNET. It does not specify, however, how the user requests that these signals be sent by User TELNET. This is an important part of the TELNET user interface.

If the local system has reserved special characters that correspond to the TELNET control signals, User TELNET can scan the data stream for these characters and translate them into appropriate TELNET commands. If this is done, the user interface should also provide a mechanism to escape the local meaning of the character so that the character can be sent as user data to the remote process. For example, if the @ character is used locally for erase line, User TELNET would translate this into ⟨IAC EL⟩. The user, however, may want to send the @ as data to the remote process. The user interface must allow TELNET to distinguish between these two uses of the character. Another way for a user to request control signals is through explicit local commands defined by the TELNET user interface. The user would escape to local mode, input the command for Interrupt Process, for example, then return to remote mode. This approach may not be as convenient for the user as typing a single character, but the command meaning is unambiguous in an environment where the user is *attached* to two processes at the same time.

6.5   EXTENDING TELNET TO SUPPORT MORE COMPLEX TERMINALS

There is a general problem with the TELNET protocol and the limitations imposed by the interfaces described previously. This is the problem of extending the TELNET service through option negotiation to support terminal-type communication that is more complex than the NVT. There are various facets of this problem. First, the process of defining a virtual terminal, that is, extracting functions common to a class of terminals and defining generic representations for those functions, is difficult for complex terminal types. For data entry or forms mode terminals, for example, manufacturers provide a very different set of capabilities for dividing the screen into fields with assigned attributes and operations, and allowing user input on a field, rather than character, basis. An attempt to define a virtual terminal that is a superset of all these capabilities is difficult, and any subset will exclude some capabilities particular users may require. Second, the transfer protocol between User and Server TELNET becomes more complex as more control signals are defined that need to be sent as TELNET commands. New commands in TELNET are often defined as subnegotiation messages. As we saw before, these are a minimum of six bytes long (a minimum of 1 byte for the command and 5 bytes for the subnegotiation header and trailer sequences). This increases transmission overhead. Processing overhead also increases, as parsing subnegotiation commands is more complex than parsing 2-byte TELNET commands. Finally, the pseudoterminal interface must provide additional capabilities that could include:

    1. A way for Server TELNET and the host process to communicate about more complex terminal control.
    2. A way to switch between terminal types for a particular TELNET connection.
    3. Adding enough intelligence to Server TELNET to negotiated an interrelated set of TELNET options and ensure that they are consistent and meaningful for the host processes.

This general problem is illustrated by the two mechanisms available for supporting data entry terminals. The first is the Data Entry terminal option [DAY77]; the second is the set of options used to support the IBM 3270 terminal protocol over TELNET [BRAD87].

The TELNET Data Entry terminal option defines another virtual terminal to replace the NVT on a TELNET connection. This Network Virtual Data Entry Terminal (NVDET) is a half-duplex, forms-mode terminal with an ASCII keyboard and an 80-character-by-24-line screen. The screen includes a cursor to indicate the next writing position. This cursor moves around the screen without disturbing the screen contents.

Once the option has been negotiated, User and Server TELNET use subnegotiation to define the forms mode facilities for editing, erasing, data transmission, and formatting. Table 6.6 shows the functions available in each of these areas. Facility subnegotiation involves each side

Table 6.6. DATA ENTRY TERMINAL FACILITIES AND FUNCTIONS

Erase		
Erase Facility Map		
	Bit Number	Facility
	4	Erase Field
	3	Erase Line
	2	Erase Rest of Screen
	1	Erase Rest of Line
	0	Erase Rest of Field
Erase Functions		
	Function	Available with Facility Bit Number
	Erase Screen	(always available)
	Erase Field	4
	Erase Line	3
	Erase Rest of Screen	2
	Erase Rest of Line	1
	Erase Rest of Field	(always available)
	Erase Unprotected	(always available)
Transmit		
Transmit Facility Map		
	Bit Number	Facility
	5	Data Transmit
	4	Transmit Line
	3	Transmit Field
	2	Transmit Rest of Screen
	1	Transmit Rest of Line
	0	Transmit Rest of Field
Transmit Functions		
	Function	Available with Facility Bit Number
	Transmit Screen	(always available)
	Transmit Unprotected	(always available)
	Transmit Line	4
	Transmit Field	3
	Transmit Rest of Screen	2

Table 6.6   (continued)

Transmit

Transmit
Functions

Function	Available with Facility Bit Number
Transmit Rest of Line	1
Transmit Rest of Field	0
Transmit Modified	(always available)
Data Transmit	5

Edit

Edit Facility Map

Bit Number	Facility
5	Incremental Cursor Addressing
4	Read Cursor Address
3	Line Insert/Delete
2	Character Insert/ Delete
1	Back Tab
0	Positive Address Only

Edit Functions

Function	Available with Facility Bit Number
Move Cursor	(always available)
Home	(always available)
Cursor Address	(always available)
Up	5 and not 0
Down	5
Left	5 and not 0
Right	5
Read Cursor	4
Line Insert	3
Line Delete	3
Char Insert	2
Char Delete	2
Back Tab	1

Table 6.6 (continued)

Format		
Format Facility/ Map		
	Bit Number	Facility
	7 (byte 0)	FN
	6	Modified
	5	Light Pen
	4	Repeat
	3	Blinking
	2	Reverse Video
	1	Right Justification
	0	Overstrike
	6 (byte 1)	Protection On/Off
	5	Protection
	4	Alphabetic Only Protection
	3	Numeric Only Protection
	0–2	Number of Intersity Levels
Format Functions		
	Function	Available with Facility Bit Number
	Repeat (data compression)	4 byte 0
	Suppress Protection	6 byte 1
	Field Separator	5 byte 1
	FN (define function keys)	7 byte 0

The remaining facility bits define acceptable values for the < format map > field of the FORMAT DATA Function. (These are the attributes of a fixed or variable field on the form.)

sending a map of the facilities it will support. The logical intersection of these becomes the facility map for the connection. Table 6.7 gives an example of this subnegotiation. Data is transferred as ASCII characters. The forms mode control signals to move the cursor and transmit selected fields, for example, are sent as subnegotiation messages. They are shown in Table 6.8.

The Data Entry terminal option is a very complex protocol. Very few implementations have been done; therefore, implementation and per-

Table 6.7.   DATA ENTRY TERMINAL FACILITY SUBNEGOTIATION EXAMPLE

User TELENET Sends	
	< IAC > < SB > < DET > < FORMAT FACILITIES > < Blinking, Protection On/Off, Protection, Alphabetic-Only Protection, Numeric-Only Protection, Intensity Levels = 3, Right Justification >
Server TELNET Sends	
	< Blinking, Protection On/Off, Protection, Numeric-Only Protection, Reverse Video, Intensity Levels = 3 >
Resulting Format Facility Map	
	< Blinking, Protection On/Off, Protection, Numeric-only Protection, Intensity Levels = 3 >

formance experience is scarce. The lack of implementations, however, is a good indication that the complexity may be too great to justify using a virtual forms mode terminal.

There is a service available with some TELNET implementations, called tn3270, that negotiates a set of TELNET options to provide support for IBM 3270 class terminals. The goal of this negotiation, however, is not to define a new virtual terminal. It is to exchange enough information about what the host and terminal can support so that native mode communication can replace the NVT. This is often called transparent operation of the TELNET protocol. This is essentially the remote access protocol described at the beginning of the chapter that can be used when the host and the terminal understand each other's native language.

The tn3270 service uses the Terminal Type [SOLO85] and the End-of-Record [POST83a] options to define the details of the terminal protocol that the terminal and the host will use. The TELNET Terminal-Type negotiation and subnegotiation sequences are shown in Figure 6.6. It then negotiates the Binary Transmission option [POST83c] in both directions. This option changes the data format from ASCII to a stream of binary bits. TELNET still translates for TELNET commands and sends option negotiation commands, but all other data is passed transparently to the terminal or the process. The assumption is that the terminal and the host understand the bit stream and will respond appropriately without a virtual terminal.

Although this transparent operation bypasses the virtual terminal part of TELNET, it highlights the fact that virtualizing a more complex

Table 6.8. DATA ENTRY TERMINAL COMMANDS

Data Entry Terminal Subnegotiation Command
IAC SB DET UP IAC SE
IAC SB DET DOWN LAC SE
IAC SB DET LEFT IAC SE
IAC SB DET RIGHT IAC SE
IAC SB DET HOME IAC SE
IAC SB DET LINE INSERT IAC SE
IAC SB DET LINE DELETE IAC SE
IAC SB DET CHAR INSERT IAC SE
IAC SB DET CHAR DELETE IAC SE
IAC SB DET READ CURSOR IAC SE
IAC SB DET REVERSE TAB IAC SE
IAC SB DET TRANSMIT SCREEN IAC SE
IAC SB DET TRANSMIT UNPROTECTED IAC SE
IAC SB DET TRANSMIT LINE IAC SE
IAC SB DET TRANSMIT FIELD IAC SE
IAC SB DET TRANSMIT REST OF SCREEN IAC SE
IAC SB DET TRANSMIT REST OF LINE IAC SE
IAC SB DET TRANSMIT MODIFIED IAC SE
IAC SB DET ERASE SCREEN IAC SE
IAC SB DET ERASE LINE IAC SE
IAC SB DET ERASE FIELD IAC SE
IAC SB DET ERASE REST OF SCREEN IAC SE
IAC SB DET ERASE REST OF LINE IAC SE
IAC SB DET ERASE UNPROTECTED IAC SE
IAC SB DET FIELD SEPARATOR IAC SE

Data Entry Terminal Subnegotiation Commands with Parameters*
IAC SB DET MOVE CURSOR
IAC SB DET CURSOR POSITION
IAC SB DET DATA TRANSMIT
IAC SB DET FORMAT DATA
IAC SB DET REPEAT
IAC SB DET SUPPRESS PROTECTION

*Parameters and IAC SE follow the command.

Server TELNET sends   User TELNET sends

1.

    IAC DO Terminal-Type

2.

                                        IAC WILL Terminal-Type

3.

    IAC SB Terminal-Type SEND IAC SE

4.

                        IAC SB Terminal-Type IS IBM-3278-2 IAC SE

Figure 6.6.   Terminal type option negotiation and subnegotiation.

terminal is a difficult and complex undertaking. This problem has been known for many years, yet transparent mode is still considered the most efficient way to provide this type of service across a network. Designers of new virtual terminal protocols should address these problems if the network world wants to move away from the lowest common denominator of service typically provided today on heterogeneous networks. One alternative is to provide new ways of defining network applications so that transactions or remote procedure calls are used to request services across the network. This would eliminate the need for imitating the user interface across the network.

APPENDIX 6A   TERMINAL TYPES

There are three basic terminal types used for character-based data entry to host processes: scroll mode, page mode, and forms mode. Terminals used for specific systems may have unique characteristics; therefore, only the general characteristics of each type will be given here.

Scroll Mode

The scroll mode terminal type is the least complex terminal type. It is based on the teletype (TTY), which uses a roll of paper that unwinds in only one direction. Once the print head is moved to the next line it cannot be moved back. Most scroll mode terminals today use screens in place of paper, but the concept is the same. Characters are displayed in lines sequentially from the top of the screen to the bottom. When the screen is filled, adding a new line causes the top line to scroll off the screen and all lines move up one position. This simulates the effect of unwinding the roll of paper.

The general characteristics of a scroll mode terminal are:

- User input is on a line basis. Lines can be either a fixed length (number of characters) or infinite length, but a system-defined newline character is always a signal that user input is complete and the host may begin processing the data.
- Host output is also on a line basis although the host may generate many lines before prompting the user for more input. If the host generates more lines than the physical screen can display, the top lines will be scrolled off the screen and possibly lost to the user.
- Communication is usually asynchronous; that is, the user can input data while host output is being written to the screen.

Page Mode

The preceding discussion of scroll mode terminals points out two disadvantages when using a screen to emulate a TTY. The first is that user input can consist of only one line. An infinite line length lessens the severity of the problem by not limiting the amount of data. There are many situations, however, when the user may wish to submit a set of commands to the host at one time without having to wait for one to execute before typing the next, or may want to type in and edit a set of commands before submitting them for processing. The second disadvantage is the potential loss of data that is scrolled off the top of the screen. With a TTY, users could read host output as fast as it was typed, and the paper held a permanent copy. With screens, users can rarely read data as quickly as it appears on the screen and any lines scrolled off the top of the screen may be lost. Page mode terminals were designed to alleviate these problems. The basic characteristics of a page mode terminal are:

1. User input can be multiple lines. Newline does not designate an end to user input, just an end to the line. Another key sequence or an out-of-band signal is used to indicate that the user input is done and the data can be processed by the host. The system must keep track of how many lines of data are part of the current input.
2. Host output is in pages, where a page is defined as the number of characters per line and the number of lines per screen the physical screen can display. The host will pause between pages until the user indicates that he or she is finished *processing* the output.
3. Communication is usually half-duplex synchronous; that is, one direction at a time. The host must have some knowledge of the amount of space left on the page. User input displayed on the screen while the host is writing a page makes screen management difficult. Therefore, half-duplex synchronous communication is preferred.

Forms Mode

Forms mode terminals are used for a special class of applications. These applications are designed so that the user inputs only the necessary data—he or she is not required to input commands to process the data or to designate the semantics of the data. This is analogous to filling out a form—you only supply the answers, the form supplies the questions and the location of the answer defines its meaning. A forms mode application will display a form on the screen. The areas, usually called fields, for user data are blank but have some attributes and semantics known to the application. Attributes can be (1) restrictions on the type of data allowed, such as numeric only; (2) display characteristics, such as reverse video or invisible; and (3) transmission attributes, such as never transmit this field (it is for the user only) or transmit only if it changes. Once the form is displayed, the user begins filling in the fields. There is no concept of a command line, and the order in which the user fills the fields is not significant. When the user finishes the form, he or she signals (with a special key or out-of-band signal) that the data be sent to the host. Usually, only the user fields are sent to the host and their transmission order defines their meaning. (For example, first field is name, second is social security number, and so on.)

The general characteristics of a forms mode terminal are:

- Host output is on a page basis, as with the page mode terminal, except the page is divided into distinct fields, each with defined attributes.
- User input is on a field basis. The application restricts the type of data entered in a field and controls how it is displayed. Order of input is not significant and local editing of user input is encouraged.
- Communication is synchronous, as with page mode terminals.

The host-to-terminal protocol becomes very complex for forms mode. In the host to terminal direction, it must define the form structure and the field attributes. This includes the location on the screen where each field belongs and how it is displayed. In the terminal-to-host direction, it must map the user input to a field identifier (this can be done by the transmission order, or by an explicit designation of a field), and it must designate whether the user input is a new form or just changed fields from a previous form. Because the terminal protocol is complex and processing is required at both the host and terminal, forms mode terminals are mainly used for specialized applications.

7

Network Management in the TCP/IP Protocol Suite

Craig Partridge* and Keith McCloghrie

Support for network management is often an afterthought in the development of a protocol suite. Certainly, network management research has lagged behind research in other areas of networking. Indeed, it is probably fair to say that research on network management is nearly a generation behind research on other topics.

In this chapter we examine the current and developing management protocols for networks using the TCP/IP protocol suite.

7.1 HISTORY OF NETWORK MANAGEMENT IN THE TCP/IP PROTOCOL SUITE

"Comprehensive" network management protocols, protocols designed to serve most or all of a protocol suite's management needs, are a new addition to the TCP/IP protocol suite. To understand why these protocols have been developed, it is worth taking a brief look at how TCP/IP networks were managed before formal management protocols were developed.

When the initial work on the protocol suite was finished in the late

*Mr. Partridge would like to acknowledge the assistance of Bolt Beranek Newman, Incorporated, which provided him the time to contribute to this book.

1970s, the only "management" protocol included was the Internet Control Message Protocol (ICMP). ICMP was designed to allow hosts and gateways to exchange control messages, in particular, messages indicating errors in datagram processing and routing, and warning of the presence of congestion. However, ICMP also includes a few basic messages that can be used for error diagnosis. The most important of these diagnostic messages are the *Echo/Echo Reply* messages. An Echo message sent to an IP system (host or gateway) requires an Echo Reply message to be sent back to the originating system. The Echo Reply message must also return any data included in the Echo message.

Using the Echo and Echo Reply messages along with various IP header options such as *Source Routing* and *Record Route* and given the ability to set some IP header fields such as the *Time-To-Live,* a very powerful program can be written to analyze network problems. Indeed, such a program is widely used throughout the ARPA Internet and is known as *ping* for Packet Internet Groper, a name coined in 1979 by Dr. David Mills of the University of Delaware. Ping can be used to observe variations in network round-trip times and loss rates which allow a manager to discover the presence of and isolate the source of network congestion in a network path. Fragmentation and reassembly problems can be traced by sending large Echo messages. Other more sophisticated observations are also possible.

Once a problem is discovered using ping, further investigations can be carried out with more specialized tools. Packet printers such as the Packet Filter [MOGUL87] can be used to examine local network traffic. Most gateways allow remote operators to log in and examine log files. Furthermore, most of the TCP/IP application protocols use ASCII data formats, which make it possible to telnet to an application port and type in commands by hand. (This last trick is particularly useful when debugging *e-mail* problems.)

In fact, the combination of ping and various auxiliary tools worked so well that for many years there was no pressure to develop new management protocols. Researchers who developed more powerful management protocols discovered that the community felt no need for them; a case in point is the Host Monitoring Protocol (HMP), which was used to manage *backbone* gateways, but never implemented in *non-backbone* gateways. There was no pressure to develop more powerful management tools until the Internet growth rate exploded in the late 1980s. This pressure resulted not just from the increased number of hosts and gateways, but also from the more complex network topologies introduced by the rapid growth.

Figure 7.1 shows how the Internet has grown. It graphs the number of IP networks attached to the Internet over time, starting in 1983. Observe that in late 1986 the growth rate suddenly became much faster. In 1987 the Internet doubled in size, from 175 to 350 active IP networks. We

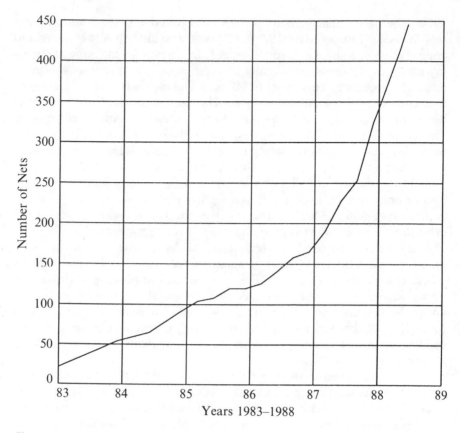

Figure 7.1. Internet growth in networks.

should also note that this number does not fully convey the impact of growth. Concurrent with the increase in IP networks has been an increase in the use of *subnetting,* the practice of combining several distinct networks together into one logical IP network. (For an example of a well-developed subnetted network, see G. Trewitt's paper on the Stanford University network [TREW88].) One way to measure the increase in subnetting is to look at the average number of hosts per network. A higher average implies increased use of subnetting. In 1983 the average number of hosts per network was about 8. By late 1987, the average was nearly 100 hosts per network. Clearly, the boom in IP networks went hand-in-hand with a boom in subnetting. This growth rate, although it has moderated slightly, continues today and is putting extraordinary management demands on the TCP/IP community.

The key management problem in a fast-growing network is training people to run it. By 1987 the training problem in the TCP/IP community had become severe. Management tools like ping are designed to be used by network experts with several years of training. They are not suitable for use by computer operators. By 1987 there was an acute shortage of experts to run networks and the community began to see cases where organizations had built networks and then had great difficulty operating those networks due to the lack of experienced personnel.

In response to the need for better and easier network management, the community encouraged several researchers to develop proposals for more comprehensive network management protocols which could be used to develop network management applications requiring less user expertise. By early 1988, three promising approaches had been developed. In February of that year, the Internet Activities Board (the group responsible for directing research on TCP/IP protocols) convened a meeting to select a future TCP/IP standard from among the three protocols. The three candidates were: The High-Level Entity Management System (HEMS) [PART 88]; the Simple Network Management Protocol (SNMP), an enhanced version of the Simple Gateway Management Protocol (SGMP); and the use of OSI's CMIP protocol over TCP/IP (CMOT).

In the end, the participants in the meeting proved unable to choose between the three proposals; each protocol had features and limitations (technical and political) that made it about equal to the other two. As a result, a compromise was fashioned. (A complete description of the meeting and its decisions may be found in RFC 1052.) The developers of HEMS volunteered to withdraw their proposal in the interest of finding a solution. The other two proposals were chosen as potential standards. The SNMP, whose developers chose to compromise on functionality and flexibility in the interest of developing a protocol that could be quickly deployed and efficiently implemented, was chosen as the current network management protocol in order to get the community out of the immediate network management crisis. The other protocol, CMOT, was an attempt to take the still-developing ISO Common Management Information Protocol (CMIP) and adapt it for use in managing networks using TCP/IP protocols. CMOT was designated the long-term management solution, contingent on demonstrations that it was suitable for extremely large datagram networks. The meeting participants further decided that, in order to aid in the eventual transition from SNMP to CMOT, both protocols would be required to use the same database of managed objects. In other words, both protocols would use the same monitoring and control variables within any host or gateway. A working group was established to define this common database.

The rest of this chapter looks at SNMP and CMOT and their common management base in more detail. We begin by introducing some basic network management concepts which are common to both protocols. We will then look at the common Management Information Base (MIB) and conclude by examining each protocol in some detail.

7.2 NETWORK MANAGEMENT CONCEPTS

Models of Network Management

As a result of the recent activity in network management and the importation of some OSI management concepts (via CMOT), the current TCP/IP model of network management is a melange formed by researchers with different perspectives.

The TCP/IP community has traditionally thought of network management in terms of the abstract operations used to support it, in particular, the monitoring and control model. The OSI community has focused more on the activities that network management is designed to support. The current TCP/IP model, influenced by CMOT, is a mix of the traditional view and the OSI approach.

The TCP/IP community has historically chosen to divide network management into two parts. *Monitoring* is the process of observing the behavior of the network and its components, both to detect problems and to support research into understanding and possibly improving the network's performance. *Control* is the process of changing the network's behavior in real-time by adjusting parameters while the network is up and running in order to improve performance or repair faults.

This dichotomy reflects the community's research background. Monitoring is generally considered a very open activity. In principle, anyone on the network should be able to monitor the network's performance or ask for information from any host or gateway. (As the TCP/IP protocol suite has became more popular commercially, there has been some pressure to reconsider this open access policy. Companies do not want their internal traffic patterns available to competitors. There is, however, an advantage to the open access policy. Experience suggests that a network in which monitoring information is universally available is much easier to keep running because more people can locate and examine a problem.) Control, on the other hand, involves changing the state of the network. Clearly, control is a privileged activity and requires some authentication that the person or system exercising control is both qualified and entitled to make changes.

In contrast, the OSI community has treated network management as an activity subdivided into a number of *functional areas,* where a functional area is a class of activities devoted to a particular purpose such as fault management or accounting. The focus of the OSI network management activity has been to identify the management needs of each functional area and standardize ways to meet those needs.

Interestingly, in practice, the methods for implementing the OSI model of functional areas and the methods for implementing the TCP/IP model of monitoring and control turn out to be very similar. Both models work in terms of application-level protocols used to effect transactions or procedure calls between managing and managed systems.

In the current TCP/IP model, management is effected through an interaction between a management application on the managing system and a management *agent* on the managed system. The agent maintains an object database of access points in the management system. These objects are standarized across systems of a particular class (e.g., hosts all support the same management objects). The management application effects monitoring and control by reading and writing (or getting and setting) the management objects in the agent using a standard management protocol. In other words, the object database provides an abstract representation of the managed system to the management application and it is the agent's responsibility to translate operations on this abstract database into real operations upon the managed system. For example, if a managing system sets an object corresponding to a *reload button* in the object database, the agent must cause the managed system to reload its networking software.

Note that although the model does not place any constraints on how many agents can be managed by one management station, the community generally would like the number to be rather high. (For example, the HEMS designers felt, after discussions with the networking community, that a single management station should comfortably be able to manage as many as a thousand agents.)

Events

One problem with managing a large number of devices from a single system is that if the number of managed devices gets very large, it is no longer possible for the management station to regularly poll each managed system. This observation naturally leads to the idea that managed systems should asynchronously notify management stations of potential problems, using special management messages called *events*. (The TCP/IP community orginally referred to such messages as *traps* and sometimes still uses this term.)

An appealing characteristic of events is that they are only sent when a problem occurs, whereas management systems that use polling find that most of their management traffic is devoted to sending polls to "healthy" systems. In other words, a lot of network bandwidth is consumed getting management information that the management station probably does not need.

All of the TCP/IP management protocols support some sort of event mechanism. They differ in how often they expect events to occur.

Methods for Managing Special Devices

Typically, the agent model described above is thought of as an exchange between two application-level processes: the management application and the management agent. Therefore, management is thought of as occurring only between systems which support the complete TCP/IP protocol suite up to the application layer.

In practice, that model has proved too limiting. Network managers want to manage all the components in their network, not just hosts and gateways. In particular, system managers want to manage specialized network devices such as modems and bridges, which do not support a full protocol suite.

There are various ways to incorporate such specialized devices into a management scheme that is based on application-level interaction. Both CMOT and SNMP use a scheme called *proxy* which was first proposed by the designers of HEMS. In the proxy approach, specialized devices are managed through a management agent on a proxy system. The proxy agent acts as an intermediary between the management application and the actual device. When requested by the management application, the proxy management agent instructs the device to perform the desired operation using the device's own management protocols. The device then returns the result to the proxy agent which in turn repackages the result into the management protocol and sends it to the management application. For example, if a management application wishes to control a modem attached to host *A*, the application sends a request to the management agent on host *A*. The agent converts the request into an instruction over the modem's control channel, gets the result of the request, and converts that result into a suitable reply to the management application. A similar approach can be used for *bridges*. By designating a *host* on the same network as the bridge, as the *proxy* for the bridge, applications can perform management operations on the bridge, even if the application is on a host several networks away.

How the agent converts the standard management protocol instructions into operations or instructions for the specialized device is left unspecified. The only requirement is that the agent support an object database that includes manageable objects for the devices for which the agent is a proxy.

In practice, proxies have been implemented in several different ways. Some proxies do protocol conversion, converting a request in the standard management protocol into a request in the device-specific protocol used by the special devices. Other proxies simply re-encapsulate the management request in a lower-level protocol. For example, the SNMP protocol can be sent over Ethernet MAC layer frames to bridges that support SNMP (RFC 1089). As a result, an SNMP proxy for a bridge can simply strip off the UDP and IP packet headers and resend the SNMP query unchanged to the bridge. Handling the reply from the bridge is simply a matter of re-encapsulating the Ethernet frame into UDP and IP for delivery to the managing application.

More recently proxy schemes have also been used to *off-load* expensive computation tasks from devices dedicated to key network functions. In particular, the SNMP community has used proxy to cache answers to commonly asked queries and to handle (expensive) authentication. Management stations ask a proxy agent for information about a device; if the proxy agent has a cached answer to the query, it uses the cache, otherwise it asks the device. Similarly, queries requiring significant processing for authentication or access-control checks can be sent to a proxy agent which does the authentication check before passing the query on to the managed agent. These different uses of proxy can be used in combination or individually.

External Data Formats

One of the key assumptions underlying the MIB or object database approach to network management is that a universal external representation of a managed system exists. In other words, there exists a way to provide a standardized system representation for management.

This assumption actually has two parts. First, it assumes that we can find an abstract representation, in the form of a MIB, for any system. This assumption is examined in more detail in the next section. The other assumption, which we look at here, is that given an abstract representation, there is a concrete way to implement that representation, which all the different systems on the network can understand and exchange. This process is called *externalization* and is achieved through the use of *external data formats*.

An external data format is a standard representation of a data object, a representation that can be understood by any machine. To use an external data format, a sending system must convert its internal representation of the object into external form before sending it to another machine. In turn, a receiving system must convert the data object from the external format it receives into its own internal representation for processing.

In the worst possible case, this representation problem is $n \times m$. All m receivers must know the n different data formats used by the senders. An $n \times m$ approach is obviously prohibitively expensive and thus almost all external data formats use a single canonical form which all systems must convert into and out of.

There are several well-known data formats suitable for this purpose, but both SNMP and CMOT use the Abstract Syntax Notation One (ASN.1), the external data format developed by CCITT and ISO.

ASN.1 is a *tagged* data format. Each data item is transferred as a triple of <type, length, value>. The *type* identifies what type of datum is encoded: integer, character, structure, boolean, etc. The *length* is the length of the value section. The *value* is the actual value itself, in a well-defined bit order. More complex data types are built recursively from simple types (e.g., to create a record, one uses a structure type whose data field contains ASN.1 objects corresponding to the fields in the record). For example, a socket type, in ASN.1, might look like Figure 7.2 where IpAddress is an ASN.1 type to represent a four-octet IP address. This is necessarily a cursory introduction. For more detail on ASN.1 and data encoding in general, see [PART88b].

7.3 INTERNET MIB AND SMI

The definition of the managed object base for TCP/IP protocol networks is divided into two parts, a Structure of Management Information (SMI) and a Management Information Base (MIB). OSI defines its object database the same way; this is not a coincidence.

The SMI

The SMI defines the general framework within which a MIB can be defined. The SMI identifies the data types that can be used in the MIB, how objects within the MIB are named and specified, and guidelines for extending the MIB. The SMI does not define any actual objects in the MIB.

In the TCP/IP protocol community, the SMI is of special importance because it has been designed to ensure that if a MIB is defined according to the SMI guideliness the MIB can be used by both SNMP and CMOT. The community was especially interested in being able to design and write applications that could be used with either SNMP or CMOT, thus easing the eventual transition from SNMP to CMOT.

Defining an SMI that accommodated both protocols proved a real challenge (see [McCL89]). For example, SNMP is designed, for efficiency reasons, to support only a very limited set of data types. As a result, the SMI is limited to four of ASN.1's eight primitive types (INTEGER, OCTET STRING, OBJECT IDENTIFIER, and NULL) and permitted only one constructed type, SEQUENCE, and further stipulates

```
TcpSocket ::= SEQUENCE {
    tcpLocalAddress -- the local IP address
        IpAddress,
    tcpLocalPort -- the local TCP port
        INTEGER (0..65535),
    tcpRemoteAddress -- the remote IP address
        IpAddress,
    tcpRemPort  -- the remote TCP port
        INTEGER (0..65535)
}
```

Figure 7.2. Example of ASN.1.

that SEQUENCES may not be nested within SEQUENCES and prohibits constructed octet strings. It required considerable deliberation to
determine that those five types were sufficient to build a useful MIB.

The OBJECT IDENTIFIER type is particularly important. It is a
structured name and is used by management protocols to name objects in
the MIB. An OBJECT IDENTIFIER is a specially encoded sequence of
integers which uniquely indentifies a node in a unique naming tree defined
by ISO. OBJECT IDENTIFIERS are typically written as a sequence of
dot-separated digits. For example, 1.3.6.1.2.1.3 identifies the type for
sysUpTime.

In the MIB, OBJECT IDENTIFIERS are used to uniquely indentify
object types. An object type defines how a piece of information is ab-
stractly encoded for transmission between managed systems (for example, that a particular field of a route structure is represented as an IP
address). In both SNMP and CMOT, the OBJECT IDENTIFIERS are
also used to name objects in the MIB (for example, to request that the
interface structure be returned). However, the protocols use different
mechanisms to identify which instance of an object is to be retrieved (i.e.,
to determine which interface's *interface structure* is to be returned).

The SMI further defines some application-specific types, built from
the five permissible ASN.1 types. The need for some of these is obvious.
For example, a standard representation for an IP address was clearly required and an *opaque* type, allowing consenting applications to exchange
arbitrary types, is clearly useful. But some of the types have more subtle
characteristics.

The *counter* type is perhaps the most interesting. A counter is a 32-
bit integer that is always increasing and which rolls over from *0xffffffff*
back to 0. Counters are used for counting packets, bytes processed, and
the like. Some network managers prefer a mechanism called *latch
counters,* which stick at *0xffffffff* until reset. However, the TCP/IP community felt very strongly that latch counters are inconsistent with allowing several applications to monitor a device simultaneously. The logic is
as follows: if multiple applications are observing a counter that latches,
then one of them must be responsible for resetting it to 0 so that all the
managing applications can continue to read useful data from the counter.
Unfortunately, if that application fails to detect that the counter has
latched and reset it, the other applications will find the counter offers no
information (the latched value never changes). If the other applications
try to reset the counter themselves, they will reset over each other's resets, causing the count to be mistakenly reset to 0 more than once, thus
losing information. *Roll-over counters* do not have this problem, they
never need to be reset. The disadvantage of roll-over counters is that after
they have rolled over a few times, it is difficult for a managing application
to learn if the counter value of 1 means that one packet has been seen or
$2^{32} + 1$ packets have been seen. The only way a management application

can distinguish between the two values is to occasionally check the counter after the agent is started. This continuous checking is a bit of a nuisance, but because the SMI defines a large counter size, it can be done infrequently.

The SMI also defines a *gauge* type which can increase or decrease and which latches *0xffffffff*. Gauges are used to measure levels, such as the current number of packets stored in a queue. As such, the latched value is useful even if it is not reset (it tells you that at some point in time the queue was larger than the system can count) and is not inconsistent with having multiple managers.

Finally, the SMI defines a timer value, called *TimeTicks,* which measures time in hundredths of a second since a given epoch. The epoch is defined on a per object basis. This type is used for timestamps and clock values and is somewhat controversial. Many experts would prefer that the MIB use absolute time values and the standard ASN.1 representations for those absolute times. Unfortunately, most systems running the TCP/IP protocol suite do not support a time synchronization protocol; the only time synchronization protocol is experimental (see RFC 1059). In the absence of synchronized time, relative timestamps are considered more useful (they provide unambiguous timestamps within a system) and with some effort such relative times can be used to construct an accurate sequence of events system-wide by comparing timestamps for known events among different machines.

The SMI also leaves out a couple of important types. One obvious limitation is the restriction on *nesting* structured types within structured types. This prohibition was intended to allow SNMP to interoperate with the MIB. The designers of SNMP felt strongly that nested structures were too expensive to process in a real-time management agent.

Another type that was left out was *thresholds.* Thresholds are values, which if exceeded, cause the agent to send events to one or more management applications. Although both SNMP and CMOT can deliver events, the working group defining the SMI felt strongly that the idea of sending events based on threshold values was, as yet, poorly understood. In particular, the group feared that threshold would cause *event floods,* situations where a managed system's threshold is repeatedly exceeded and the system sends out a continuous stream of events which inundates the network. Such event floods have been observed on several networks, most notably the ARPANET. Event floods have the perverse characteristic that they are generally caused by network congestion and, because the event floods cause more data to be sent, usually make the congestion problem even more severe.

It is possible that additional types will be added, and a relaxation of some of these restrictions could occur in future versions of the SMI, as lessons are learned through implementation experience.

The MIB

The MIB defines the actual management objects which are operated upon by the management protocol. It also defines what protocol operations may be applied to each object. For example, it defines an object that represents TCP Connections Blocks (TCBs) and decrees that remote applications can read this object, but not change it. (Changing a TCB is forbidden because allowing third parties to change TCP connection states while a connection is in progress can invite disaster.)

The first version of the MIB (which is currently the standard) is intentionally small; only 126 management objects are defined. Most of the objects are required of all systems; a few are required only of gateways.

The MIB was limited in size because the TCP/IP community believed that it was important to get the MIB deployed as soon as possible to deal with the looming network management crisis. A smaller MIB was considered to be less of an imposition on TCP/IP protocol vendors, who had to re-instrument their systems to support the MIB. In retrospect this decision appears to have been correct. Most major manufacturers deployed a MIB within six months of the release of the specification.

Many people are suprised by the notion of a MIB that is required of all systems. They find it difficult to believe that very different implementations can be made to provide a consistent MIB. However, experience with the TCP/IP MIB suggests this is not as difficult as it sounds. A careful reading of the protocol standards makes it clear that all implementations must provide certain types of functionality (routing tables and protocol control blocks are two good examples). It is then possible (although not easy) to define a MIB representation of that common functionality which can be used across all implementations.

In part because of the decision to limit the size of the MIB, the MIB working group set strict guidelines to ensure that the objects included in the standard were, indeed, useful. In particular, the group required that any object in the MIB be shown to be:

1. Essential for either fault or configuration management.
2. Useful in some implementations of the protocol suite (an experimental implementation was considered acceptable).
3. General in its utility. In particular, implementation-specific objects were excluded.

The working group further agreed to limit the MIB's effect on protocol efficiency by avoiding objects which were redundant (e.g., a value that could be derived from another in the MIB) and limiting the number of counters or objects that had to be updated by critical sections of code (for example, the primary path through any layer of the network stack).

The MIB is divided into eight groups: the *System Group,* the *Inter-*

faces Group, the *Address Translation Table,* the *IP Group,* the *ICMP Group,* the *TCP Group,* the *UDP Group,* and the *EGP Group.*

The System Group is used to represent information about the system on which the protocol suite is running, in particular, information about the system's manufacturer and software revision, as well as how long the system has been up. At some point in the future this group will probably be expanded to include information about system load level and memory management.

The Interface Group presents generic information about each network interface on the system. A large amount of information is stored about each interface, including the number of inbound and outbound data errors found, the number of broadcast, multicast, and unicast packets sent, the number of packets received and sent, and the maximum transmission unit of the device. In practice, this definition has proved useful but inadequate and there are plans to enchance it so that device specific information (such as Ethernet frame errors and FDDI interval timers) can be represented.

The Address Translation group contains the mappings between IP addresses and subnetwork-specific addresses that all IP systems must support. Examples of such tables include the ARP table on Ethernets and the X.121 mapping table needed on X.25 networks that support IP.

The IP Group stores information about the IP layer. This information is generally much the same as the information kept for interfaces: datagrams received and sent, counts of datagrams with errors, and the like. In addition, the layer contains addressing information as well as control variables that permit remote applications to adjust the default IP Time-To-Live and manipulate the IP routing tables.

The ICMP Group, the TCP Group, and the UDP Group all store information about their particular protocol. This information includes aggregate counts of datagrams received and sent, counts of particular types of messages received, and in the case of TCP, protocol control blocks. One interesting problem with control blocks that the current MIB does not address is what to do with a control block after the connection is closed. Currently, the MIB provides no mechanism for representing inactive control blocks, but this is known to be inadequate. If a user complains to a network manager that his or her connection failed, the information the manager wants most is the old control block for the broken connection because it contains all the state information for the connection at the time it failed.

The EGP Group is required only of these systems (i.e., gateways) which support the Exterior Gateways Protocol, the routing protocol used to link autonomous systems.

The MIB does not include any management information for applications such as TELNET, FTP or SMTP. Management information for applications was left out for a variety of reasons, of which two were paramount. First, requiring vendors to instrument applications for the MIB would have made it substantially more difficult to implement. Most implementations of the TCP/IP protocol suite already collected management information for the transport layer and below and had some mechanism for retrieving management information that could be adapted to support the MIB. The MIB designers knew of no system which instrumented its applications, perhaps because lower-layer protocols are typically part of the operating system and therefore relatively easy to access, whereas applications can have multiple instantiations in processes, which are harder to manage. Second, because the community had no experience with managing applications, the MIB working group felt that defining standard objects for managing applications would clearly violate its "prior experience" rule.

Case Diagrams

One interesting by-product of the development of the TCP/IP MIB was a method of diagramming MIBs, a method termed *Case diagrams* for Prof. Jeffery D. Case of the University of Tennessee, Knoxville, who developed them.

A key problem in defining a MIB is making sure that all the error conditions will be tracked so that if there is an error, somewhere in the MIB, some object will reflect the fact that the error occurred. Unfortunately, a tedious list of MIB object definitions is an inefficient way to make sure that the errors are recorded. What is really needed is a *flow* or *state diagram*, with each path labeled with the name of the object that records information about that path. Another problem is ensuring that all implementations record the same information at the same place in the processing sequence (if they record information at very different places, the values from two implementations will not be comparable). Case diagrams attempt to solve both problems.

An example Case diagram is shown in Figure 7.3. It illustrates the inbound IP layer of the TCP/IP MIB. There is a main path from the interface layer to the transport layer. An arrow leaving the main path indicates an error condition or flow (in the case of fragmentation) that must be accounted for. Arrows into the main path indicate cases where data is reinjected into the main path and should be counted. The arrows also show the relative positions at which an object is updated, which allows us to keep implementations consistent.

The figure also illustrates one drawback of Case diagrams, as they are currently designed—there is no way to represent global errors or transitions. For example, datagrams may be dropped at any point in the main processing path, not just at the point indicated on the diagram.

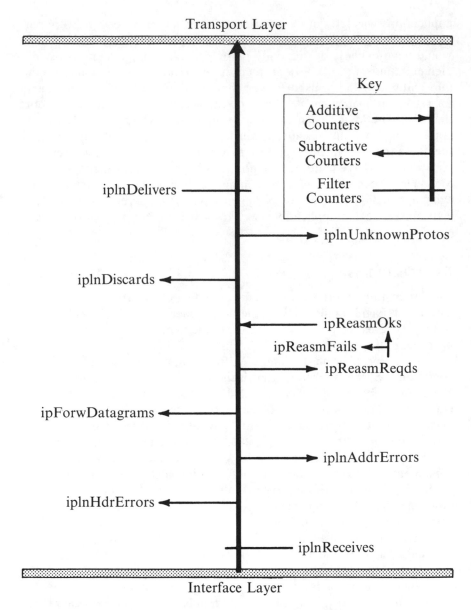

Figure 7.3. Case diagram for IP Input.

7.4 SNMP

Philosophy

The Simple Network Management Protocol (SNMP) is specified in RFC-1098. It was designed, as its name implies, to optimize the processing of a few simple operations upon which network management can be built. Initially, the primary motivation for keeping SNMP simple was to allow network management implementations to be implemented quickly to meet the immediate needs of the Internet, but other benefits have also been realized through this approach.

Simplicity allows management implementations in agents to be smaller and more efficient. This allows agents to spend the majority of their (often) limited memory and processing resources on performing their primary functions, rather than on the processing of management requests.

As and when management requires more complexity, the designers' philosophy was to burden the management station, rather than the agents, with implementing that complexity. In this way, any significant management processing needs are performed in management stations for which network management is a primary function.

Another design goal of SNMP was to be robust under adverse network conditions. In fact, in contrast to the goals of non-management protocols, it is more important for network management to work under adverse conditions than under normal conditions, particularly for fault and performance management when diagnosing and rectifying the causes of the adverse conditions. Network management protocols are most valuable and need to work efficiently when a network is performing poorly.

These goals led to SNMP being *transaction-based* and *datagram-oriented*. Being datagram-oriented removes any need for a set-up phase prior to requesting protocol operations, and datagram-oriented SNMP has no "connection" that can fail under adverse conditions. Also, management applications have full control over retransmitting requests; therefore, different applications can employ different strategies. A vitally important request can be retransmitted many times until (hopefully) it eventually succeeds, as opposed to a routine periodic query for which a single failure is of little consequence.

However, because it is datagram-oriented, SNMP requires protocol messages to be sent wholly contained within a single datagram. In practice, this imposes a size restriction on requests. The size restriction follows the general TCP/IP model of limiting datagrams to fit within an 576 byte IP datagram, unless it is somehow known that a larger size can be accomodated.

In SNMP, the asynchronous messages generated by agents and sent to management stations on specific occurrences (e.g., link down) are called *traps*. SNMP defines only a limited number of traps because they are intended to alert a management station to a problem area. It is the responsibility of the management station to intensify its management operations on that or other nearby agents, to diagnose what conditions exist, and to monitor for improvement or deterioration. This philosophy is called *trap-directed polling*.

Protocol Stack

The standard method of encapsulating SNMP requests for transmission across a TCP/IP-based network is to use the User Datagram Protocol (UDP). An alternative would have been to have SNMP run on top of a transaction-based protocol, but no such standard existed in 1988.

The option of using TCP was rejected on several grounds: TCP is more complicated than UDP; TCP is not datagram-based; TCP requires connection-state information to be maintained if connections are long-lived; and TCP requires more overhead if connections are set-up/torn-down as and when required.

SNMP uses two UDP ports: 161 and 162. Port 161 is the agent's port to which the management station sends requests; port 162 is the port at a management station to which an agent sends traps.

The SNMP protocol is specified using ASN.1; that is, the format of the protocol messages exchanged between protocol entities is described using the ASN.1 specification language, and the data portion of UDP datagrams which carry the protocol messages contains ASN.1 encodings. However, care was taken in specifying the ASN.1 syntax in order to simplify the requirements on the ASN.1 parser needed by an implementation; in particular, there are no context-specific tags.

Conformance with SMI

SNMP conforms to the requirements placed on a management protocol by the TCP/IP-standard SMI. The variables which can be manipulated by SNMP are those which occur as instances of non-aggregate object types specified according to the rules set out in the SMI. This includes not only versions of the TCP/IP-standard MIB, but also experimental or proprietary extensions to the MIB which can be specified using object identifiers.

SNMP does not allow access to aggregate object types (i.e., access to a whole table); rather, access must be to instances of the individual object types within the aggregate object. Thus, to retrieve a whole table, all elements of that table must be retrieved individually. In effect, SNMP views the MIB as a flat space and provides access only to the individual leaves of the MIB tree.

The SMI also requires that a conformant management protocol provide a means of identifying object instances. SNMP does this by appending an instance identifier at the end of the object identifier. For those object types which do not occur within an aggregate object type, there can be only one instance; SNMP uses an instance identifier of "0" for such objects. For example, the MIB object sysUpTime has the object identifier 1.3.6.1.2.1.3; because there is only one instance of this object, the object identifier used to identify its object instance for SNMP is 1.3.6.1.2.1.3.0.

In contrast, there can be multiple instances of those object types which occur within an aggregate object. For these objects, SNMP defines a sequence of one or more values as the instance identifier. The particular sequence used is dependent upon the object to be identified. For example, the MIB object ifDescr has the object identifier 1.3.6.1.2.2.2.1.2; this object occurs within an entry in the Interfaces Table. There is an instance of this object for each agent's interfaces. The object identifier used to identify the object instance for the first interface is 1.3.6.1.2.2.2.1.2.1.

Protocol Data Units

All SNMP protocol messages begin with two fields of header information followed by a message-type specific format (see Figure 7.4). The header fields are the protocol version number and the community name. The

```
snmpMessage Message ::=
    {
        version version-1,
        community "public",
        data {
            get-response {
                request-id 42,
                error-status noError,
                error-index 0,
                variable-bindings {
                    {
                        name 1.3.6.1.2.1.1.0,    -- sysDescr
                        value {
                            simple {
                                string "unix",
                            }
                        }
                    }
                    {
                        name 1.3.6.1.2.1.3.0,    -- sysUpTime
                        value {
                            application-wide {
                                ticks 360000,    -- one hour
                            }
                        }
                    }
                }
            }
        }
    }
```

Figure 7.4. Example of an SNMP message.

protocol version number is handled exactly as in any other protocol. The community name will be explained later.

SNMP defines five message types: Get-Request, Get-Next-Request, Get-Response, Set-Request, and Trap. There is, by design, some commonality between these types. For example, there is only one "response" type message, even though there are three "request" type messages. This is because the same response message type is used for each of the request types.

The commonality is also evident in the content and format of the different message-type specific formats. In particular, each of them contains a sequence of variable bindings, where each binding consists of the name and value of an object (the name of an object is its object identifier including the appended instance identifier). Note that because SNMP views the MIB as flat, there is no restriction on what combinations of objects may be named in the variable bindings of a single request.

In addition, all but the Trap type contain a request-id, an error-status, and an error-index. The value of request-id in a request serves to distinguish it from other requests in progress. When generating a response, the value of request-id in the response is set equal to the value of request-id in the request; this serves to resolve ambiguity in matching responses with requests when a management station has multiple concurrent requests in progress.

Some of these common fields (the error-status, the error-index, and the value fields in the variable bindings) are redundant in request messages. In these cases, the fields are present but their values are ignored. Their presence provides for greater similarity of syntax between the message types, which allows for more optimal parsing techniques in the agents, and may provide the opportunity for agents to generate responses in situ (i.e., in the same buffer as the incoming request). They also help when composing requests for many objects, by knowing how many objects can be included in the variable bindings of each request without causing the error condition which results from a response being larger than can be sent in a single datagram.

Another commonality is that each of the requests are atomic; that is, the specified operation is to be applied either to all or to none of the objects named in the variable bindings. Therefore, before the operation is put into effect, all error-checking must be performed for all the objects named in the request.

Lexicographical Ordering

Because of the dynamics of the set of objects in an agent's MIB, a management protocol needs a mechanism by which a management station can search for and retrieve objects without specifying them by name. SNMP provides this through its concept of having a lexicographical ordering of all object instances in the agent's MIB. This ordering is by object identifier (including the appended instance identifiers). By having an ordering, the management station can supply an object identifier and ask for the object instance which occurs next in the ordering.

For example, the first few objects defined in the standard MIB (version 1), for an object with two interfaces, are shown in Table 7.1 listed in their lexicographical order, with their SNMP instance identifiers appended.

Thus, a management station can obtain lexicographically next values as shown in Table 7.2.

Note that because SNMP views the MIB as having no hierarchy, the lexicographical ordering takes no account of the end of tables in the MIB. There is only one object which does not have a lexicographically next object (the object which is lexicographically last in the agent's MIB).

Message Types

The Get-Request operation names a set of objects and requests that the agent generate a Get-Response containing the values of those objects.

Table 7.1.   LEXICOGRAPHICAL ORDERING OF OBJECTS

Object	Object Identifier
sysDescr	1.3.6.1.2.1.1.0
sysObjectID	1.3.6.1.2.1.2.0
sysUpTime	1.3.6.1.2.1.3.0
ifNumber	1.3.6.1.2.2.1.0
ifIndex.1	1.3.6.1.2.2.2.1.1.1
ifIndex.2	1.3.6.1.2.2.2.1.1.2
ifDescr.1	1.3.6.1.2.2.2.1.2.1
ifDescr.2	1.3.6.1.2.2.2.1.2.2

Table 7.2.   LEXICOGRAPHICAL-NEXT OBJECTS

Object Identifier	Lexicographical-Next Objects
1.3.6.1.2	1.3.6.1.2.1.1.0
1.3.6.1.2.1.1	1.3.6.1.2.1.1.0
1.3.6.1.2.1.1.0	1.3.6.1.2.1.2.0
1.3.6.1.2.1.1.1	1.3.6.1.2.1.2.0
1.3.6.1.2.1.3	1.3.6.1.2.1.3.0
1.3.6.1.2.1.3.0	1.3.6.1.2.2.2.1.1.1
1.3.6.1.2.2	1.3.6.1.2.2.2.1.1.1
1.3.6.1.2.2.2.1.1.1	1.3.6.1.2.2.2.1.1.2
1.3.6.1.2.2.2.1.1.2	1.3.6.1.2.2.2.1.2.1

Each object named must exactly match an object instance available in the agent's MIB.

The Get-Next-Request operation also requests that the agent generate a Get-Response containing the values of a set of objects. However, in this case the objects are not specifically named. Instead, for each of the object names in the variable bindings, it is the (name and) value of the lexicographically next object which is returned in the Get-Response.

The Set-Request operation requests that each of the objects named in the variable bindings be set to the values specified. After success (or failure) the agent generates a Get-Response to confirm (or deny) that the new values were set (see Table 7.3). Only some of the objects in the MIB can be set to new values. For objects which are parameters, the purpose of the Set-Request is to give them new values. Action-type objects, which can be set to a particular value to request a specific action, are also possible with SNMP. For example, an object called reBoot could be defined in an agent's MIB, which when set to the value 1, would cause the agent to restart itself.

There are three special circumstances which occur when setting object instances within an aggregate object type. First, SNMP provides no way to differentiate between the creation of a new object instance and the modification of an existing object instance. The typical way this is implemented is that an *agent* assumes a *modify* is requested if the instance already exists, and a *create* otherwise. Second, when creating a new instance (e.g., a new entry in the IP Routing Table), some agents require that values be supplied (in the one Set-Request) for all objects within the new entry; other agents may be able to supply default values for some of the objects. Third, for deletion of an entry in a table, an object instance of any object within an entry can be set to the ASN.1 type NULL.

The final message type is the Trap. It is generated by an agent to send an asynchronous notification to a management station of the occurrence of some significant event. The message includes a number of fields to identify which agent generated the trap and when, and what type of event occurred (see Table 7.4). The ubiquitous variable bindings are also present; in this case, the objects and their values are used to supply additional information about the event. For example, a Link-Down trap re-

Table 7.3. SNMP ERROR CODES

Error-type	Value	Description
noError	0	Success
tooBig	1	Response too large to fit in single datagram
noSuchName	2	Requested object unknown/unavailable
badValue	3	Object can not be set to specified value
readOnly	4	Object can not be set
genErr	5	Some other error occurred

Table 7.4.   SNMP TRAP CODES

Trap-type	Value
coldStart	0
warmStart	1
linkDown	2
linkUp	3
authenticationFailure	4
egpNeighborLoss	5
enterpriseSpecific	6

quires that the first object in the variable bindings be the ifIndex object instance identifying the particular interface which went down. However, for the most part, the contents of the variable bindings on traps are agent-specific.

Community Names

One of the fields in the header of an SNMP message is the community name. SNMP uses the community name for three separate purposes: authentication/privacy, access control, and proxy identification.

In concept, a network management system based upon SNMP consists of overlapping communities. An agent belongs to a set of such communities. Different communities use different authentication and privacy techniques. The agent may provide access for a specific community to only a subset of its MIB, and the agent may belong to a community only in its role as being a proxy agent for some other device(s).

In practice, all that is required is to determine how many different combinations of authentication/privacy, access control, and proxy are required for SNMP access to the agent, and then assign a community name to each. All of these are then configured into the agent, and the appropriate subsets into the management station(s) for which SNMP access to the agent is valid, together with the appropriate parameters. Except for *proxy* (see below), any commonality of community names between different agents is merely coincidental and irrelevant.

Typically, an agent will use the same community name in generating a response as was used in the corresponding request. In addition, the agent needs to be configured with a community name for each management station to which it will send traps.

Authentication and Privacy

Authentication and privacy is an area for which a complete solution could not be devised within the time frame in which SNMP needed to be deployed. *Hooks* were provided in the protocol for an initial "trivial" scheme and provision was made for the later addition of more sophisticated schemes. This was proved to be adequate while the majority of management is concerned with monitoring. The more sophisticated schemes will be required before network adminstrators are likely to allow a significant amount of control via network management.

To implement authentication and privacy, received SNMP messages are passed to an authentication procedure together with the message's community name, source, and destintation addresses. The authentication procedure's role is to determine if a message is authentic, perform any authentication related transformations on the query, and return the resulting message. Processing would then continue using the message in its revised form. Note that in the event that privacy were in use, the data passed to the authentication procedure would be encrypted, and the data returned would be unencrypted. Another procedure performs the role in reverse during the generation of a SNMP message.

At the time of this writing, the only authentication and privacy mechanism defined is *trivial* authentication. Any community name which indicates trivial authentication has no privacy and is always declared authentic. Thus, any SNMP message with a valid community name is authentic. Effectively, the community name becomes a password (which appears unencrypted in every message).

It is expected that other authentication mechanisms will be defined, possibly including a method based on the Kerberos system [STEI88].

Access Control

The purpose of access control is to provide different management capabilities to different management stations. The details of defining the number of differentiations and what they allow is an agent-specific implementation matter. The protocol provides the concept that the community name indicates the subset of the MIB to which the request can have access and the type of access allowed. Different types of access are *read-only, read-write, write-only,* and *not-accessible.* Note that write-only can actually be useful in a few situations; for example, storing a password into a MIB variable.

Some fairly sophisticated access control policies are possible using the schemes outlined above. In keeping with SNMP's simple model, it is not appropriate to burden an agent with any such schemes requiring significant processing or memory resources. However, such a capability can be provided by having requests processed through an intermediate proxy agent. In this scenario, the authentication scheme(s) used between the originating entities and the proxy agent would be different from that used between the proxy agent and the real agent. The proxy agent would have the superset of capabilities to individual network operators or interested network users, and would only pass on requests to the agent which passes the sophisticated access control.

Proxy

The uses for proxy have already been mentioned: protocol translation, offloading of repetitive queries, and offloading of sophisticated authentication and access control. In each of these circumstances, the proxy agent acts as an intermediary between the entity originating a request and the agent whose MIB is being accessed. Typically, such a proxy agent will be acting as an intermediary for many agents and will also have its own MIB. So it needs to be able to determine which MIB a received request is trying to access.

The use of an intermediary proxy agent does not change the originating entity's procedures; it still generates the request using the community name appropriate for the agent whose MIB the request is to access. Therefore, by using different community names for different agents, the proxy agent can use the community name to determine which agent's MIB is being accessed.

Loss of Protocol Messages

With the standard encapsulation of SNMP messages within UDP datagrams, the underlying protocol stack provides no protection against the loss of SNMP messages. With the request and response type messages, recovery can be handled by the management station because it can detect loss by the lack of response (after some time-out period). For Get-Requests and Get-Next-Requests, the management station can simply retry by re-transmitting the request for some number of times; if none of these succeeds, it can assume that either the agent has gone down or that connectivity to the agent has been lost.

Recovery from no response to a Set-Request is also possible, although a little more tricky, in that the station should probably (depending on what objects are being set) issue a Get-Request to determine if the sets took effect before re-issuing the Set-Request.

In contrast, traps are unreliable; that is, there is no protocol message sent in response to a trap, and there is no way to know if they ever arrived at the management station. This is an important point to realize when planning a network management system based on SNMP. Effectively, traps can be used only as an early warning system; there must be a secondary way to discover that a significant event occurred. One way to do this is to have the management station poll the agent for status at an appropriate frequency.

Thresholds

Thresholds are really a MIB issue, rather than a protocol issue, and there is provision in SNMP to allow enterprise-specific extensions to the set of traps. A trap could be generated when a Counter increases by more than some threshold value within some time period or a Gauge reaches some threshold value. However, the use of thresholds in agents is contrary to the spirt of SNMP which endeavours to keep the agent's network management role simple. Thresholds are still possible within the SNMP spirit though, if the inspection of values for a threshold exceeded condition is done in the management station. In this case, the additional network traffic will generally be of more concern than the additional load on the agent.

7.5   CMOT

Philosophy

Unlike other protocols, work on defining network management standards began in the International Standards community at about the same time as it did in the Internet. Because most people believe that transition from TCP/IP to OSI protocols will happen in the future, some vendors questioned the rationale of developing protocol standards for both at the same time. Rather they reasoned, Why not take the early versions of the OSI standards and adapt them to operate in TCP/IP internets? After all, the OSI network management standards were being viewed as the means to manage not only OSI networks, but other networks (e.g., telecommunications networks) as well. Then, as transition of all network protocols to OSI occurred, network management would be easier because it would already be part way there. Although OSI standards were not yet fully developed, they would have progressed at least beyond their embryonic stage by the time they were adapted for use with TCP/IP. There would still be some risk as to the kind of changes that can occur in an OSI standard in its transition through the various stages of becoming an International Standard (IS). However, implementing an early version should at least be a convenient stepping stone to the eventual IS version.

CMIP is the Common Management Information Protocol. The use of the term "common" refers to the fact that the protocol is used to support work in all five functional areas of OSI network management: Fault Management, Configuration Management, Performance Management, Security Management, and Accounting Management. Each of these functional areas has its own set of requirements, but each is based on there being a common underlying framework: the Common Management Information Service (CMIS) through which management stations and agents communicate with each other using the CMIP.

The CMOT specification, RFC-1095, has been declared a co-standard with SNMP for network management of TCP/IP internets. This specificiation is based on the Draft International Standard (DIS) version of CMIP. (DIS is the penultimate status prior to becoming an international standard.)

As with most OSI protocols, OSI's network management strategy is to encompass just about all possible requirements. Thus, CMIP specifies a full range of functionality with an emphasis on versatility (in contrast to SNMP's emphasis on simplicity). However, this does not mean that every agent or management station need implement all functionality specified in the protocol. The CMOT specification defines a number of subsets, called *functional unit groups,* and requires that conformant systems implement at least one of these functional unit groups. Then, during operation, protocol entities negotiate (i.e., exchange information) about which functional unit groups they support when they first start communicating and thereby determine the common subset of functionality which both of them support.

CMIP is transaction-based and connection-oriented. Being connection-oriented is a consequence of being an OSI application protocol (layer 7 in the OSI Reference Model). All recently defined OSI application protocols are based on the notion of establishing an "association" between the communicating application entities. Such associations are naturally connection-oriented with association establishment and release. CMIP performs to this model. However, being connection-oriented poses a problem which CMIP leaves as an implementation-specific matter: How long should associations remain open? It is not practical to leave them open indefinitely, because that would require the management station to maintain associations for every agent it is managing, which in CMOT's case, includes a presentation connection and possibly a TCP connection. A management station does not want to open and close an association every time it has a request to send, nor does an agent every time it has an event to send.

Application Service Elements

OSI application layer protocols are built using Application Service Elements (ASEs). CMIP uses three ASEs: the Association Control Service Element (ACSE), the Remote Operations Service Element (ROSE), and the Common Management Information Service Element (CMISE). ACSE provides standard mechanisms for the establishment and release of associations. ROSE provides standard mechanisms for request-response transactions. CMISE provides the Common Management Information Service (CMIS) to network management applications.

Some form of Directory Service Element (DSE) is also needed to convert system names (in OSI terminology, Application Entity Titles) into

```
|                                             |
|     Management Application Processes        |
+---------------------------------------------+
|                  CMISE                      |
+------+--------------------------------------+
| DSE  |     ACSE        |        ROSE         |
+------+--------------------------------------+
|     Lightweight Presentation Protocol       |
+---------------------------------------------+
|       TCP       |          UDP              |
+---------------------------------------------+
|                   IP                        |
+---------------------------------------------+
```

Figure 7.5. The CMOT protocol stack.

presentation addresses. For the present, the DSE is a local matter; for example, it could be implemented using local table look-up.

The Lightweight Presentation Protocol

To perform their functions, ASCE and ROSE request service from the underlying Presentation Services (provided by layer 6, the presentation layer). It is at this point that CMOT diverges from CMIP. With CMIP, the Presentation Services used by ACSE and ROSE are provided by pure OSI stack (layers 1 through 6). CMOT uses the Lightweight Presentation Protocol (LPP) instead (see RFC-1085). LPP supports a subset of the OSI Presentation Services running over the TCP/IP transport protocols. The subset supported is just enough to provide the set of services used by ACSE and ROSE.

The philosophy behind CMOT's use of LPP is that the use of Presentation Service allows CMIP to be implemented just as it would be over a pure OSI stack, but LPP replaces all the excess capabilities (some would say baggage) of Presentation and Session Services which CMIP does not need.

The TCP/IP transport protocol used by LPP can be either TCP or UDP. The choice between TCP and UDP is made dynamically according to a Quality of Service parameter provided by the management application process when it intializes its communication with a remote entity. TCP is chosen by requesting "high" Quality of Service. UDP is provided when a "low" Quality of Service is requested.

Presentation Services provides a connection-oriented service and needs to exchange information (e.g., the presentation context) in PDUs when setting up the presentation connection. LPP defines a set of PDUs to serve this function, which includes not only presentation layer information, but also information which would normally be carried by the OSI Session layer. These same PDUs are exchanged whether TCP or UDP is selected. In the UDP case, the LPP sets-up a "low-quality" connection (i.e., it leaves the responsibility for the reliability of data PDUs up to the application), although LPP does retransmit, if necessary, its own connection establishment PDUs.

CMOT leaves the choice of TCP or UDP up to the management application. It is expected that systems within a LAN environment are likely to choose UDP, whereas systems in a WAN environment might choose TCP. One drawback to having two choices is the issue of non-interoperability between systems choosing TCP and those choosing UDP. The solution to this probably requires a general-purpose management station which implements both and uses DSE to determine which protocol to use for specific agents.

CMOT Profile

In OSI, a protocol specification typically provides optional features and leaves some necessary parameters/values unspecified. Which optional features are to be implemented, and the specification of necessary values, is typically contained in a *profile*. RFC-1095 serves as the profile for CMOT. In particular, RFC-1095 specifies that CMOT use ports 163 and 164 of both UDP and TCP. Port 163 is the port used by a management station; port 164 is the port used by an agent.

Conformance to SMI

OSI network management views the MIB as having more structure than is provided by the TCP/IP-standard SMI. The OSI SMI introduces three hierarchies of objects: the registration hierarchy, the containment hierarchy, and inheritance hierarchy. The registration hierarchy and the inheritance hierarchies are used only in defining MIB objects. Thus, they are not applicable to CMOT, which must use MIB objects defined using the TCP/IP-standard SMI. The containment hierarchy is used by OSI network management in identifying object instances, which is left by the TCP/IP SMI as a protocol-specific matter. Thus, CMOT, in order to conform to the TCP/IP SMI, defines a mapping from RFC-1065 to OSI's containment hierarchy.

OSI's SMI specifies that network management is performed through the use of CMIP operations acting on *managed objects,* where a managed object is defined as an instance of an object class. Each object class is defined as having (among other things) a set of attributes. Thus, a managed object exists as an object instance having the set of attributes defined by its object class. It is these attributes which have values. One (or more) attributes must be defined as the object class's *distinguished attribute(s)*. The distinguished attribute(s) are chosen such that specifying their value(s) uniquely identifies which managed object is being referenced. The extra structure of OSI's SMI occurs because object classes can be contained within other objects classes. The containment hierarchy, of interest to CMOT, defines this hierarchy of the object classes.

In order to identify (or to name, in OSI terminology) a managed object of an object class which is contained in another, the value(s) of its distinguished attribute(s) must be specified, as well those of its containing object class and those of all other object classes above it in the containment hierarchy. A pairing of distinguished attribute(s) and their value(s) used to name an instance of a managed object class is called a *relative distinguished name*. The set of relative distinguished names needed to name an object is called a *distinguished name*. A relative distinguished name can be empty if there is only one instance of that object class.

The mapping between the TCP/IP SMI and the containment hierarchy is achieved by mapping those object-types defined in a TCP/IP MIB as *leaf nodes* to attributes and *non-leaf node* object-types to object classes. The mapping of the first version of the TCP/IP-standard MIB (RFC-1066) to object classes is shown in Figure 7.6. The mapping of leaf nodes within RFC-1066's system group to attributes of the system object class is shown in Figure 7.7.

OSI's SMI specifies that events and actions be defined as a part of an object class's definition. RFC-1095 does not define any events or actions in its interpertation of RFC-1066, because none are defined in RFC-1066.

Protocol Operations

For its protocol, CMOT (currently) uses the DIS version of CMIP. It is expected that CMOT will upgrade to use the IS version of CMIP at some

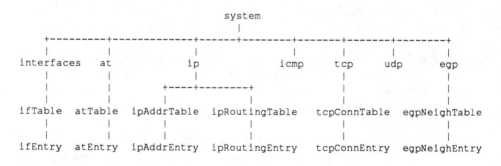

```
                             system
                                |
   +---------+--------------+------+---------+-------+--------+--------+
   |         |              |      |         |       |        |        |
interfaces  at             ip     |       icmp     tcp      udp      egp
   |         |              |      |         |       |        |
   |         |        +----+--------+        |       |        |
   |         |        |             |        |       |        |
 ifTable  atTable  ipAddrTable  ipRoutingTable    tcpConnTable  egpNeighTable
   |         |        |             |                |          |
   |         |        |             |                |          |
 ifEntry  atEntry  ipAddrEntry  ipRoutingEntry    tcpConnEntry  egpNeighEntry
```

Figure 7.6. Mapping of RFC-1066 to CMOT containment hierarchy.

```
system OBJECT CLASS
        CONTAINS {
                -- the following are attributes of this object class
                sysDescr,
                sysObjectID,
                sysUpTime
        }
```

Figure 7.7. Mapping of RFC-1066's system group to attributes.

time in the future. The lag in time between the ISO approval of the IS version of CMIP and its adoption by CMOT will probably be a function of how much change there is between the DIS and IS versions.

CMIP as a protocol supports the service provided by CMIS. This service provides a network management application with the following primitives: M-INTIALIZE, M-GET, M-SET, M-CREATE, M-DELETE, M-ACTION, M-EVENT-REPORT, M-ABORT, and M-TERMINATE. Note that the same CMIS service is provided both in a management station and in an agent. While it is unlikely that a management station will send event-reports to an agent, CMIS does provide for this capability.

Table 7.5 gives the functionality of the CMIS primitives. The M-INTIALIZE, M-ABORT, and M-TERMINATE do not map to CMIP protocol operations, but instead map directly to ACSE service primitives. Each of the other CMIS primitives maps to an exchange of CMIP PDUs which are sent using a combination of ROSE's RO-INVOKE, RO-RESULT, and RO-ERROR primitives (RO-REJECT is also used in some error situations).

The CMIS primitives which map onto ROSE services can be either confirmed or unconfirmed (see Table 7.6). If confirmed, the receiver of the request (the Responder, in OSI terminology) is required to send back a response which confirms the service, indicates whether the operation was successful, and (in the case of M-GET) contains the retrieved values.

Some of the requests can operate on multiple object instances. When they do, a separate response must be sent in its own CMIP PDU for each object instance. These are "linked" together, with the last being the service confirmation.

If the set of attributes to be retrieved is omitted from a M-GET, then all attributes of the selected object instance(s) are to be retrieved. This

Table 7.5.   **FUNCTION OF CMIS PRIMITIVES**

CMIS primitives	Used to:
M-INTIALIZE	Establish an association.
M-EVENT-REPORT	Send an asynchronous notification to a management station of occurrence of some significant event.
M-GET	Retrieve values of a specified set of attributes.
M-SET	Set values of a specified set of attributes.
M-CREATE	Create a new object instance, supplying all necessary attribute values.
M-DELETE	Delete existing object instances.
M-ACTION	Perform an operation on object instances (i.e., an operation other than setting values of attributes).
M-ABORT	Abort an association.
M-TERMINATE	Gracefully terminate an association.

Table 7.6. REQUEST-RESPONSE FEATURES OF CMIS PRIMITIVES

CMIS primitive	Confirmed/Unconfirmed	Operates on Object Instances
M-EVENT-REPORT	either	no
M-GET	confirmed	one or more
M-SET	either	one or more
M-CREATE	confirmed	one
M-DELETE	confirmed	one or more
M-ACTION	either	one or more

allows one CMOT request to be able to retrieve all objects defined within a RFC-1066 table entry.

CMIP provides two choices concerning the synchronization of performing the specified operation when it involves multiple object instances or attributes. The two choices are: *atomic* and *best effort.* Atomic requires that no other operation of significance to network management can be allowed to occur during the processing of the whole CMIP request. Best effort means that the agent will do its best to achieve atomicity but does not guarantee it.

Selection of Objects Instances

Most of the CMIP PDUs require that a managed object be identified. The format of a CMIP PDU allows for the specification of only one object class and one object-instance. In response PDUs, these uniquely specify the managed object. However, a request PDU can optionally select a set of object classes and specify that the requested operation be performed on a selected set of object instances of those object classes. This is achieved through the use of *scoping* and *filtering.*

Scoping is the means to select a set of object classes. The way this works is that the request PDU specifies a *unique object class* (called the base managed object class) plus a *scope parameter.* The scope parameter (see Table 7.7) selects some subset of the base managed object class and the object classes contained within it. Some values of the scope parameter specify a "level" below the base object class; this concept of level is in reference to the containment hierarchy.

Filtering is the means to select a set of object instances. When filtering is used, the CMIP PDU contains a set of filters to be applied to all object instances of all object classes selected by the scope parameter. Filters may be grouped using the logical operators AND, OR, and NOT. Each filter may be a test for equality, ordering, or presence on the attributes of an object instance. Only object instances for which the combined filters evaluate to TRUE are subject to the operation requested by the PDU.

Table 7.7.   VALUES OF THE SCOPE PARAMETER

Value	Meaning
0	Only the base object class.
+2	The base object class and all subordinate classes.
+1	All object classes one level below the base object class.
−n	All object classes n levels below the base object class.
omitted	Only the base object class.

```
{
    userData {                                          -- LPP
        ro-Result {                                     -- ROSE
            invokeID 42,
            {
                operation-value m-Get (3),              -- CMIP
                argument {
                    baseManagedObjectClass {
                        globalForm system { 1.3.6.1.2.1 }
                    },
                    baseManagedObjectInstance {
                        distinguishedName {
                            relativedistinguishedName { }
                    },
                    currentTime "19890426215429.300000Z",
                    attributeList {
                        attribute {
                            localID 1,                  -- sysDescr
                        },
                        attributeValue "unix",
                    }
                    attributeList {
                        attribute {
                            localID 3,                  -- sysUpTime
                        },
                        attributeValue 360000,          -- one hour
                    }
                }
            }
        }
    }
}
```

Figure 7.8.   Example of a CMOT PDU.

Proxy

CMOT also encompasses the concept of proxy. Its only difference from SNMP's handling of proxy is the way the agent on which the protocol operation is to be performed is identified. CMOT uses its containment concept for this. Because all MIB items are contained within the system object class (see Figure 7.6), the object instance in a proxy request will include the distinguished attribute of the system object class in order to identify which system (i.e., which agent) the request references.

Future Issues

CMIP does define a field in its PDUs for access control, but no standard is yet defined for its use. CMOT implementations will probably encode an unencrypted password here, until more sophisticated authentication and access control mechanisms are defined.

OSI's SMI defines a number of ASN.1 types for use as Timemarks, Counter Thresholds, Gauge Thresholds, etc., along with algorithms by which events are generated when threshold conditions are exceeded. Specific thresholds are defined as attributes in an OSI MIB. CMOT is not able to use these until provision is made for them in the TCP/IP SMI.

7.6   COMPARISON OF SNMP AND CMOT

The essence of the comparison between SNMP and CMOT is based on arguing the cost/benefit trade-offs of having the underlying primitives be simpler or more complex. It is interesting to note that these are basically the same arguments used in the comparison between RISC versus CISC instruction sets. However, the environments are not necessarily the same. Even though the arguments are similar, the trade-offs themselves are different.

Certainly from a network operator's perspective, SNMP and CMOT are equivalent in as much as the same applications in the network management station can be built on top of either. As such, equivalent functionality can be provided in a management station using either (or indeed both, if the management station is managing a mixed set of agents).

The essential differences between the two protocols are:

- They have radically different philosophies on how to divide functionality between agents and management stations. For simple queries between the station and the agent, the two protocols provide roughly the same functionality. In this case, the extra load on the agent required by CMOT is unwarranted. However, CMOT supports features (e.g., the use of scoping and filtering) which allow the management station to ask more complicated queries. The same functionality can be achieved through SNMP queries, but normally requires several queries and a greater amount of information to be sent over the network. However, the processing cost to the agent of the multiple SNMP queries is probably less than the processing required for a single complex CMOT query.

- From a network bandwidth perspective, CMOT tends to cause less background load on the network during normal operations because the agents typically monitor themselves and send event/trap messages in case of trouble. With SNMP, a management station needs to query the agents for their status more often. On the other hand, the bandwidth load from SNMP is more predictable and, in particular, more controllable from the management station (which can be very important under abnormal network conditions).

- SNMP is datagram-oriented; CMOT is connection-oriented. Some experts believe that this will make it easier for SNMP to handle larger networks, with each management station able to handle more agents, and will allow SNMP to be more robust under adverse network conditions. Only time and full-scale use of CMOT will tell if this is true. As of May 1989, there were too few implementations of CMOT (and none widely deployed), so a proper test of this question may still be some time in the future.

It is also worth noting that OSI's network management allows greater structure to be placed on the objects contained in the MIB. However, this is not available to CMOT since it shares a common SMI and MIB with SNMP, and so those aspects of SMIP which take advantage of this are of no value to CMOT (i.e., CMOT has functionality it can not use).

In summary, both protocols have their good points and their proponents. Unfortunately, the technical arguments between them have become more of a "religious" issue with political overtones. It would have been better to have had only a single standard protocol, but the reality is that both will be used for network management of TCP/IP-based internets.

Citations

McCL89. McCloghrie, K., Rose, M.T., and Partridge, C. *Defining a Protocol-Independent Management Information Base*. In Integrated Network Management: Proc. of the IFIP TC 6/WG 6.6 Symp. on Integrated Network Management. Edited J. Westcott and B. Meandzija.

MOGUL87. Mogul, Jeffrey C., Rashid, Richard F., and Accetta, Michael J. *The Packet Filter: An Efficient Mechanism for User-Level Network Code.* In Proc. Eleventh ACM Symp. on Operating Systems Principles. November 1987, Austin, Texas.

PART88. Partridge, C. and Trewitt, G. *The High-Level Entity Management System (HEMS)*. In IEEE Network. Vol. 2, No. 2. March 1988.

PART88b. Partridge, C. and Rose, M.T. *A Comparison of External Data Formats*. Proc. IFIP TC 6 Working Symp. Edited E. Stefferud and O. Jacobsen. Irvine, CA. October 1988.

STEI88. Steiner, J. G., Newman, C., and Schiller, J. I. *Kerberos: An Authentication Scheme Service for Open Network Systems*. Proc. 1988 Winter USENIX Conf. Dallas, Tx. February 1988.

TREW88. Trewitt, G. *Topological Analysis of Local-Area Internetworks*. In Proc. ACM SIGCOMM '88. Stanford, CA. August 1988.

A

The Open Systems Interconnection Reference Model

Throughout this book, reference is made to both the concepts and the specifics of the open systems interconnection (OSI) reference model. For the reader unfamiliar with the OSI model, this appendix provides a brief overview. Greater detail can be found in another book in this series [STAL90b].

A.1 MOTIVATION

When work is done that involves more than one computer, additional elements must be added to the system: the hardware and software to support the communication between or among the systems. Communications hardware is reasonably standard and generally presents few problems. However, when communication is desired among heterogeneous (different vendors, different models of same vendor) machines, the software development effort can be a nightmare. Different vendors use different data formats and data exchange conventions. Even within one vendor's product line, different model computers may communicate in unique ways.

As the use of computer communications and computer networking proliferates, a one-at-a-time special-purpose approach to communications software development is too costly to be acceptable. The only alternative is for computer vendors to adopt and implement a common set of conventions. For this to happen, a set of international or at least national standards must be promulgated by appropriate organizations. Such standards have two effects:

- Vendors feel encouraged to implement the standards because of an expectation that, because of wide usage of the standards, their products would be less marketable without them.
- Customers are in a position to require that the standards be implemented by any vendor wishing to propose equipment to them.

It should become clear from the ensuing discussion that no single standard will suffice. The task of communication in a truly cooperative way between applications on different computers is too complex to be handled as a unit. The problem must be decomposed into manageable parts. Hence, before one can develop standards, there should be a structure or *architecture* that defines the communications tasks.

This line of reasoning led the International Organization for Standardization (ISO) in 1977 to establish a subcommittee to develop such an architecture. The result was the *Open Systems Interconnection* reference model, which is a framework for defining standards for linking heterogeneous computers. The OSI model provides the basis for connecting *open* systems for distributed applications processing. The term open denotes the ability of any two systems conforming to the reference model and the associated standards to connect.

Table A.1, extracted from the basic OSI document [ISO84] summarizes the purpose of the model.

A.2 CONCEPTS

A widely accepted structuring technique, and the one chosen by ISO, is *layering*. The communications functions are partitioned into a vertical set of layers. Each layer performs a related subset of the functions required to communicate with another system. It relies on the next lower layer to perform more primitive functions and to conceal the details of those functions. It provides services to the next higher layer. Ideally, the layers should be defined so that changes in one layer do not require changes in the other layers. Thus, we have decomposed one problem into a number of more manageable subproblems.

The task of the ISO subcommittee was to define a set of layers and the services performed by each layer. The partitioning should group functions logically, should have enough layers to make each layer manageably

Table A.1. PURPOSE OF THE OSI MODEL [ISO84]

The purpose of this International Standard Reference Model of Open Systems Interconnection is to provide a common basis for the coordination of standards development for the purpose of systems interconnection, while allowing existing standards to be placed into perspective within the overall Reference Model.

The term Open Systems Interconnection (OSI) qualifies standards for the exchange of information among systems that are "open" to one another for this purpose by virtue of their mutual use of the applicable standards.

The fact that a system is open does not imply any particular systems implementation, technology or means of interconnection, but refers to the mutual recognition and support of the applicable standards.

It is also the purpose of this International Standard to identify areas for developing or improving standards, and to provide a common reference for maintaining consistency of all related standards. It is not the intent of this International Standard either to serve as an implementation specification, or to be a basis for appraising the conformance of actual implementations, or to provide a sufficient level of detail to define precisely the services and protocols of the interconnection architecture. Rather, this International Standard provides a conceptual and functional framework which allows international teams of experts to work productively and independently on the development of standards for each layer of the Reference Model of OSI.

Table A.2. PRINCIPLES USED IN DEFINING THE OSI LAYERS [ISO84]

1. Do not create so many layers as to make the system engineering task of describing and integrating the layers more difficult than necessary.
2. Create a boundary at a point where the description of services can be small and the number of interactions across the boundary are minimized.
3. Create separate layers to handle functions that are manifestly different in the process performed or the technology involved.
4. Collect similar functions into the same layer.
5. Select boundaries at a point that past experience has demonstrated to be successful.
6. Create a layer of easily localized functions so that the layer could be totally redesigned and its protocols changed in a major way to take advantage of new advances in architectural, hardware or software technology without changing the services expected from and provided to the adjacent layers.
7. Create a boundary where it may be useful at some point in time to have the corresponding interface standardized.
8. Create a layer where there is a need for a different level of abstraction in the handling of data (e.g., morphology, syntax, semantics).
9. Allow changes of functions or protocols to be made within a layer without affecting other layers.
10. Create for each layer boundaries with its upper and lower layer only.

Similar principles have been applied to sublayering:

11. Create further subgrouping and organization of functions to form sublayers within a layer in cases where distinct communication services need it.
12. Create, where needed, two or more sublayers with a common, and therefore minimal functionality to allow interface operation with adjacent layers.
13. Allow bypassing of sublayers.

small, but should not have so many layers that the processing overhead imposed by the collection of layers is burdensome. The principles by which ISO went about its task are summarized in Table A.2. The resulting OSI reference model has seven layers, which are listed with a brief definition in Table A.3. Table A.4 provides ISO's justification for the selection of these layers.

Table A.3 defines, in general terms, the functions that must be performed in a system for it to communicate. Of course, it takes two to communicate, so the same set of layered functions must exist in two systems. Communication is achieved by having the corresponding *(peer)* layers in two systems communicate. The peer layers communicate by means of a

Table A.3. THE OSI LAYERS

Layer	Definition
1. Physical	Concerned with transmission of unstructured bit stream over physical link; involves such parameters as signal voltage swing and bit duration; deals with the mechanical, electrical, and procedural characteristics to establish, maintain, and deactivate the physical link
2. Data link	Provides for the reliable transfer of data across the physical link; sends blocks of data (frames) with the necessary synchronization, error control, and flow control
3. Network	Provides upper layers with independence from the data transmission and switching technologies used to connect systems; responsible for establishing, maintaining, and terminating connections
4. Transport	Provides reliable, transparent transfer of data between end points; provides end-to-end error recovery and flow control
5. Session	Provides the control structure for communication between applications; establishes, manages, and terminates connections (sessions) between cooperating applications
6. Presentation	Performs generally useful transformations on data to provide a standardized application interface and to provide common communications services; examples: encryption, text compression, reformatting
7. Application	Provides services to the users of the OSI environment; examples: transaction server, file transfer protocol, network management

Table A.4. JUSTIFICATION OF THE OSI LAYERS [ISO84]

---

a. It is essential that the architecture permit usage of a realistic variety of physical media for interconnection with different control procedures (e.g., V.24, V.25, X.21, etc.). Application of principles 3, 5, and 8 [Table A.2] leads to indentification of a *Physical Layer* as the lowest layer in the architecture.

b. Some physical communication media (e.g., telephone line) require specific techniques to be used to transmit data between systems despite a relatively high error rate (i.e., an error rate not acceptable for the great majority of applications). These specific techniques are used in data-link control procedures, which have been studied and standardized for a number of years. It must also be recognized that new physical communication media (e.g., fibre optics) will require different data-link control procedures. Application of principles 3, 5, and 8 leads to identification of a *Data Link Layer* on top of the Physical Layer in the architecture.

c. In the open systems architecture, some systems will act as the final destination of data. Some systems may act only as intermediate nodes (forwarding data to other systems). Application of principles 3, 5, and 7 leads to identification of a *Network Layer* on top of the Data Link Layer. Network-oriented protocols, such as routing, for example, will be grouped in this layer. Thus, the Network Layer will provide a connection path (network-connection) between a pair of transport-entities, including the case where intermediate nodes are involved.

d. Control of data transportation from source end-system to destination end-system (which is not performed in intermediate nodes) is the last function to be performed to provide the totality of the transport-service. Thus, the upper layer in the transport-service part of the architecture is the *Transport Layer,* on top of the Network Layer. This Transport Layer relieves higher layer entities from any concern with the transportation of data between them.

e. There is a need to organize and synchronize dialogue, and to manage the exchange of data. Application of principles 3 and 4 leads to the identification of a *Session Layer* on top of the Transport Layer.

f. The remaining set of general interest functions are those related to representation and manipulation of structured data for the benefit of application programs. Application of principles 3 and 4 leads to identification of a *Presentation Layer* on top of the Session Layer.

g. Finally, there are applications consisting of application processes that perform information processing. An aspect of these applications processes and the protocols by which they communicate comprise the *Application Layer* as the highest layer of the architecture.

---

set of rules or conventions known as a *protocol*. The key elements of a protocol are:

- *Syntax:* Includes such things as data format and signal levels
- *Semantics:* Includes control information for coordination and error handling
- *Timing:* Includes speed matching and sequencing

Figure A.1 illustrates the OSI model. Each system contains the seven layers. Communication is between applications in the systems, la-

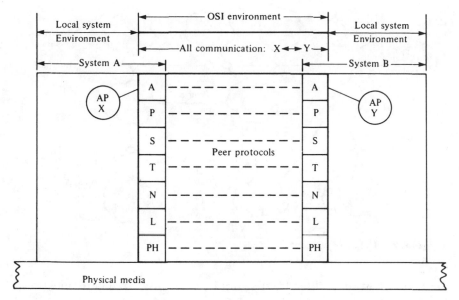

Figure A.1.   The OSI environment.

beled AP X and AP Y in the figure. If AP X wishes to send a message to AP Y, it invokes the application layer (layer 7). Layer 7 establishes a peer relationship with layer 7 of the target machine, using a layer 7 protocol. This protocol requires services from layer 6, so the two layer 6 entities use a protocol of their own, and so on down to the physical layer, which actually passes the bits through a transmission medium.

Note that there is no direct communication between peer layers except at the physical layer. Even at that layer, the OSI model does not stipulate that two systems be directly connected. For example, a packet-switched or circuit-switched network may be used to provide the communications link. This point should become clearer below, when we discuss the network layer.

The attractiveness of the OSI approach is that it promises to solve the heterogeneous computer communications problem. Two systems, no matter how different, can communicate effectively if they have the following in common.

- They implement the same set of communications functions.
- These functions are organized into the same set of layers. Peer layers must provide the same functions, but note that it is not necessary that they provide them in the same way.
- Peer layers must share a common protocol.

To assure the above, standards are needed. Standards must define the functions and services to be provided by a layer (but not how it is to

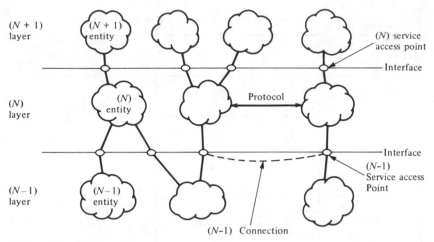

Figure A.2. The layer concept.

be done—that may differ from system to system). Standards must also define the protocols between peer layers (each protocol must be identical for the two peer layers). The OSI model, by defining a 7-layer architecture, provides a framework for defining these standards.

Some useful OSI terminology is illustrated in Figure A.2. For simplicity, any layer is referred to as the *(N) layer,* and names of constructs associated with that layer are also preceded by (N). Within a system, there are one or more active entities in each layer. An *(N) entity* implements functions of the (N) layer and also the protocol for communicating with (N) entities in other systems. An example of an entity is a process in a multiprocessing system. Or it could simply be a subroutine. There might be multiple identical (N) entities, if this is convenient or efficient for a given system. There might also be differing (N) entities, corresponding to different protocol standards at that level. Each (N) entity implements a protocol for communicating with (N) entities in other systems. Each entity communicates with entities in the layers above and below it across an interface. The interface is realized as one or more *service access points* (SAPs).

To clarify these terms as well as some functions common to all layers, refer to Figure A.3. The functions we wish to discuss are:

- Encapsulation
- Segmentation
- Connection establishment
- Flow control
- Error control
- Multiplexing

First, consider the most common way in which protocols are realized, which is by a process of *encapsulation*. When AP *X* has a message

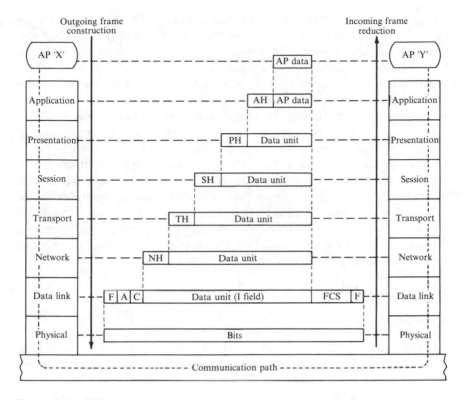

Figure A.3. OSI operation.

to send to AP *Y,* it transfers those data to a (7) entity in the application layer. A *header* is appended to the data that contains the required information for the peer layer 7 protocol; this is referred to as an encapsulation of the data. The original data, plus the header, is now passed as a unit to layer 6. The (6) entity treats the whole unit as data, and appends its own header (a second encapsulation). This process continues down through layer 2, which generally adds both a header and a trailer, the function of which is explained later. This layer 2 unit, called a *frame,* is then transmitted by the physical layer onto the transmission medium. When the frame is received by the target system, the reverse process occurs. As the data ascend, each layer strips off the outermost header, acts on the protocol information contained therein, and passes the remainder up to the next layer.

At each stage of the process, a layer may segment the data unit it receives from the next higher layer into several parts, to accommodate its own requirements. These data units must then be reassembled by the corresponding peer layer before being passed up.

When two peer entities wish to exchange data, this may be done with or without a prior *connection.* A connection can exist at any layer of the hierarchy. In the abstract, a connection is established between two

(N) entities by identifying a connection endpoint, (N-1) CEP, within an (N-1) SAP for each (N) entity. A connection facilitates flow control and error control. *Flow control* is a function performed by an (N) entity to limit the amount or rate of data it receives from another (N) entity. This function is needed to ensure that the receiving (N) entity does not experience overflow. *Error control* refers to mechanisms to detect and correct errors that occur in the transmission of data units between peer entities.

   Multiplexing can occur in two directions. *Upward* multiplexing means that multiple (N) connections are multiplexed on, or share, a single (N-1) connection. This may be needed to make more efficient use of the (N-1) service or to provide several (N) connections in an environment where only a single (N-1) connection exists. *Downward* multiplexing, or *splitting,* means that a single (N) connection is built on top of multiple (N-1) connections, the traffic on the (N) connection being divided among the various (N-1) connections. This technique may be used to improve reliability, performance, or efficiency.

A.3 LAYERS

Physical Layer

The *physical layer* covers the physical interface between devices and the rules by which bits are passed from one to another. The physical layer has four important characteristics:

- Mechanical
- Electrical
- Functional
- Procedural

Examples of standards at this layer are RS-232-C, RS-449/422/423, and portions of X.21.

Data Link Layer

Although the physical layer provides only a raw bit stream service, the *data link layer* attempts to make the physical link reliable and provides the means to activate, maintain, and deactivate the link. The principal service provided by the link layer to the higher layers is that of error detection and control. Thus, with a fully functional data link layer protocol, the next higher layer may assume virtually error-free transmission over the link. If communication is between two systems that are not directly connected, however, the connection will comprise a number of data links in tandem, each functioning independently. Thus, the higher layers are not relieved of an error control responsibility.

   Examples of standards at this layer are HDLC, LAP-B, LAP-D, and LLC.

Network Layer

The basic service of the *network layer* is to provide for the transparent transfer of data between transport entities. It relieves the transport layer of the need to know anything about the underlying data transmission and switching technologies used to connect systems. The network service is responsible for establishing, maintaining, and terminating connections across the intervening communications facility.

It is at this layer that the concept of a protocol becomes a little fuzzy. This is best illustrated with reference to Figure A.4, which shows two stations that are communicating, not via direct link, but via a packet-switched network. The stations have direct links to the network nodes. The layer 1 and 2 protocols are station-node protocols (local). Layers 4 through 7 are clearly protocols between (N) entities in the two stations. Layer 3 is a little bit of both.

The principal dialogue is between the station and its node; the station sends addressed packets to the node for delivery across the network. It requests a virtual circuit connection, uses the connection to transmit data, and terminates the connection. All of this is done by means of a station-node protocol. Because packets are exchanged and virtual circuits are set up between two stations, however, there are aspects of a station-station protocol as well.

There is a spectrum of possibilities for intervening communications facilities to be managed by the network layer. At one extreme, the simplest, there is a direct link between stations. In this case, there may be little or no need for a network layer, because the data link layer can perform the necessary functions of managing the link. Between extremes, the most common use of layer 3 is to handle the details of using a communication network. In this case, the network entity in the station must

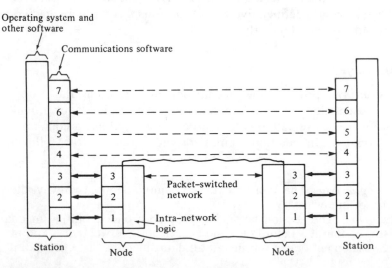

Figure A.4. Communication across a network.

provide the network with sufficient information to switch and route data to another station. At the other extreme, two stations might wish to communicate but are not even connected to the same network. Rather, they are connected to networks that, directly or indirectly, are connected to each other. One approach to providing for data transfer in such a case is to use an internet protocol (IP) that sits on top of a network protocol and is used by a transport protocol. IP is responsible for internetwork routing and delivery, and relies on a layer 3 at each network for intranetwork services. IP is sometimes referred to as "layer 3.5."

The best known example of layer 3 is the X.25 layer 3 standard. The X.25 standard refers to itself as an interface between a station and a node (using our terminology). In the context of the OSI model, it is actually a station-node protocol.

Transport Layer

The purpose of layer 4 is to provide a reliable mechanism for the exchange of data between processes in different systems. The *transport layer* ensures that data units are delivered error-free, in sequence, with no losses or duplications. The transport layer may also be concerned with optimizing the use of network services and providing a requested quality of service to session entities. For example, the session entity might specify acceptable error rates, maximum delay, priority, and security. In effect, the transport layer serves as the user's liaison with the communications facility.

The size and complexity of a transport protocol depends on the type of service it can get from layer 3. For a reliable layer 3 with a virtual circuit capability, a minimal layer 4 is required. If layer 3 is unreliable, the layer 4 protocol should include extensive error detection and recovery. Accordingly, ISO has defined five classes of transport protocol, each oriented toward a different underlying service.

Session Layer

The *session layer* provides the mechanism for controlling the dialogue between presentation entities. At a minimum, the session layer provides a means for two presentation entities to establish and use a connection, called a *session*. In addition it may provide some of the following services:

- *Dialogue type:* This can be two-way simultaneous, two-way alternate, or one-way.
- *Recovery:* The session layer can provide a checkpointing mechanism, so that if a failure of some sort occurs between checkpoints, the session entity can retransmit all data since the last checkpoint.

Presentation Layer

The presentation layer offers application programs and terminal handler programs a set of data transformation services. Services that this layer would typically provide include:

- *Data translation:* Code and character set translation
- *Formatting:* Modification of data layout
- *Syntax selection:* Initial selection and subsequent modification of the transformation used

Examples of presentation protocols are text compression, encryption, and virtual terminal protocol. A virtual terminal protocol converts between specific terminal characteristics and a generic or virtual model used by application programs.

Application Layer

The *application layer* provides a means for application processes to access the OSI environment. This layer contains management functions and generally useful mechanisms to support distributed applications. Examples of protocols at this level are virtual file protocol and job transfer and manipulation protocol.

A.4 PERSPECTIVES ON THE OPEN SYSTEMS INTERCONNECTION MODEL

Figure A.5 provides two useful perspectives on the OSI architecture. The annotation along the right side suggests viewing the seven layers in three parts. The lower three layers contain the logic for a host to interact with a network. The host is attached physically to the network, uses a data link protocol to reliably communicate with the network, and uses a network protocol to request data exchange with another device on the network and to request network services (e.g., priority). The X.25 standard for packet-switched networks actually encompasses all three layers. Continuing from this perspective, the transport layer provides a reliable end-to-end connection regardless of the intervening network facility. Finally, the upper three layers, taken together, are involved in the exchange of data between end users, making use of a transport connection for reliable data transfer.

Another perspective is suggested by the annotation on the left. Again, consider host systems attached to a common network. The lower two layers deal with the link between the host system and the network. The next three layers are all involved in transferring data from one host to another. The network layer makes use of the communication network

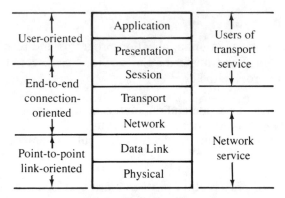

Figure A.5. Perspectives on the OSI architecture.

facilities to transfer data from one host to another; the transport layer assures that the transfer is reliable; and the session layer manages the flow of data over the logical connection. Finally, the upper two layers are oriented to the user's concerns, including considerations of the application to be performed and any formatting issues.

B

Error Detection

B.1   THE ERROR DETECTION PROCESS

Any data transmission process is subject to errors. In transmitting across a data link, signal impairments, such as attenuation, distortion, noise, and interference, may alter the contents of a unit of data (see [STAL88] for details). In transmitting across a network or an internet, these link errors may also occur. In addition, logical or software errors may occur as the data unit is routed and switched through the network or internet.

Because of the potential for errors, a number of protocols include an error detection mechanism, which allows a receiving protocol entity to determine if any errors have occured in data transmitted by a peer sending protocol entity.

The error detection procedure is illustrated in Figure B.1. On transmission, a calculation is performed on the bits of the protocol data unit (PDU) to be transmitted; the result is inserted as an additional field in the PDU. On reception, the same calculation is performed on the received bits and the calculated result is compared to the value stored in the incoming PDU. If there is a discrepancy, the receiver assumes that an error has occurred. This procedure is used both on IP datagrams and TCP segments. In the case of IP, a datagram in error is discarded. In the case of TCP, the damaged segment is discarded, but will eventually be retransmitted by the sending TCP entity.

Transmitter

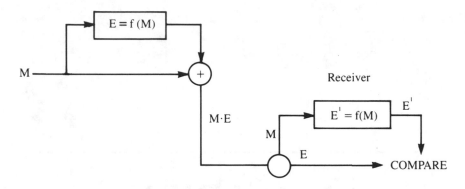

M = Message

$E, E^{'}$ = Error-detecting code

f = Error-detecting code function

Figure B.1. Error detection.

The error-detecting calculation used by IP and TCP is based on one's-complement addition. This concept is explained next, followed by a definition of the error-detection calculation.

B.2   ONE'S-COMPLEMENT ADDITION

One's-complement addition is a calculation performed on binary integers. To define the addition algorithm, we must first look at the way in which integers may be represented in binary form.

The simplest form of binary representation for integers is the *sign-magnitude representation*. In this representation, the leftmost (most significant) bit is a sign bit, with zero for positive and one for negative. The remaining bits hold the magnitude of the integer. Thus,

$$00010010 = +18$$
$$10010010 = -18$$

So, an 8-bit word can represent values in the range -127 to $+127$.

Note that with sign-magnitude representation, there are two representations for zero:

$$00000000 = 0$$
$$10000000 = -0 \text{ (sign-magnitude)}$$

One drawback to this representation is that addition and subtraction require a consideration of both the signs of the numbers, and their relative magnitude, in order to carry out the required operation. An alternative is one's-complement representation. This representation still makes use of a leftmost sign bit, so that it is easy to distinguish positive values from negative values. It differs from sign-magnitude in the way in which the other bits are interpreted, and leads to simpler algorithms for addition and subtraction.

To introduce the concept, we need to distinguish between an operation and a representation. To perform the *one's-complement operation* on a set of binary digits, simply replace 0 digits with 1 digits and 1 digits with 0 digits. Thus

$$X = 01010001$$
$$\text{one's-complement of } X = 10101110$$
$$Y = 10101110$$
$$\text{one's-complement of } Y = 01010001$$

Note that the one's complement of the one's complement of a number is that number.

Now, the *one's-complement representation* of binary integers is as follows. Positive integers are represented in the same way as in sign-magnitude representation. A negative integer is represented by the one's complement of the positive integer with the same magnitude. For example,

$$+18 = 00010010$$
$$-18 = \text{one's complement of } +18 = 11101101$$

Note that since all positive integers in this representation have the leftmost bit equal to 0, all negative numbers necessarily have the leftmost bit equal to 1. Thus the leftmost bit continues to function as a sign bit.

In ordinary arithmetic, the negative of the negative of a number gives you back the number. For consistency, this should be true in one's-complement representation, and it is. For example,

$$-18 = 11101101$$
$$+18 = \text{one's complement of } -18 = 00010010$$

As with sign-magnitude, one's complement has two representations for zero.

$$00000000 = 0$$
$$11111111 = -0 \text{ (one's complement)}$$

We can now turn to a consideration of one's-complement addition. It should be intuitively obvious that the simplest implementation of addition for signed binary integers is one in which the numbers can be treated as unsigned integers for purposes of addition. With that in mind, we can immediately reject the sign-magnitude representation. For example, these are clearly incorrect:

$$0011 = +3$$
$$+1011 = -3$$
$$\overline{1110} = -6 \text{ (sign-magnitude)}$$

$$0001 = +1$$
$$+1110 = -6$$
$$\overline{1111} = -7 \text{ (sign magnitude)}$$

For sign-magnitude numbers, correct addition (and subtraction) are relatively complex, involving the comparison of signs and relative magnitudes of the two numbers.

With one's-complement addition, however, the straightforward approach, with a minor refinement, works:

$$0011 = +3$$
$$+1100 = -3$$
$$\overline{1111} = 0 \text{ (one's complement)}$$

$$0001 = +1$$
$$+1001 = -6$$
$$\overline{1010} = -5 \text{ (one's complement)}$$

This scheme will not always work unless an additional rule is added. If there is a carry out of the leftmost bit, add 1 to the sum. This is called an *end-around carry*. For example:

$$1101 = -2$$
$$+1011 = -4$$
$$\overline{1\ 1000}$$
$$\underline{\qquad 1}$$
$$1001 = -6 \text{ (one's complement)}$$

$$0111 = +7$$
$$+1100 = -3$$
$$\overline{1\ 0011}$$
$$\underline{\qquad 1}$$
$$0100 = 4 \text{ (one's complement)}$$

A further discussion of these topics can be found in [STAL90a].

B.3   APPLICATION TO IP AND TCP

For the IP error detection operation, the entire header of an IP datagram is viewed as a block of 16-bit binary integers in one's-complement representation. For purposes of computing the checksum, the checksum field in the header is set to all zeros. The checksum is then formed by performing a one's-complement addition of all the words in the header, and then taking the one's complement of the result.

The identical computation is performed for TCP. In this case, the computation is performed on the words comprising the segment header, the segment data, and a "pseudo header" that includes the source address, destination address, TCP's protocol identifier, and the length of the TCP segment. If a segment contains an odd number of octets, the last octet is padded on the right with zeros to form a 16-bit word. As with the IP algorithm, the checksum field itself is set to zero for the calculation. [BRAD89] is a discussion of techniques for computing the checksum.

C

List of Acronyms

ARP	Address Resolution Protocol
ARPANET	Advanced Research Projects Agency Network
CCITT	International Telegraph and Telephone Consultative Committee
DDN	Defense Data Network
DOD	Department of Defense
EGP	Exterior Gateway Protocol
FTAM	File Transfer, Access, and Management
FTP	File Transfer Protocol
GGP	Gateway-to-Gateway Protocol
IGP	Interior Gateway Protocol
ICMP	Internet Control Message Protocol
IP	Internet Protocol
ISO	International Organization for Standardization
NAP	Network Access Protocol
NBS	National Bureau of Standards
OSI	Open Systems Interconnection
PSN	Packet-Switching Node
RARP	Reverse Address Resolution Protocol
SMTP	Simple Mail Transfer Protocol

SNMP	Simple Network Management Protocol
TCP	Transmission Control Protocol
UDP	User Datagram Protocol
VTP	Virtual Terminal Protocol

References

BARC81 Barcomb, D. *Office Automation*. Bedford, MA: Digital Press, 1981.

BOGG80 Boggs, D., Shoch, J., Taft, E., and Metcalfe, R. Pup: An Internetwork Architecture. *IEEE Transactions on Communications*, April 1980.

BRAD87 Braden, R. 3270 Over TELNET. Presented at *TCP/IP Interoperability Conference*, March 1987.

BRAD89 Braden, R., Borman, D., and Partridge, C. "Computing the Internet Checksum." *Computer Communications Review*, April 1989.

CERF83 Cerf, V., and Cain, E. The DoD Internet Architecture Model. *Computer Networks*, Vol. 7, 1983.

CLAR82 Clark, D. *Name, Addresses, Ports, and Routes*. RFC814, July 1982. Reprinted in [DCA85].

CLAR88 Clark, D. "The Design Philosophy of the DARPA Internet Protocols." *Proceedings, SIGCOMM 88 Symposium*, August 1988.

COME85 Comer, D., and Peterson, L. Issues in Using DARPA Domain Names for Computer Mail. *Proceedings, Ninth Data Communications Symposium*, 1985.

COME87 Comer, D. *Operating System Design, Volume II: Internetworking with Xinu*. Englewood Cliffs, NJ: Prentice-Hall, 1987.

COME88 Comer, D. *Internetworking with TCP/IP: Principles, Protocols, and Architecture*. Englewood Cliffs, NJ: Prentice-Hall, 1988.

CROC82 Crocker, D. *Standard for the Format of ARPA Internet Text Messages*. RFC 822, August 1982.

DALA81 Dalal, Y., and Printis, R. 48-bit Absolute Internet and Ethernet Host Numbers. *Proceedings, Seventh Data Communications Symposium*, 1981.

DALA82 Dalal, Y. Use of Multiple Networks in the Xerox Network System. *Computer,* October 1982.

DAVI77 Davidson, J., et al. The ARPANET TELNET Protocol: Its Purpose, Principles, Implementation, and Impact on Host Operating System Design. *Proceedings, Fifth Data Communications Symposium,* 1977.

DAVI88 Davidson, J. *An Introduction to TCP/IP.* New York: Springer-Verlag, 1988.

DAY77 Day, J. *TELNET Data Entry Terminal Option.* RFC732, September 1977. Reprinted in [DCA85].

DCA83a Defense Communications Agency. *Military Standard Internet Protocol.* MIL-STD-1777, August 12, 1983. Reprinted in [DCA85].

DCA83b Defense Communications Agency. *Military Standard Transmission Control Protocol.* MIL-STD-1778, August 12, 1983. Reprinted in [DCA85].

DCA83c Defense Communications Agency. *Defense Data Network X.25 Host Interface Specification.* December 1983. Reprinted in [DCA85].

DCA84a Defense Communications Agency. *Military Standard File Transfer Protocol.* MIL-STD-1780, May 10, 1984. Reprinted in [DCA85].

DCA84b Defense Communications Agency. *Military Standard Simple Mail Transfer Protocol.* MIL-STD-1781, May 10, 1984. Reprinted in [DCA85].

DCA84c Defense Communications Agency. *Military Standard TELNET Protocol.* MIL-STD-1782, May 10, 1984. Reprinted in [DCA85].

DCA85 Defense Communications Agency. *DDN Protocol Handbook.* Menlo Park, CA: DDN Network Information Center, SRI International, December 1985.

DEUT86 Deutsch, D. Electronic Mail Systems. In *Digital Communications,* T. Bartee, editor, Indianapolis, IN: Sams, 1986.

ENNI83 Ennis, G. Development of the DOD Protocol Reference Model. *Proceedings, SIGCOMM '83 Symposium,* March 1983.

FINL84 Finlayson, R., Mann, T., Mogul, J., and Theimer, M. *A Reverse Address Resolution Protocol.* RFC903. June 1984. Reprinted in [DCA85].

HIND83 Hinden, R., Haverty, J., and Sheltzer, A. The DARPA Internet: Interconnecting Heterogeneous Computer Networks with Gateways. *Computer,* September 1983.

HIRS85 Hirscheim, R. *Office Automation.* Reading, MA: Addison-Wesley, 1986.

ISO84 International Organization for Standardization. *Basic Reference Model for Open Systems Interconnection,* ISO 7498, 1984.

JACO88 Jacobson, V. "Congestion Avoidance and Control." *Proceedings, ACM SIGCOMM '88,* August 1988.

KARN87 Karn, P., and Patridge, C. "Improving Round-Trip Estimates in Reliable Transport Protocols." *Proceedings, ACM SIGCOMM '87,* August 1987.

KORB83 Korb, J. *A Standard for the Transmission of IP Datagrams over Public Data Networks.* RFC 877, September 1983. Reprinted in [DCA85].

LEIN85 Leiner, B., Cole, R., Postel, J., and Mills, D. The DARPA Internet Protocol Suite. *IEEE Communications Magazine,* March 1985.

MARI79 Marill, T. Why the Telephone Is on Its Way Out and Electronic Mail Is on Its Way In. *Datamation,* August 1979.

MCCO88 McConnell, J. *Internetworking Computer Systems: Interconnecting Networks and Systems.* Englewood Cliffs, NJ: Prentice-Hall, 1988.

MILL84 Mills, D. *Exterior Gateway Protocol Formal Specification*. RFC 904, April 1984. Reprinted in [DCA85].

NBS86 National Bureau of Standards. *Proposal to U.S. Industry to Assist the National Bureau of Standards and the Defense Communications Agency in the DOD Transition to the Use of OSI Products*. ICST/SNA 86-6, February 1986.

NRC85 National Research Council. *Transport Protocols for Department of Defense Data Networks*. February 1985.

PADL83 Padlipsky, M. A Perspective on the ARPANET Reference Model. *Proceedings, INFOCOM '83*. April 1983. Reprinted in [PADL85].

PADL85 Padlipsky, M. *The Elements of Networking Style*. Englewood D. The ARPA Internet Protocol. *Computer Networks*, No. 5, 1981. Reprinted in [DCA85].

PLUM82 Plummer, D. *An Ethernet Address Resolution Protocol*. RFC 826, November 1982. Reprinted in [DCA85].

POST80 Postel, J. *User Datagram Protocol*. RFC 768, 28 August 1980. Reprinted in [DCA85].

POST81a Postel, J., Sunshine, C., and Dogen, D. The ARPA Internet Protocol. *Computer Networks*, No. 5, 1981. Reprinted in [DCA85].

POST81b Postel, J. *Internet Control Message Protocol*. RFC792, September 1981. Reprinted in [DCA85].

POST83a Postel, J. *TELNET End of Record Option*. RFC 930, December 1983. 1983. Reprinted in [DCA85].

POST83b Postel, J., and Reynolds, J. *TELNET Echo Option*. RFC 857, May 1983. Reprinted in [DCA85].

POST83c Postel, J., and Reynolds, J. *TELNET Binary Transmission Option*. RFC 856, May 1983. Reprinted in [DCA85].

POST85 Postel, J. Internetwork Applications Using the DARPA Protocol Suite. *Proceedings, INFOCOM '85*, 1985.

POST88 Postel, J., and Reynolds, J. *A Standard for the Transmission of IP Datagrams over IEEE 802 Networks*. RFC 948, February 1988.

POTT77 Potter, R. Electronic Mail. *Science*, March 19, 1977.

SELV85 Selvaggi, P. The Development of Communications Standards in the DoD. *IEEE Communications Magazine*, January 1985. Reprinted in [DCA85].

SHEL82 Sheltzer, A., Hinden, R., and Brescia, M. Connecting Different Types of Networks with Gateways. *Data Communications*, August 1982. Reprinted in [DCA85].

SOLO85 Solomon, M., and Wimmers, E. *TELNET Terminal Type Option*. RFC930, January 1985. Reprinted in [DCA85].

STAL86 Stallings, W. The DOD Communication Protocol Standards. *Signal*, April 1986.

STAL90a Stallings, W. *Computer Organization and Architecture Second Edition*, New York: Macmillan, 1990.

STAL90b Stallings, W. *Handbook of Computer-Communications Standards, Volume 1: The Open Systems Interconnection (OSI) Reference Model and OSI-Related Standards Second Edition*, New York: Macmillan, 1990.

STAL88 Stallings, W. *Data and Computer Communications*. 2nd Ed. New York: Macmillan, 1988.

SUNS78 Sunshine, C., and Dalal, Y. Connection Management in Transport Protocols. *Computer Networks,* No. 2 1978.

SUNS81 Sunshine, C. Transport Protocols for Computer Networks, in *Protocols and Techniques for Data Communication Networks,* F. Kuo, editor. Englewood Cliffs, NJ: Prentice-Hall, 1981.

TANG86 Tang, D., et al. *A Gateway Architecture Between SMTP and MHS.* National Bureau of Standards, ICST-SNA-86-11, December 1986.

TOML75 Tomlinson, R. "Selecting Sequence Numbers." *Proceedings, ACM SIGCOMM/SIGOPS Interprocess Communications Workshop,* March 1975.

WALL86 Wallace, M., et al. *A Gateway Architecture Between FTP and FTAM.* National Bureau of Standards, ICST-SNA-86-6, March 1986.

ZHAN86 Zhang, L. Why TCP Timers Don't Work Well. *Proceedings, SIGCOMM'86,* August 1986.

Index

Biographies

WILLIAM STALLINGS

William Stallings is a frequent lecturer and the author of numerous technical papers and books in the fields of data communications and computer science. In addition to the three-volume *Handbook of Computer-Communication Standards*, his Macmillan books include *Data and Computer Communications, Local Networks: An Introduction*, and *Computer Organization and Architecture*. He is also author of *Computer Communications: Architecture, Protocols, and Standards, Local Network Technology, Integrated Services Digital Networks*, and *Reduced Instruction Set Computers*, all from the IEEE Computer Society Press.

Dr. Stallings received a Ph.D. from M.I.T. in computer science and a B.S. from Notre Dame in electrical engineering. He is an independent consultant. His clients have included the Government of India, the International Monetary Fund, the National Security Agency, IBM, and Honeywell. He has been vice president of CSM Corp., a firm specializing in data processing and data communications for the health-care industry. He has also been director of systems analysis and design for CTEC, Inc., a firm specializing in command, control, and communications systems.

ANTHONY MICHEL

Anthony Michel is a manager of special projects in the Development and Engineering Division of BBN Communications Corporation of Cambridge, Massachusetts. He was a designer of parts of the early ARPAnet Packet Switch (the IMP) and has had a continuous role in the development of the DARPA Internet since its inception. Currently, he leads a group which produces specialized network access devices and internetwork gateways. He also is a codeveloper of the "DDN Technology Seminar," which is presented periodically to industry and government. He consults and lectures widely on the architecture of data networks. He has a particular interest in the development of testing methodologies for internetwork systems and protocols. Mr. Michel holds a B.S.E.E. from M.I.T. and an M.S.E.E. from Northeastern.

PAUL MOCKAPETRIS

Paul Mockapetris is currently project leader at USC Information Sciences Institute, Marina del Rey, CA. He is a member of the DARPA Internet Engineering Task Force and the Distributed Systems Advisory Board Task Force on Naming. He participated in the development of the SMTP protocol and has implemented servers for SMTP. He defined and authored the specification for the Domain Name System, and implemented a version of the system. His current research interests are high speed networks and distributed naming and database systems.

Dr. Mockapetris received a Ph.D. from the University of California at Irvine in information and computer science, and B.S. degrees in electrical engineering and physics from M.I.T.

SUE McLEOD

Sue McLeod is a group leader in the Data Networks Department at the MITRE Corporation in McLean, Virginia, where she is manager of a project to provide local area and long-haul network expertise for a large government network procurement. Her work experience includes implementation of virtual terminal and file transfer protocols, including TELNET, for local area networks and long-haul DOD networks. As a member of the ANSI committee on Application Layer Protocols, she participated in the completion of the ISO virtual terminal standard. She is co-author of a paper entitled "ISO Virtual Terminal Protocol and Its Relationship to MIL-STD TELNET," presented at the IEEE Computer Society Computer Networking Symposium in November 1986. Sue holds a B.S. from Colby College in Waterville, Maine.

CRAIG PARTRIDGE

Craig Partridge received his B.A., M.Sc. and expects shortly to receive his Ph.D. from Harvard University. For the past several years he has been a research scientist at BBN Systems and Technologies Corporation, where he has worked on various projects in networking and distributed systems. His current interests include very high speed networks, information services and network management. He is also editor of ACM SIGCOMM *Computer Communication Review* and a member of the Internet Engineering and End-to-End Services Task Forces.

KEITH McCLOGHRIE

Keith McCloghrie is the director of software engineering at the Wollongong Group Inc. His responsibilities include the development of network management as weli as TCP/IP products for a variety of computer systems. He was coauthor of *RFCs 1065 and 1066*. He has also participated in the Internet Engineering Task Force's SNMP Extensions Working Group and the Netman (CMOT) Working Group. McCloghrie received his B.Sc. in Mathematics from the University of Manchester in England.